Art Therapy Research in Practice

ANDREA GILROY

ART THERAPY RESEARCH IN PRACTICE

PETER LANG
Oxford · Bern · Berlin · Bruxelles · Frankfurt am Main · New York · Wien

Bibliographic information published by Die Deutsche Nationalbibliothek
Die Deutsche Nationalbibliothek lists this publication in the Deutsche Nationalbibliografie; detailed bibliographic data is available on the Internet at http://dnb.d-nb.de.

A catalogue record for this book is available from the British Library.

Library of Congress Cataloging-in-Publication Data

Art therapy research in practice / Andrea Gilroy (ed.).
p. ; cm.
Includes bibliographical references and index.
ISBN 978-3-03911-994-3 (alk. paper)
1. Art therapy. I. Gilroy, Andrea, 1949-
[DNLM: 1. Art Therapy. WM 450.5.A8]
RC489.A7A7835 2011
616.89'1656--dc22

2010051073

ISBN 978-3-03911-994-3

Cover image: Aggressive Bodies: 'Rebecca' Beating 'Becky'

Hochfeldstrasse 32, CH-3012 Bern, Switzerland
info@peterlang.com, www.peterlang.com, www.peterlang.net

Contents

List of Figures and Tables ix

Plates xi

ANDREA GILROY

Introduction: N=1: Practitioner Research in Art Therapy 1

PART ONE Researching Art Therapy with Children 17

FRANCES PROKOFIEV

1 'I've been longing and longing for more and more of this': Researching Art Therapy in the Treatment of Children with Developmental Deficits 19

UWE HERRMANN

2 The Tangible Reflection: A Single Case Study Investigating Body Image Development in Art Psychotherapy with a Congenitally Blind Client 39

HILARY HOSEA

3 The Brush's Footmarks: Researching a Small Community Art Therapy Group 61

ELIZABETH STIRLING

4 Collaboration, Education, Frustration: Integrating Art Therapy into the School Setting 81

ANDREA GILROY

Commentary: Art Therapy with Children 107

PART TWO Researching Art Therapy with People who have Learning Disabilities 115

BARRIE DAMARELL

5 Shaping Thoughts: An Investigation into the Cognitive Significance of Image-Making for People with Learning Disabilities 117

ROBIN TIPPLE

6 Art Therapy and Diagnostic Assessment 139

ELIZABETH ASHBY

7 Resourceful, Skilful and Flexible: Art Therapy with People who have Severe Learning Disabilities and Challenging Behaviour 159

ANDREA GILROY

Commentary: Art Therapy with People who have Learning Disabilities 181

PART THREE Researching Art Therapy with Adults 187

KEVIN JONES

8 Art 'fer-a-Pee'. An Exploratory Randomised Controlled Trial (RCT) of Group Based Art Therapy as an Adjunctive Treatment for People with a Diagnosis of Schizophrenia 189

CHRIS WOOD

9 The Evolution of Art Therapy in Relation to Psychosis and Poverty 211

JACKY MAHONY

10 Artefacts Related to an Art Psychotherapy Group: The Therapist's Art Practice as Research 231

SALLY SKAIFE

11 Maps and Mess: Group Members' Experience of the Relationship between Art and Talk in an Art Therapy Group 251

ANDREA GILROY

Commentary: Art Therapy with Adults 269

References 275

Notes on Contributors 299

Index 303

List of Figures and Tables

All artworks are reproduced by kind permission of the artist. Unless stated otherwise, all photographs, tables and diagrams are copyrighted by the chapter's author.

Figures

4.1	Model of Project	91
4.2	Reasons for Referral	94
4.3	Understanding of Art Therapy	97
4.4	Nursery Nurses' Responses to Liaison Time	98
4.5	Teachers' Responses to Liaison Time	99
4.6	Nursery Nurses' Responses to Art Therapy Service	100
4.7	Teachers' Responses to Art Therapy Service	100
4.8	Parents' Responses to Art Therapy Service	101
6.1	Surfer	148
6.2	The Camel	150
6.3	The Golf Club	152
7.1	Collaborative Work	169–70
8.1	Flow Chart of RCT	195
8.3	Art Fer a Pee	208

Tables

4.1	Project Description	95
4.2	Aims and Outcomes	102
5.1	Analysis of Image Type	128
5.2	Participants' Non-Marking Activity	129
5.3	Participants' Vocalisations	130
7.1	Employers	165
7.2	Theoretical Orientation	166
7.3	Professional Support	166
7.4	Difficulties with Service Provision	167
9.1	Correlation of Recovery Rates from Schizophrenia with Average Unemployment Rates in the USA and UK during Four Periods of the Twentieth Century	217

Plates

1.1 Visual Form of Gesture

1.2 Monoprint

1.3 Free Action Painting

1.4 'Jackson Pollock', 1950. Photograph by Hans Namuth.
Courtesy Centre for Creative Photography, University of Arizona, copyright 1991, Hans Namuth Estate

1.5 Picture-folding (Action Painting)

1.6 Painting in Primary Colours and Black

2.1a Auxiliary Bodies: 'Helpful Somethings'

2.1b Auxiliary Bodies: 'Helpful Somethings'

2.2 Changing Bodies: 'Gyroscopic Self Figure'

2.3 Passive Victim Bodies: 'Torn between Mother and Teacher'

2.4 Container Bodies: 'Ambivalence'

2.5 Aggressive Bodies: '"Rebecca" Beating "Becky"'

2.6 Integrated Bodies: 'Negotiation'

2.7 Transformed Bodies: 'The Destroyed Body'

2.8 Father Bodies: 'Mask Pleading for Acceptance'

2.9 Reconciliation: 'Medusa Surrendering'

8.2 Collage

10.1 Installation View, *Algebra*, Private Exhibition, 2002

10.2 Installation View, *Artefacts 1*, Private Exhibition, 2000

10.3 Harrow Kiln Site: Jacky Mahony Opening a One-off Kiln, 1972.
Photograph by Jay Myrdal

10.4 Jacky Mahony, *Carved Bowl*, 1972, celadon glaze, 44 cm diameter. Photograph by Jay Myrdal

10.5 Jacky Mahony, *Knitting Grayscale*, handspun Shetland wool, commercial cashmere yarn, knitting needle, safety pins

10.6 Installation View, *Artefacts 2*, Private Exhibition, 2000

ANDREA GILROY

Introduction: N=1: Practitioner Research in Art Therapy

This book aims to inform readers about the latest evidence from innovative art therapy research. It shows how, through engaging with research that derives from clinical work, practice and research can mutually inform one another in lively, interesting and useful ways. Projects range from the microanalysis of interactions between clients, their art and the art therapist to investigations of art therapy services and an unpacking of the inside story of a Randomised Controlled Trial (RCT).

The book is divided into three parts addressing art therapy research with children, with people who have learning disabilities and adults. Chapters follow the same structure, each author beginning with 'how it all began' before going on to situate their research in a critical context and describing the research methods they chose to investigate their particular research question. Methods of data collection and analysis are outlined, several contributors discussing innovative use of visual methods and case study approaches to their research. Each chapter concludes with authors' reflections about the influence of their research on what they do, articulating a reflexive loop that moves from practice to research and then from research back into practice.

A distinguishing feature of this book is the collaboration between the editor and the contributing authors. When the chapters were in final draft, authors in Parts One, Two and Three met, having read each other's chapters, to discuss their research with each other and with me; these were recorded, transcribed and sent to the authors for comment. Our conversations identified themes across the chapters and explored and elaborated the research findings particular to each part of the book. As our meetings and conversations progressed it became evident that key themes resonated across the book as a whole. These were to do with the art in art therapy: its communicative power, its capacity to contain important material that can remain unspoken and the importance of art's physical materiality in relation to bodily experiences. A key theme was the current political context of art therapy provision in Britain. Three editorial commentaries, situated at the end of each part of the book, draw on these conversations, relating contributors' research to the wider art therapy literature and, given our discussions, to government policies too. The nature of these and the many other exchanges that I have had with the contributors about their chapters and the commentaries has made my editorial role an enjoyable and collaborative one. I thank them for this and for their patience with my editorial obsessions. I would also like to thank our Commissioning Editor, Nick Reynolds at Peter Lang, for publishing our 'intriguing' book.

It has long seemed to me that art therapists are natural researchers. Practitioners will have acquired many of the necessary research skills of observing, describing, documenting, distilling and interpreting data in their everyday clinical work. Critical reflection permeates the daily routine. Gathering clinical data from different sources is nothing new. All of this makes research an accessible, empowering and eminently do-able activity that can be incorporated into art therapists' routine practice. I suggest that every art therapist has the potential to become a practitioner researcher, to be a single subject: the N=1.

Art therapy practice generates many rich and compelling questions. Practitioner research gives art therapists an opportunity to investigate these questions, to examine particular preoccupations, to explore processes and phenomena that have caught the eye and to spend time with a particularly interesting topic or case. What characterises practitioner research is, as McLeod (1999) has said, an intensive analysis of a particular aspect of practice, an emphasis on enhancing practical understanding of clinical work and high levels of investment in a topic. This is plain to see in these authors' narratives of their research experiences when they describe how they travelled from a deepening curiosity about someone or something to the emergence of findings that have real implications for art therapy practice and service provision. They demonstrate, for example, the importance of the physical materiality of art-making in art therapy with children (Prokofiev, Chapter One; Hosea, Chapter Three) and adults (Mahony, Chapter Ten;

Skaife, Chapter Eleven). They show how art therapy 'fills something in' for children who have developmental deficits (Prokofiev, Chapter One; Herrmann, Chapter Two) and enables thought for those with learning disabilities (Damarell, Chapter Five). Contributors evidence the significance of all the communications in art therapy (Tipple, Chapter Six) and the outcomes of a Randomised Controlled Trial which demonstrated the effectiveness of group art therapy with people diagnosed as schizophrenic (Jones, Chapter Eight). They unpack the relationship between poverty, mental health and art therapy (Wood, Chapter Nine) and explore art therapy services for people with severe learning disabilities and children in mainstream education (Ashby, Chapter Seven; Stirling, Chapter Four).

This research enters the public domain at a time when the demand for 'evidence' of an intervention's clinical and cost effectiveness underpins all provision in the public sector. Building the evidence base of art therapy is more critical now than ever before. In this Introduction I therefore set the scene with a brief outline of Evidence-Based Practice (EBP) that explains the continuing dominance of RCTs. Before you head for the hills please read on to see how these are but a part of the research field and how practitioner research can bridge the research-practice 'gap', particularly through a case study approach to research and the use of visual methods. At the end of this Introduction I map the chapters themselves. I hope that what follows will show how you – the practitioner, the N=1 – can make a contribution to art therapy's evidence base.

Evidence-Based Practice

EBP is a cyclic process which requires that all interventions in health, social, educational and criminal justice systems are based on research that has demonstrated their effectiveness. It requires that practitioners constantly update their knowledge of research so that they can ensure that 'best practice' is delivered that will lead to the best outcomes. Healthcare practitioners are also required to demonstrate that they have actually implemented what the research recommends; this is achieved through two quality assurance procedures: clinical guidelines – which distill findings from research and make recommendations about treatment – and audit. EBP therefore draws a linear equation between a person, their diagnosis, research and the treatment they receive. EBP pervades the discourses and policies of Britain's public services and increasingly determines the interventions and treatments that are resourced by public funds. In these particularly hard-pressed, credit-crunched times, the pressure to provide empirical research that will support the continuing delivery of all kinds of services has increased, especially those for marginalised groups delivered by specialist practitioners such as art therapists. (See Gilroy, 2006 for further description and critical discussion of EBP.)

Those interventions whose evidence base is well established, such as cognitive behaviour therapy (CBT) have, as a direct consequence of the implementation of EBP in Britain's mental health services, expanded exponentially in recent years, but all is not well in the EBP world as far as art therapy and many other public sector practices are concerned. This is because the only acceptable form of research within the EBP paradigm is a RCT – the 'gold standard' of 'scientific evidence'. Other kinds of quantitative research are of lesser value; qualitative research is usually excluded. This kind of 'big' research occurs in a political arena (McLeod, 1999), requires significant funding and huge numbers of people to be randomly assigned either to groups that receive the intervention or to other, non-intervention or 'control' groups. The results of both groups are measured and compared using standard tests and statistics to see if those who received the intervention do better than those who did not. The method derives from medicine and takes a positivist approach, based on the principles of the natural sciences (biology, physics and chemistry) which assume that the same patterns of response will always occur, given the same conditions. This approach is well-suited to physical treatments and to manualised psychological interventions that consider the body and the mind as organisms; when something goes wrong there is a cause which can be identified and an intervention that can be made to rectify the problem. However, the human mind is highly individualistic and does not always operate in such a mechanistic, cause and effect way, being influenced by relationships, experiences, cultures and socio-political contexts.

The dominance of RCTs in EBP in the psychological therapies (as well as in general medicine, education and social care) is vigorously contested. McLeod (1999), for example, argues that RCTs are privileged because their structure fits bio-behavioural systems of psychiatric diagnosis. Further, as Westen et al (2004) and many others have pointed out, RCTs require particular conditions: clients with a single diagnosis, the use of a manualized therapy and a 'treatment package', often administered for relatively short periods of time that are determined by the project's funding. Their nature also requires practice to be precisely articulated and then delivered exactly as it has been described, in laboratory-like conditions. This means that RCTs rarely reflect the norms of everyday clinical work. Further, clinical approaches that do not accede to medical and behavioural models need other forms of research investigation, not only to identify what is effective but also to understand the processes of interventions that are based in relationship. Nonetheless, clinical guidelines about all treatments, including those for mental health problems, are issued by powerful organisations like the National Institute for Clinical Health and Excellence (NICE, see www.nice.org) and the Cochrane Collaboration (see www.cochrane.org.uk) based solely on RCTs, creating a situation that can lead '... to a state of affairs where the methodological tail wags the clinical dog' (Westen et al., 2004: 642).

This is not to say that quantitative research in general, and RCTs in particular, cannot and should not be done in art therapy. Indeed I have suggested elsewhere (Gilroy and Lee, 1995; Gilroy, 2006) that art therapists' focus on building a respectable body of rich, descriptive literature and inductive research has been to the detriment of outcome research. This is not to say that inductive research, undertaken by practitioners, should be neglected. Far from it. In my view such research is critical to art therapy's evidence base, not only because it is an essential precursor to the empirical research that EBP requires but also because it has intrinsic worth. Inductive research is cumulative. It builds slowly and steadily. It often involves a personal journey for the practitioner researcher. It accesses the practitioner's tacit knowledge, describing practices, developing theories and exploring new ideas, all the while seeking to describe possibilities and exploring questions that art therapists want to investigate in order to enhance their practice rather than provide answers to EBP's questions about 'what works'. It is here that the N=1 practitioner researcher has a definitive role to play, doing research that comes from the ground up, which travels, as Westen et al (2004) have suggested, from the clinic – and, in art therapy's case, the studio – to the RCT laboratory.

There are many research methods that can be used in art therapy, as I have described elsewhere (Gilroy, 2006) and summarise below.

- Action: cycles of action and reflection
- Collaborative: co-researching, subjective, experiential
- Case studies: clinical – experimental, descriptive, exploratory, case series; social – the 'bounded' case and/or system
- Ethnographic: observation and description of people and/or events in their natural environment
- Hermeneutic: interpretation of texts
- Heuristic: experiential discovery using self and others Phenomenological: observation and definitive description
- Historical/archival: texts and objects, primary and secondary sources
- Interviews: structured, semi-structured, open
- Randomised Controlled Trials (RCTs) and controlled group studies: measurement of treatment outcomes
- Surveys: questionnaires gathering quantitative and/or qualitative data
- Visual: looking, writing, curating, making

Some entail an enormous amount of data collection and analysis and, usually, several researchers – which can include art therapists (as in Jones, Chapter Eight) – who bring to the research table expertise that goes beyond the routines of clinical work. Others are suited to small-scale, inductive, research. Here art therapists can, like the contributors to this book, draw on their transferable skills and incorporate research into their everyday work, especially when it comes to a case study approach to practitioner research.

Case Studies

A case study is 'a study of the singular, the particular, the unique' (Simons, 2009: 3). In the research traditions of the psychological therapies a 'case' is usually understood to refer to a person or a group; the 'study' is of the background, development, processes and outcomes of therapeutic work, either in a narrative or an experimental form. In other research traditions in the social sciences e.g. anthropology, history and sociology, case studies take different forms; a case study could be of a person or a group but it could equally be of a classroom, an organisation, a service, a system or a country. Generally speaking a case study approach to research is understood as a method through which the particular can be systematically explored. Art therapy draws on all these approaches to case study, there being no 'correct' way of using case studies as a research approach.

Therapeutic work has long been conceived as a research method in psychoanalysis, psychotherapy and counselling. As McLeod (1994) describes, key figures in the history of these disciplines have, through publication of classic case studies, demonstrated the distinctiveness of their approach. These have acted as a starting point for subsequent research, either through the accumulation of further case studies which confirm or challenge the conclusions of earlier work or which lead into larger-scale, quantitative research. A similar model applies in art therapy. However, case studies have been critiqued because of their subjectivity and inherent bias and because of difficulties with generalisation beyond the individual case. In response to such criticism approaches have been developed which differentiate between an 'ordinary', descriptive case study (like that written during art therapy training) and systematic case study research. These methods can readily be applied to a wide range of art therapy research questions by the practitioner researcher. It only requires one: one client or one group, and one practitioner researcher.

In this book practitioner researchers have drawn primarily on the 'clinical' tradition of case studies but they have also used a social science approach to the 'bounded system' of a case (Simons, 2009: 29): of participative action research in an organisation (Stirling, Chapter Four), an historical study of a discrete set of art therapy practices (Wood, Chapter Nine) and a survey of a group of art therapists (Ashby, Chapter Seven). Practitioner researchers have used the 'clinical' approach to research their own practice (see Prokofiev, Chapter One; Mahony, Chapter Ten) or another's (Skaife, Chapter Eleven). This kind of practitioner research can be retrospective and draw on the different kinds of documents, artworks, recordings and interviews that are part of a case (Herrmann, Chapter Two; Tipple, Chapter Six) or they can also be part of ongoing practice (Hosea, Chapter Three). An experimental session, an art therapy group and a 'self-study' of the lived experience of a RCT (respectively Damarell, Chapter Five; Skaife, Chapter Eleven; Jones, Chapter Eight) all draw on different approaches to case study.

Positivist approaches to case study research in the psychological therapies usually evaluate change through well-established psychological, behavioural and social outcome measures, the therapy being delivered in carefully controlled conditions with measures being administered before, during and after therapy and at follow-up too; measures can also be collected weekly, for example after each session, or even daily. This approach, stemming from psychology, uses an ABA design, 'A' being the before and after measures, 'B' the therapy. It can involve the practitioner researcher in the administration of the measures or, if this sits uncomfortably with the practitioner, can be done in co-operation with colleagues in the multi-disciplinary team. Alternatively the practitioner's 'natural' activities can be reframed into a research method. For example, Greenwood and Loewenthal (2005) suggest a hermeneutic approach that breaks routine practice into a series of stages that can be reflected upon. The therapist's process notes forms stage one; reflection on these with a supervisor and a subsequent re-writing comprises stage two where additional meanings will emerge; the practitioner researcher subjects this to a further hermeneutic analysis, stage three, where yet further meanings evolve that are different from those originally conceived in the cultural domain of the clinical work. Such naturalistic inquiry into 'real life' situations invites not only the analysis of different kinds of documents and artefacts but also participant observation and interviewing of the different participants that creates another layer of texts for further analysis. Add artworks into the picture and the research process gets richer as recording, looking and artwriting create another kind of hermeneutic frame, hermeneutics meaning to describe, discover and interpret the meanings of texts in terms of the cultures and contexts in which they are written, received, read and understood.

Case studies can take a narrative form, be an experiment, involve collaboration with one or more participants or combine quantitative and qualitative approaches. Whatever the approach, the informed consent of all participants is a must, whether the research is concurrent or in retrospect. Ethical approval is another must. These are complex issues, the governance of which has changed rapidly in recent years and, although increasingly rigorous, it varies across sectors and so it is always best to check with local requirements and statutory policies. Completing ethics applications and designing consent forms requires careful thought and precision about the aims and objectives of the research, the processes and procedures involved, the ways in which the practitioner researcher intends to gather and analyse data, how clients and other participants will be protected and how the findings will be disseminated.

Having gathered piles of texts, recordings, original artworks and/or documentation of same, the practitioner researcher then has to analyse them. Data analysis of different kinds – of case material, interview transcripts, artworks and so on – involves a process of immersion, reflection, selection and perhaps categorization of the data prior to its conceptualization as 'findings' and their final interpretation. This can be done in different methodological frameworks, depending on the research approach e.g. phenomenological or heuristic, or be analysed using different forms of content or discourse analysis and grounded theory (Corbin and Strauss, 2008; Sharmaz, 2006). This requires careful, detailed work but it allows the practitioner researcher to unpack the processes, events and artworks that have, for example, contributed to change as a result of art therapy.

Visual Research

Generally speaking, visual research methods comprise four approaches that can be utilised in art therapy practitioner research, namely looking, artwriting, curating and art-making. Not all have been used by the contributors to this book but I outline them here in order to indicate how they are being developed in art therapy practitioner research.

Retrospective looking at clients' artworks is a well-established part of routine practice in art therapy; introducing systematic procedures into this reflexive process enables it to be construed as a research method, as Schaverien has usefully outlined (1992, 1993). Rose (2001) takes another approach, proposing a tripartite structure that enables artworks to be analysed through three sites: of the work's production, consideration of the thing itself and how it is viewed or 'audienced'. Both approaches to visual analysis have a natural 'fit' with the habitual practices of art therapists and provide us with useful research tools, as Prokofiev (Chapter One) and Herrmann (Chapter Two) show.

This kind of detailed looking generates description and often a text; an example can be found in Mahony (Chapter Ten). This is key and leads us to the next visual method: artwriting. To my mind the 'thick descriptions' of artworks are an 'ekphrasis' – a verbal evocation of an artwork – which can be analysed in various ways, e.g. through the layers of iconographical analysis proposed by Panofsky (1972) or a grounded theory approach (Sharmaz, 2006). 'Artwriting' has become a contemporary investigative and creative genre that includes the artist/writer/practitioner/researcher's subjectivity in an heuristic and situated approach to art (e.g. Clark 2006; Elkins, 2001) in relation to how it is seen and understood which has much to offer the art therapy practitioner researcher (Gilroy, 2008).

It is acknowledged that the context in which artworks are viewed and how they are displayed influences how they are seen (Berger, 1972; Woolf, 1993). This suggests that clients' artworks can be explored through visual displays – thematic, chronological and/or iconographical. A reflexive engagement with looking through a curatorial process of organising and display of artworks made in art therapy can invite different kinds of viewing and audiencing through which new meanings can be found (see Herrmann, Chapter Two; Mahony, Chapter Ten). Research supervision has taught me the value of this, especially of deconstructing what seems to be a developmental, chronological 'canon' in the display of artworks in art therapy. We know, for example, that retrospective exhibitions of artists' works do not necessarily follow the chronology of a life; why, therefore, should consideration of clients' artworks always follow the chronology of the sessions? A curator may structure a show around events, places, themes, media and other, content-related themes, and so inform the audience about the person of the artist in relation to their works, their context of production in terms of history, geography, peers and so on through visual juxtapositions. Taking a similar curatorial approach to the display and audiencing of clients' art in art therapy could, I suggest, offer another visual research method through which we can find things out. Such displays can be private to the practitioner but could be extended in various ways, depending of course on individual circumstances, for example to the client and perhaps to the supervisor and/or multi-disciplinary team. Clients could curate and/or co-curate displays of their work with the art therapist in different locations, within and outside the host organization, which could be considered in terms of what they enable or inhibit. Visual displays could also be accompanied by videoed or taped recording, perhaps combining the curatorial process and subsequent audiencing with an in-depth, collaborative exchange with the client as co-researcher, either as part of the ending or at a follow-up meeting, as Herrmann describes (Chapter Two).

Finally we come to art-making as a visual research method. Art therapists know through experience that making art is a means through which we find things out, be it about ourselves, our worlds or each other. Making art leads to new thinking, to discovery. Thus there is an irreducible logic that it too should be a method of research-based inquiry. It can take several forms. Art practice itself can be construed as a means of inquiry (Sullivan, 2005; Irwin and de Cosson, 2004). It can also be part of a practitioner researcher's creative and/or reflexive process about their research. Research respondents, participants and co-researchers can also make art in order to access and convey data or to disseminate findings (Bagley and Cancienne,

2002). And of course, as in social research, art can provide a means of visual documentation of the social context and many other aspects of therapeutic work through film, photography and so on (Banks, 2001; Pink, 2001; Prosser, 1998).

Mapping the Book

Part One focuses on art therapy practitioner research with children. The first chapter is by Frances Prokofiev who describes single case research in a mainstream primary school with a child whose deep engagement in the art process led to rapid changes in his cognitive and emotional development. A retrospective review of his art demonstrated the importance of Prokofiev's containment of the child's sensuous, tactile art-making. This, coupled with thinking about merging and separation in the art of Jackson Pollock, leads her to suggest that a supportive, containing approach is more effective with children who have developmental deficits than one that focuses on the interpretation of visual and other material, and indeed that art therapy therefore serves to repair and 'fill something in'. In Chapter Two, Uwe Herrmann also draws on a retrospective, single case approach, this time in collaboration with his client who, at the end of therapy, became a co-researcher. A panoramic, sensory and visual display of the subject's sculptures – the 'case' being that of a blind adolescent – together with Herrmann's careful documentation of the visual material and their recorded, collaborative review sessions, investigate clinical outcomes in terms of body image development, aesthetic and sensory issues in relation to the blind client and the sighted art therapist. Chapter Three, by Hilary Hosea, also explores participative research, on this occasion about an art therapy group. Here the art therapist used video to discover how attunement was promoted through the sharing of art-based 'vitality' between parents and their very young children, the project's success leading to the development of new services. The last chapter in Part One, by Elizabeth Stirling, also addresses the development of art therapy services in a new area of provision. Chapter Four describes a participative action research project which investigated the difficulties and the potential of introducing art therapy into mainstream education. The organic, collaborative nature of the research method and the project's focus on supporting those involved enabled a positive response to art therapy. The difficulties inherent in trying to establish a new service in sectors that remain unfamiliar with art therapy are all too apparent but so too are ways in which problems can be overcome.

Part Two addresses art therapy practitioner research with people who have learning disabilities. Chapter Five, by Barrie Damarell, describes innovative research that demonstrates, through detailed analysis of video recorded experimental meetings, how the non-mark making movements and accompanying vocalisation of learning disabled clients whilst making art enhances their capacity for thought. He shows how particular kinds of movement relate to different levels of consciousness, 'styles' of art and to early bodily experiences. In Chapter Six, Robin Tipple uses a hermeneutic approach to conduct a detailed investigation of an art therapy assessment with a child on the autistic spectrum. Tipple's analysis of the video-recorded interactions, documents and images relating to a single case show how the child and his art works were 'produced' in a social interaction which is determined as much by the family, the service and the art therapist as by the child's inner world. Our attention then turns to the impact of working with people who have severe learning disabilities and challenging behaviours. In Chapter Seven, Elizabeth Ashby describes the debilitating impact of her clinical practice and how it led her to do a survey-based investigation of other art therapists working with the same client population. Key strategies for the development of best practice are identified that relate directly to the influence of the environment on practitioners' ability to work effectively and efficiently.

Researching art therapy with adult clients is the focus of Part Three which begins, in Chapter Eight, with Kevin Jones' description of working on – or perhaps in – an RCT. He outlines the findings from a trial of group art therapy with people diagnosed as schizophrenic, namely the reduction of negative symptoms and the increased inclusion of ethnic minority clients in art therapy. However, unlike 'bog standard' reports of RCTs, this narrative takes the reader into the heart of the research as the author describes his encounters with clients' poverty and deprivation in his role as researcher and of class, ethnicity and gender as practitioner. Chris Wood, in Chapter Nine, also uses a case example to describe the reality of her client's poverty and distress. She uses a dialectical, historical method to locate and describe the 'bounded case' of art therapists who have worked throughout the profession's history with people with severe and enduring problems. Wood suggests that the contemporary elaboration of the role and function of art in art therapy offers a powerful explanatory paradigm which situates the profession and its practices within a social and political context. The practitioner research described in Chapter Ten, by Jacky Mahony, speaks again to the art in art therapy, telling the story of an investigation of the significance of the art therapist's art to the creative art experience of clients in an art psychotherapy group. A visual heuristic approach includes art practice and visual display and shows how clients with severe and complex problems were able to overcome their difficulties through their deep engagement with making art. The final chapter, Chapter Eleven by Sally Skaife, explores the tension between art and interactive dialogue in art therapy as experienced by the members of another's art therapy group. Questionnaires and interviews, which enabled Skaife to discover how clients resolved this tension through visual 'mapping', while being powerfully expressive, were found to have left much unspoken.

What of the impact of their research on these practitioners? In our collaborative conversations contributors said that research relieved some of the isolation that is, we agreed, an issue for many art therapists and certainly enabled the development of their practice and their capacity to think about what they do. Some spoke about writing and how certain research traditions, for example those of EBP or academic scholarship, seemed to require a particular kind of 'voice'; an important realisation had been that this could be challenged and that writing could be a source of data or a means to researcher reflexivity. The research process was not always easy and, like the 'slow labour' of making art that Mahony (Chapter Ten) describes, takes time and effort, but it is manageable. Doing research that derives from, sits alongside and then feeds back into practice had been immensely rewarding, was certainly empowering and contrasts with what has been described as 'quick and dirty' health service research which, though it quickly replies to the questions asked by stakeholders, does not tackle the issues practitioners want to address (Milton, 2002). Research, as Herrmann remarked, was 'very much a wake-up call… Some part of my thinking being kissed back into life'. Hosea continued:

> It (research) does allow you to examine things and give yourself space in a way that nothing else has done. Nothing else has done that, It's so rich and it's so satisfying and it allows you to be far more relaxed about what you're doing and far more inventive and flexible and all the things that you should be doing with art processes when you might be becoming a rigid art therapist if you're not careful. It allows you to flow and go with the flow, and unwind and go in different directions which is deeply beneficial to the people you're working with.

Some art therapy clients stay in our minds. It may be that the images were particularly striking, that the transference relationship was strong, that the client's story was especially moving or their journey amazingly fast or very long. Art therapy may have been particularly effective, succeeding when other interventions had failed, or the client may have embodied something about the ordinary, everyday clinical work of an art therapist that usually goes unsung. Some teams may have worked together especially well; some spaces might have been particularly conducive to art therapy. It is worth exploring why particular people, artworks, events and places have stayed in the practitioner's mind, distilling what it is that has captured the imagination or stimulated curiosity and then developing it into a research question. This can lead to stimulating, inductive, practitioner research that is close to the heart of the art therapist who becomes a researcher and which makes a real contribution to art therapy's evidence base. I hope that the eleven stories that come next will intrigue and inspire you, our reader, to follow in their footsteps. It is all at the fingertips of the art therapy practitioner researcher.

PART ONE

Researching Art Therapy with Children

FRANCES PROKOFIEV

1 'I've been longing and longing for more and more of this': Researching Art Therapy in the Treatment of Children with Developmental Deficits

Abstract

This chapter researches the artwork from a two-year retrospective single case study of a nine-year old boy to discover whether important experiences missed in early development can be compensated for by the art process in art therapy. Close study using a retrospective review of the pictures and theory about the development of children's drawing as well as the rationale behind Pollock's art process, helps to identify meaning and development in the artwork and make links between changes in the art process and personal development in the world outside art therapy sessions.

Key Words

maternal deprivation; developmental deficits; art process; self experiences; retrospective review.

How it all Began: from Practice to Research

This research developed from thirteen years work as an art therapist in an inner London mainstream primary school and builds on material from my research-based MA (Prokofiev, 2002). Typical referrals for art therapy in the school were children with difficulty accessing learning because of their emotional needs, including some with behavioural problems and a level of disturbance which implied chronic insecure or disorganised attachments and consequential developmental deficits.

I was interested to find that many of the more damaged children, as well as those less traumatised but without a sense of their own efficacy and an impaired sense of self, readily responded to a non-directive approach to art therapy in a room set aside for the purpose. Their early experience affected their ability to make a positive attachment in therapy but my role in setting clear boundaries was important. They became absorbed in experimenting with sensuous materials, experiencing their impact on them as if for the first time and clearly finding meaning and self-enhancement in the art practice they developed. It seemed that the art process itself had the potential to fill in something that had been missed in the early environments of their lives. This is echoed in Killick (2000: 99) who found that the concreteness of the art therapy room fostered the emergence of a sense of self in severely disturbed adult patients in a psychiatric setting.

One nine-year-old child I worked with, whom I will call Paul, puzzled me by the fairly rapid changes he was able to make in response to the art therapy environment despite the severity of his symptoms. His early infancy was catastrophically insecure because of inconsistency of care and his mother's depression, and there were concerns about all his early milestones. His literacy and numeracy were very delayed and he could not take part in classroom discussion, being unable (as I later understood) to form ideas. He reacted to the smallest stressor in school, including new work or his mother leaving him in the morning, by immediate hyper-arousal and flight and could not respond to normal soothing. His face showed no affect and, although he could be aggressive with other children, on the whole he was very 'flat' and detached. It is important to stress that in very developmentally delayed children their experience is so fragmented as to make them feel unintegrated and unaware of themselves as a whole person. However, two years of art therapy enabled Paul to make remarkable changes. I wanted to discover how this had come about.

The Context of the Research

In recent years there has been an increase in papers about art therapy with children whose development has been disrupted and delayed by early pre-verbal experience. Some of these children's symptoms are made more complex and entrenched through subsequent institutionalisation (Rabiger, 1990; Henley, 2005) and through abuse, particularly repeated sexual abuse (Murphy, 2001; Case, 2002, 2005; O'Brien 2003, 2004). Many patients are, or have been in the 'Looked-After' system.

One of the challenges in this work is that trust in the therapeutic relationship is hard to establish because of fear in the transference caused by adverse attachment experience. The fear can also be strongly felt in the countertransference as high anxiety (Meyerowitz-Katz, 2003). The reader is made aware too of how tired and 'absent' the therapist can become in the presence of a child who wants to avoid feeling and thinking (Case, 2002; Meyerowitz-Katz, 2003). Art therapists have to be sensitive to these children's states, often witnessing and mirroring activities rather than interpreting in the early stages, or else seeking ways to promote the beginnings of relationship, as in the ball games with a child described by Case (2008).

A significant link between these case studies is that the children's lack of early containment implies that they are concrete in their use of art and play materials as they have not reached the stage of being able to imaginatively symbolise or conceive of an 'as if'. Some of the art products are described as 'mess' and understood as an outpouring of fragmented experience demonstrating the children's lack of a sense of coherence in their lives and the desire to evacuate their feelings, 're-presenting' them rather than symbolising them (Thomas, 1998; O'Brien, 2004). Aldridge (1998) connects the 'food' and 'shit' mixtures made of visceral materials by her patients, with the art of contemporary artists whose similar themes express their inner states in powerful images; this helped her understand her young patients. Case (2002, 2005) on the other hand, describes a child who initially stopped short of using art materials at all until experiences of observing nature outside the art room window alongside his therapist helped to animate him and stimulate growth.

Some of the literature sets out to show how art therapy can aid the transition to symbol formation through the containment offered in art therapy (Case 2002, 2005; Meyerowitz-Katz, 2003). Meyerowitz-Katz suggests that the concrete nature of art materials supports the assimilation of containment, implying that it is repeated experience of interacting with materials that helped her four-year-old patient internalise boundaries and understand that there is an inside and outside (of himself). She shows that she had to be proactive to enable a shift in her patient's therapy, placing paper in the way of his mindless pouring of paint so that a shape was formed on its containing surface. Alvarez writes that the perspective from which experience is viewed may make experience more accessible for children who have a difficulty in learning from a human object (1992: 79). She also comments on the value of assimilating experience through the visual modality when the patient has difficulty in listening to verbal interpretations.

What is missing in the art therapy literature is a detailed examination of how different aspects of making art in art therapy can help a child access a range of experiences missed in early life which can support a better sense of self. This is the area I chose to study. The research question I began with was: 'What elements in Paul's art process supported change and repair of developmental deficits caused by early maternal deprivation?'

In order to investigate developmental deficits and their repair, I had to revisit what factors are needed for normal development and what, in contrast, maternal deprivation implies. In the early months of life it is the relationship with the mother or primary caregiver which provides infants' experience of their environment. The degree to which this person can be consistently available and sensitively attuned to the baby, adapting to their needs and providing stimulation but not over-stimulation, affects the child's future mental health, their trust in the world and their cognitive and emotional development, including their personality (Bowlby, 1953; Winnicott, 1971). Bowlby (1953) coined the term 'maternal deprivation' to describe the state which absence of adequate, in-tune nurture represents. Bion (1962) suggested that the development of the ability to think, understand feelings and find meaning in the world are dependent on the primary carer's in-tune containment in the first two years. In the last fifteen years, research linking neuro-science to attachment theory has extended understanding by demonstrating that secure attachment is implicit in linking neural pathways in the right hemisphere of the brain in the first two years of life, when a huge growth spurt occurs (Schore, 1994). Among other things, this establishes self-regulation of the emotions and understanding of the whole lexicon of facial expressions and their meanings as experienced in the mother's face (the foundation for understanding others' intentions towards them in future life). Absence of secure attachment therefore impacts on what has been described as the 'hardwiring' of the brain (ibid.) and affects future social functioning.

Stern (1985), who used infant observation research to study early development of self, describes how early mother-infant exchanges show the mother not only mirroring but sensitively elaborating on her baby's gestures: a proto-conversation ensues which develops the baby's sense of self as communicator, one who experiences intersubjectivity with another. His theory of the infant's developing sense of self in the first two years of life, a period which is largely pre-verbal (1985: 8–9), describes a range of self-experiences without which mental health is threatened. These include a sense of agency, without which paralysis or non-ownership arises; a sense of physical cohesion, without which there is fragmentation of body experience; a sense of the self as having continuity in time, without which there can be a sense of dissociation or 'not going on being'; and a sense of self as having feelings, without which there is dissociation. In good-enough circumstances the child also experiences and internalises a subjective self, which can achieve intersubjectivity with another and without which there is loneliness or psychic transparency; a sense of self as a creator of organisation, without which there is psychic chaos; and finally a sense of self as a transmitter of meaning, without which the individual is excluded from culture and lacks validation of personal knowledge. The level of deprivation implied by absences of some or all of these self-experiences is very serious and paints a picture of an isolated and confused individual who has no sense of the meaning or intention of people's actions or of his own relationship to the world. This is compounded by feeling that he has no control over his own actions or any ability to make things happen. Underlying all this, as attachment theory explains, the insecurely attached child experiences a constant anxious tension because of the threat that their environment poses as they have no expectation that anyone can help them.

On the face of it, it would seem that Stern's selves could well be experienced reparatively in the art process of art therapy by patients who have missed responsive and creative interactions with their primary carers. Stern makes an interesting suggestion that, once the verbal domain and the verbal self has been reached, there is a split in the child's sense of self with the verbal self gaining precedence, making it much more difficult for him or her to access the preverbal domains where there is a more 'immediate level of relatedness' because they are less readily shareable. This has implications for the therapeutic treatment of pre-verbal disturbances to which the non-verbal nature of art therapy might be considered naturally suited. With this in mind, a second research question can therefore be asked: 'Can art therapy provide self experiences which have been missed in early development?'

Pine (1986), in his model of 'the borderline child to be', describes other factors that are missing when a child's early experience has been traumatic, including a lack of libidinal drives that stimulate step-by-step development. He sees this as the result of the child lacking experience of their needs being satisfied by a specific, longed-for other. With no expectation of gratification, a sense of emptiness and lack of drive pervades. Kut-Rosenfeld and Sprince (1965: 504) suggest that what may be needed in therapy for the borderline child with developmental deficits is 'to stimulate temporary phase dominance so that the material of that phase can be worked through, therefore allowing a move forward (or back) to the next relevant material'. A third research question I therefore asked was: 'Can engagement with art materials offer gratification of a sense of unfulfilled need, leading to a drive to invest in the art process that might kick-start other sorts of development outside the art therapy room?' I thought this might be particularly likely because the tactile quality of art materials permits regression to the sensuous experiences of the pre-verbal phase.

Method

I justified my choice of Paul's case as suitable for retrospective research because there were such profound changes (McLeod, 2001) and because I wanted to improve my practice through deeper understanding of what had enabled the changes to occur. Furthermore, the quantity of art works allowed an in-depth study of Paul's art practice which was important in relation to my hypothesis: that the practical nature of the art process within art therapy was a key factor in the treatment of children with developmental deficits.

I used a qualitative methodology based on the retrospective investigation of a single case. I hoped that detailed description and findings would clarify what happened with Paul and elicit principles that could inform practice in art therapy with children with similar presenting problems. The concept of case study research as the study of the particular serving to illuminate the general is supported in research literature providing that the case selection is justified (Higgins, 1993; McLeod, 2001; Denscombe, 2003). An advantage of this approach is that the detailed investigation involved makes it possible to discover how different parts of the material affect each other and why certain outcomes happen, rather than just identifying what they are (Denscombe, 2003). Single case study research is familiar in art therapy (Dalley, 1979, 1980; Schaverien, 1991; O'Brien, 2004; Case, 2005) and has been encouraged as an important and valid means to develop and share clinically relevant knowledge and re-evaluate existing theories in the profession (Gilroy, 1996, 2006; Edwards, 1999).

This chapter focuses on one aspect of my research and its findings: the visual research which explored the art process and its role in supporting the repair of developmental deficits. Data from Paul's art therapy includes all the artworks, my process notes, records of meetings with his mother, teachers and SENCO and associated review papers and reports.

Analysing the Visual Data

I felt challenged by the task of finding meaning in the artwork because it was non-figurative and during the sessions it had seemed such a meaningless outpouring. The first tool I considered was a retrospective review, which Schaverien (1993) has described as arranging the artwork chronologically or by theme in order to identify movement in the art process that implies therapeutic change. There are four stages in her process of analysing the visual data (Schaverien, 1993; Gilroy, 2006):

Stage 1. A systematic analysis of the shape, form and colour of the marks in each picture (i.e. as objective an approach to the pictorial data as possible.
Stage 2. Documentation of any changes in the use of figures in the artwork.
Stage 3. Reference to change in the therapeutic process as recorded in the process notes.
Stage 4. Where the patient's comments are available, a comparison between the patient's and therapist's experiences.

Paul had made forty paintings on paper and a cupboard full of containers with mixtures. It was not easy to review the mixtures coherently as they often defied labelling and were not really intended to have separate identities. As for the works on paper, I had assumed that the *process* of painting was more important for Paul than the finished object. Also Matthews (1986) warns against focusing too much on the end product of young children's artwork on the grounds that their process can just as likely be an expression of movement in space. Although a retrospective review had been useful to Schaverien (1991, 1993), whose adult patient worked figuratively, I wondered if the same method would be viable in an analysis of artwork which was neither representational nor symbolic. However, there was a particular attraction in trying to conduct a review of the paintings in chronological order because of my question about whether the experience of gratification in art-making could stimulate a developmental process. I had observed how

Paul had been absorbed in the art process from the beginning and his 'longing for more and more of this' six months into therapy demonstrated the way it appeared to fill a need in him, so I thought I would attempt a review of the paintings, leaving the mixtures in the background of the research. My intention was that the review would be an examination of the development of the pictures as concrete works, investigating signs of cognitive and emotional development in any changes in his process, including signs of developing ability to symbolise.

I also researched the literature on children's early drawing development which I thought might be relevant to understanding development in Paul's art. The middle period in Paul's work reminded me of Pollock's action painting and so I investigated what Pollock said about his painting process. Similar sources are used in Tipple (1992) to cast light on his study of a patient with severe learning difficulties, another example of a case where apparently repetitive, non-figurative paintings prompted the need to find theoretical frameworks which could throw light on the meaning of the patient's process.

Ehrenzweig's explanation of the making of a piece of art as a three-stage process (1967) was a useful benchmark against which to measure Paul's art process at different points in his art therapy. He describes:

Stage 1. A schizoid projection of unconscious parts of the self into the picture.

Stage 2. A stage of unconscious integration on an undifferentiated manic level (the 'oceanic state' or state of being merged with the picture).

Stage 3. A final depressive stage where the picture is seen as having a separate existence.

I began by placing the paintings chronologically on a large floor space and set about looking at the quality of the marks in Paul's pictures. It became clear that in order to understand the meaning of an individual work, I had to think of it as part of a process: I needed to be aware of the body of work as a whole. This meant that I had to switch from looking at an individual picture to stepping back to see the whole group, and then go back to the individual picture again. Most of the pictures were large, measuring sixty by eighty four centimetres; taking photographs of them and reducing their size made the process of viewing the whole work simpler. My version of Schaverien's 'Stage 1' was therefore closely linked with 'Stage 2', the documentation of changes in the figures in the artwork. At this point, I consulted my process notes only in relation to Paul's manner of using the materials. Later on I checked the dates of the pictures against my case notes, cross-referencing these with my reviews with the teachers and Paul's mother and against my notes of the dialogue in therapy sessions. This was 'Stage 3' of Schaverien's reviewing process when I looked to see if there were connections between changes in Paul's art-making and personal change outside the sessions. Here I was estimating the effectiveness of art therapy.

Findings

A rigorous examination of each painting had helped me to identify discrete stages and their function and I became aware of how pictures related to each other, dividing them into types. I referred to literature on the developmental stages of art in young children's development to help me (Dubowski, 1984; Willats, 1997; Matthews, 1986, 1999, 2003; Atkinson, 2002). Because of the limited space of this chapter, I will confine the report of my findings to three stages: Paul's use of art materials at the beginning of therapy; findings relating to pictures from the middle period; and a stage I think of as the watershed, represented by one painting made towards the end of art therapy in which symbolic communication is achieved.

My first finding was that the pictures were very different from each other, even when a similar method was used, and that there was more of a developmental process going on in the sequence than I had observed during the sessions. I was able to observe the range of feeling that was embodied in the quality of marks for the first time, now that I was freed from the countertransference. I reflected that when a child shows no affect in his facial expression, it is hard to be conscious of feeling that might nevertheless be projected into the artwork. Henley (2005) also notes this.

Beginnings

My finding in the pictures of the first three months was that Paul's painting process was a spontaneous application of marks on paper, often a visual equivalent of a different kind of gesture and feeling, exemplified by Plate 1.1, a splatter painting on A3 paper which had been pinned to the easel.

It was executed with energy and perhaps a sense of irritation, reminiscent of Pollock's action painting approach. Part of Pollock's interest was to dialogue with the picture surface in an activity that was also a pursuit of self (Gottlieb, 1976). This is what seemed to be happening here and in subsequent paintings by Paul during the first year of art therapy. Another early picture at this time was composed of crossed lines painted with the energy of his whole arm; another, an amorphous splodge of paint, the result of pressing and rolling paint onto paper with a lump of clay. Through experiment Paul soon discovered the monoprint and that a form could be reproduced that was a mirror of the original (Plate 1.2).

In art therapy, Paul retreated from the figurative artwork that he was capable of doing in the classroom, to something much more immediate and for which he expressed a hunger.

These pictures show Paul's work as essentially comparable to early experimental graphic work of young children for which there seems to be an innate drive (Dubowski, 1984). This drive is likely to have been precluded in a child like Paul, whose beginnings were unfavourable. Simon (1992) shows the developmental value of mark-making when she observes a fourteen month infant using a pen, consciously repeating movements that were initially accidental, thereby demonstrating his awareness of the effects of his actions and that he could experiment and control them. Matthews (1986, 1999) describes how young children use art and other materials experimentally to explore the workings and patterns of their environment and find meaning, discovering that the same effects can be seen across different modes. Judging by the driven nature of Paul's attitude to using the room and its materials, I presumed that he too was using the materials to find meaning and patterns in the way the world works, as well as seeing the impact of his movements and feelings made concrete in his artwork.

Although my focus was on the two dimensional work alone, I understood that Paul's experimental mixture-making was part of the same activity. Through experiencing his impact on the materials in his first gestural pictures, Paul discovered an ability to use tools in different ways. From these beginnings a logical sequence of stages in his art production was generated but always with the potential to return to a style used before; moving on did not imply that past ways of working had lost their value.

The Middle Stage of Art Therapy

After nine months of art therapy, Paul's painting had reached a stage exemplified by Plate 1.3.

Here he was engaged in an interactive relationship with his picture and instead of painting on the easel, he had progressed to placing his paper on the floor where the flow from paint bottles could be aided by gravity. No longer simply spontaneous, he exerted some control in the way he directed the bottle of paint and when he decided to stop but he also enjoyed the lack of total control he had over the liquid paint. I could observe how absorbed he was by his interaction with the materials, gazing at the resulting image as it built up on paper in a way that was reminiscent of Pollock in photographs of him at work (Plate 1.4).

When the paper was sufficiently covered to please him, Paul moved on to the next art activity. By this point in art therapy, Paul had also discovered the technique of picture-folding (Plate 1.5) which could be understood as a step towards introducing structure to his image-making as it meant he could reliably produce a simple but balanced form out of something which was originally amorphous; he was extending his agency while still confining his interest to the process itself. It was after he had discovered this art process that Paul began to summon me to look at his work with him to share his surprise.

It seemed he now sought the affirmation of joint gazing which may be a missed experience in children like Paul whose early life has been affected by trauma so that the normal joint looking with mother has not been part of development (Isserow, 2008). This simple interaction that was repeated between us many times in art therapy was in fact a means to realise that the same emotional reaction can be felt by another person and that sharing on this level brings a sense of being known and empathising.

Paul was developing ideas in his work now, and with this came a greater degree of intent than in the simpler pictures of the first three months. He would also sometimes give his pictures a title, which Dubowski and James (1998) suggest marks a development in the realm of imaginative thought.

My analysis led me to question why Paul went from one art activity to the next in the early and middle phases of art therapy, giving so little attention to the finished work. In terms of Ehrenzweig's theory, it seemed that Paul's art process emphasised the first two stages, in particular the second, oceanic stage in the process. For a boy who had suffered maternal deprivation, the oceanic state offered an experience of symbiosis or being at one with an object. Instead of taking pleasure in the final stage in the process, where the separate existence of the painting was acknowledged, Paul went as quickly as possible from a state of being merged with one painting to starting a new one, evidently finding fulfilment of need in this – perhaps a relief from the psychic isolation of an insecurely attached infant. Ehrenzweig (1967) suggests that this third phase is attenuated in 'modern art' too (by which he implies Abstract Expressionists). Pollock's description of his action painting as an 'easy give and take' between artist, paper and materials in which 'there is no beginning and no end' (Chipp, 1968: 546), explains this art process well.

A Watershed

Plate 1.6 appeared three quarters of the way through art therapy and surprised me at the time by the suddenness of its new method. It was a highly structured and considered painting, marking a change in the therapy and a new stage of cognitive and emotional growth. Thinking again about the meaning of Paul's art process and why one way of working might follow another, the middle stage could be seen as a natural bridge to this new position as Paul was already introducing conscious thought to his process. Plate 1.6 was unique in taking two sessions to make. Paul used the motif of what looks like an eye or lozenge shape and, with a very small brush, composed the picture using a system that he developed and applied throughout. His sense of what result he wanted developed as he worked and Paul knew when it was finished. There was more consciousness in the composition.

He painted black shapes that he gave a blue inside, thus creating a container-and-contained motif. Smaller black lozenges were given a red outline that made the shapes more balanced in size; this began to create a homogeneous feel to the whole image. He took care with placement, seeking a certain kind of balance. Then red lozenges were added and this time acquired black interiors. The use of primary colours and black gave the picture intensity and impact. The final stroke was to add the yellow as a background, intuitively finding the third primary colour; this allowed Paul to re-state the shape of the lozenges. The yellow ground performed a unifying function, linking the shapes and giving the impression of cells floating. It was a highly achieved painting and marked a move into symbolism where Paul had formed his materials to communicate an idea. Thinking psychodynamically, one might describe the picture as representational of his feeling a sense of internal integration. Paul said nothing about the picture but we stood and admired it, exchanging pleased expressions that spoke without words. Schaverien describes this phase as a stage of 'familiarisation' (1991). Unlike the period when he was merged with his painting, Paul saw this picture as a separate entity. This enhanced his self-esteem through identifying himself as its creator (Schaverien, 1991). After this painting, further symbolic pictures were made in the last five months before Paul left the school, some of them expressing his feelings about ending, which we could now discuss.

Changes in the Classroom and at Home

Other findings draw on the differing texts associated with Paul's case. In our first meeting Paul's mother described how poor his coordination and fine motor control were; this was reiterated in an occupational therapy report which noted his hand tremor when he was under pressure to perform tasks. In art therapy, where there was an absence of pressure to perform, Paul managed delicate manipulative tasks, including cutting with scissors. His physical involvement in painting, from the early gestural pictures onwards, must also have supported a growing sense of physical cohesion and ownership of his body and movements which, as Stern points out, is deficient when early nurture has not created this through handling and responding to the baby as a whole person (1985).

Five months into art therapy, Paul's mother was excited to tell me in one of our regular reviews that he was happier and also more confident to try things rather than fearing failure. He was expressing a new curiosity about the world and asking her lots of questions. My process notes and the images from the early months leading up to this meeting indicate that Paul had, by then, been making experimental mixtures in containers for two months and that, building on his early gestural paintings where he relished the sensuousness of thick and dripping paint, had just made his first folded pictures. This was a developmental advance: folding a painted image implies less passivity and more active manipulation of a work. On a personal level, greater confidence and more sense of his own agency were implied and this is what Paul's mother reported.

At the same time, Paul's teacher said in a review that his anxious flights from the classroom had stopped. I think this indicates that his experimental interaction with art materials in a safe environment and questioning me about my own experience was already transforming his internal model of reality into something more solid and shareable where taking risks did not present such a threat.

There was another important change in the classroom after just over a year of art therapy when Paul began to form and communicate his own ideas. In another review his teacher reported that Paul was now participating in classroom discussions for the first time. The timing of this was linked with the painting of Plate 1.6 which I described as introducing a new, symbolic stage in his art-making where Paul discovered and developed an idea. Paul's art development was therefore directly linked to the development of his mentalizing process.

There was also a change in the intimacy of our relationship by this later stage, which I had recorded in my process notes, as Paul began to allow and value my empathy which, in the first year of art therapy, would have been experienced as a threatening impingement. A new element of humour appeared between us as Paul recognised that relationship could be a source of pleasure.

Discussion

I set out to discover what aspects of making art might help children like Paul to access experiences missed in early life and asked what aspects of Paul's art process supported change and repair of developmental deficits. A key observation was that Paul was able to regress and find gratification in the use of tactile materials in a spontaneous way which helped him discover a sense of agency. This observation also answers another of my research questions about whether engagement with art materials could offer gratification of a sense of unfulfilled need because, as his enthusiastic engagement in art therapy showed, even before I understood what his process was about Paul was telling me he was 'longing and longing for more and more of this'. He said that the reason he liked art therapy was 'because I can do what I want', which might be interpreted as doing what had meaning for him and what he needed.

It appeared that the opportunity to use materials stimulated a missing drive to creativity which enabled Paul to engage in a developmental process that he could work through at his own pace, without fear of impingement by the therapist. He found meaning at every level of discovery in the art process before moving on to subsequent levels, as new skills and understandings were reached and built on. This shows how art therapy can perform the reparative function which Kut-Rosenfeld and Sprince suggest are needed by children with developmental deficits (1965).

Paul's process started concretely with spontaneous marks that mirrored his gestures and feelings, enabling him to feel less fragmented and more connected, in concrete terms, with his physical and emotional self. In this way my question about whether art therapy can provide self-experiences which have been missed in early life is partially answered. He handled materials in an experimental way that connected him with his environment, aroused his curiosity and increased the sense of meaning in his experience. He finally reached a symbolic stage where he was able to structure experience and impose his own meanings on it, at which point his art became a communicative process. His subsequent sense of ownership of his work led to increased self-esteem and sense of himself as a communicator. All these elements link to other aspects of self: self as communicator and as a creator of organisation together with a sense of continuity or going on being that were developed through regular sessions and the solidity of the therapeutic alliance that helped him experience being known and held in mind.

One of the deficits noted at the beginning was Paul's lack of ability to think and form ideas. From the moment he began to find structure in the art therapy and repeated meaningful activities, the art process was clearly triggering ideas which he acted on. While initially Paul gained a sense of immediate and primitive gratification in swirling paint on paper or mixing tactile materials in pots, evacuating and representing material as Thomas (1998) and O'Brien (2004) describe, there was increasing interplay between unconscious and conscious mark-making as time went on and as his sense of mastery and omnipotence increased. This research has shown how Paul's achievement in the art process was immediately reflected in the way he became able to function at a higher level in his life outside the art therapy room, just as in Meyerowitz-Katz (2004), where four-year-old Alex started to communicate more at home once he could interact more with his therapist in sessions, even though the focus of their conversation was uniquely about the art process.

Through investigation and application of theories on the development of self, on attachment theory and on normal development in general, this research suggests that at the same time as the art materials helped Paul develop his ability to find meaning in the world and create his own meanings, they also provided him with essential self-experiences as described in Stern (1985); this had been precluded by his early insecure attachment to his mother.

Paul's stronger sense of self and his growing sense of the world as more predictable, gained from his art-making experience, reduced the immediacy of his spiralling anxiety quite quickly; this affected the rigidity of his defences and allowed him to relate to me a little more, experiencing what Stern described as a subjective self. This matches Meyerowitz-Katz' finding that her four-year-old client became less defended and able to form an alliance with her once he felt he had some control in his art process (a sense of control that was made more obvious because it was in the form of concrete marks and therefore visible).

The changes and progress were possible because, as Paul told me early on, he found the room and art therapist quiet and calm. He was able to relax vigilance and be creative, which implied his sense of being safe.

From Research into Practice

When I was working with Paul I had faith in the process but did not fully understand the therapeutic nature of his activities. This research clarified the elements that supported change and why, and equipped me for future work in the field. In particular I was made aware of the value of experiment and repetition in concrete art activity for children who need to discover their own agency and find meaning in the world around them. The results of this retrospective review also showed how important it is to be aware that if art is not symbolic it must be reviewed as a concrete body of work if meaning is to be found.

Both this study and the other literature I have referred to indicate that the art therapist working in this field is vulnerable to countertransference feelings of being overwhelmed by meaninglessness that is hard to contain (which is of course the child's experience). Knowing this to be a potential factor is an important and strengthening insight for my future work with similarly deprived children.

The research also indicates the kind of art therapy environment that may stimulate the child with developmental deficits to engage in the art therapy process. Materials with sensory qualities including water, sand, liquid paints and glue, as well as a selection of containers and general collection of junk materials, are indicated as valuable or even essential to this process. My research also alerted me to the possibility that feelings from which the patient wishes to distance himself can be embodied or tried out in the artwork.

Art therapy in the treatment of children with early trauma leading to developmental deficits needs a different approach from work within the context of normal development. I learnt that, because part of the work in therapy with children with developmental deficits is about giving them the opportunity to find meaning in their interactions with the materials and stimulating the development of thinking, and because the development of the art process has an important function in terms of providing experience of normal progression (of one thing leading to another at a pace that is manageable to the child), this is work that cannot be rushed. It must synchronize with the child's pace. Interpretations that put the child in touch with feelings too early, promote a spiralling anxiety and create an experience of the original primary relationship that he or she wants to avoid; this can inhibit their engagement in the early stages of art therapy. What the child needs is an experience of what has been missed pre-verbally. Therefore a non-directive approach, where he or she can experiment and experience their own efficacy whilst also feeling confirmed and contained, is indicated. However, it should be acknowledged that some art therapists who work with children who have suffered prolonged neglect or abuse (Rabiger, 1990; Henley, 2005) favour a more structured approach which avoids a regression that they describe as counterproductive.

While the topic of this research was art therapy in the repair of developmental deficits, my study of the role and function of the art process has drawn attention to the way in which the art process offers a range of the self-experiences that Stern describes (1985). This important aspect of art therapy is available to all art therapy clients and could be given fresh attention by the profession.

These findings suggest that the opportunity to engage in art therapy offers a more optimistic prognosis for highly anxious and insecurely attached children with developmental deficits than a therapeutic intervention that relies heavily on dialogue in the therapeutic relationship. This research has demonstrated how Paul was able to begin a process of dramatic change through relating to the materials unharried, with the art therapist playing a bit part in the background (not withstanding the important containment provided) until he had made enough progress to enter into a fuller relationship. This maintained his engagement and was the concrete means of strengthening a stronger core of self.

This research confirmed my hypothesis that the art process in art therapy supports the repair of developmental deficits. I was able to demonstrate the central role of the art materials in the art therapy of a child who could not symbolise and show how the changes evolved and were linked to changes in the child's behaviour at home and in school.

UWE HERRMANN

2 The Tangible Reflection: A Single Case Study Investigating Body Image Development in Art Psychotherapy with a Congenitally Blind Client

Abstract

This chapter summarizes a retrospective single case study of art therapy with a congenitally blind adolescent who developed sculptures concerned with her body-self image, its structure and its boundaries. Our collaborative scrutiny of her sculptures followed the closing of a five year therapeutic process. Discerning eight body image groups, this investigation deepened my client's understanding of her biography and sculptures and enabled her to achieve an increasingly differentiated and integrated image of her body-self. The client's clay modelling closely related to her growing ego functioning. This resulted in theory building, an elaboration of a visual research methodology, and a change in my therapeutic practice with the blind.

Key Words

art psychotherapy; retrospective single case study; collaborative research; art-based visual research; congenital blindness; modelling; body image; sensory filter; tactile mirror.

How it all Began: from Practice to Research

In 1991, establishing an art therapy service at a German state school for blind entailed professional isolation: I was the only art therapist on site and, seemingly, the only one working in this field in Europe. Three years into my work, I observed how long-term art therapy successfully addressed the high rate of psychological disturbances in congenitally blind clients, often with the emergence of sculptural self-representations. I wondered how blindness impeded the individual's emerging body-self concept and how sculptural body conceptualization aided the formation of a sense of self. To improve the effectiveness of my clinical work, I needed a deeper understanding of this phenomenon which, given my isolation, only research into my own practice could provide.

The Context of the Research

In order to formulate my research question I needed to establish what was known about blindness and the body in art therapy and in psychoanalysis. As I reviewed the literature the term 'body image' caught my attention. This concept represents the individual's continuous demarcation from the external world, the ability to distinguish between 'me' and 'not – me', inside and outside body boundaries, based on body perceptions and on the internalized, reciprocal relationship between the body and the environment. The psychoanalytic literature stresses the crucial role of vision in forming an image of one's body:

> In constructing a body image, vision offers a unique advantage that no other sensory mode can duplicate: ... the picture by its nature can unite in one percept, or as a memory flash, all the attributes and parts into a whole. (Adelson and Fraiberg, 1973: 559)

The authors argue that the blind child must compose a body image through non-visual perceptions. However, these alternative sensory means differ from the unifying mode of the visual image as they do not instantaneously replicate the body or its parts as a whole gestalt. Most psychoanalytic researchers had found body image distortion in congenitally blind clients and linked these problems to the frequent occurrence of lags in ego development and its organizing functions (Warren, 1984). This link between the two phenomena might explain why the more widely used term 'body image' is interchangeable with 'body-self' or 'body-ego'. Omwake and Solnit (1961) are perhaps most outspoken on the relationship between body image disturbance and ego development. They believed that blindness prevented the construction of a sensory filter, a visual psychic image of body boundaries, which resulted in a weakness of repressive abilities that protect the child's ego. Though psychoanalytic authors strongly connect body image and ego development in theory, there was no reference to working with body image in practice. However, Warren (1984) observed a general lack of 'substitute experiences' to assist body image development in the blind and of accompanying procedures to assess the effectiveness of interventions (98).

Although art educator Victor Lowenfeld pioneered artwork with the blind (1934, 1939), literature on art therapy and blindness is scarce. Kramer (1971, 2000), Rubin (1978) and Henley (1991) have paid particular attention to the art process and describe a strengthened feeling of self and self-acceptance in art therapy with the blind; previously I had described how suppressed anger and retaliatory wishes at the sighted were explored in the clay modelling of the blind (Herrmann, 1995). Both Henley and Kramer (1979) underscored the particular suitability of clay for the blind and how it facilitated object relations.

Assisting body image construction and ego development through clay modelling with the blind seemed largely unexplored. However, art therapy has undertaken such work with other client populations (Killick and Greenwood, 1995; Levens, 1995). These authors all mention the psychoanalyst Gisela Pankow (1981) who used modelling with psychotic patients. A disturbance in the symbolising functions of the ego was known to interfere with verbal analytic therapy. Pankow pioneered an assisted construction of the patient's body image through a third object, outside the therapist's and the patients' bodies, before verbal psychoanalysis commenced. Through an exploration of the lost relationship between form and content of their bodies, patients were able to achieve a 'dynamic structurization' of their body image (170) which Pankow regarded as paramount to the restoration of a capacity to symbolise.

Pankow pointed out that, unlike the schizophrenic, neurotic patients experience the body as symbolically dismembered, although still as one entity. She distinguished between two functions of body image: a spatial function concerned with the dialectics between body parts and the whole on a formal level, and another where body image operates as a depiction of personal content.

The gap in the literature was clear and revealed how this study might provide a novel outlook in an under-researched and under-practiced field. Psychoanalysis with the blind, while noting body image disturbance, had not worked with sculpture. Art therapy had addressed body image with other populations, but not with the blind. I wondered if the role of sculpture in enhancing body image and ego structures could be investigated more deeply in the work of one of my congenitally blind patients and distilled three research questions from the reviewed literature:

1. Can forms of body image representation be identified in a blind individual's sculptures in art therapy?
2. Can these body image representations be linked to the client's ego development?
3. Do the client's sculptures provide a substitute for the organizational function of sight?

Method

Given the paucity of literature and the immediacy of my work at the school, I chose the single case study method as most appropriate to explore these questions in depth. I had a particular patient in mind who was shortly to end art therapy. Her sculptures exuded a striking physicality, indicating that they might concern issues of 'body' and 'self', yet the specifics of their vast variations and interconnections remained obscure as the end of therapy approached.

Rebecca, a sixteen-year-old, congenitally blind girl, had come for weekly, non-directive art therapy sessions for five years and five months. The case material, or data, fell into three distinct sets:

1. Rebecca's 63 clay sculptures.
2. My case notes containing descriptions of one hundred and eight sessions, Rebecca's sculptures and verbatim accounts of our conversations.
3. Two imminent retrospective review sessions with Rebecca which I planned to audio-tape and transcribe as part of the ending of art therapy.

A single case study analyses variance within one case (Chassan, 1979; Warren, 1984; Hilliard, 1993; McLeod, 1994). For art therapy, Gilroy (1992) points to the possibilities of this qualitative research model for theory building as 'cumulative evidence' (235). Similarly, Edwards (1999) highlights its place alongside quantitative research and its strengths involving the client's, the therapist's, and the supervisor's voices. He, like Gilroy (1996, 2006), has called for a sound procedure in following through the study. McLeod (2001) points to examples of rigorously analysed individual case narratives and underscores the case study's 'storytelling' nature as a valid method of gaining insight into the nuts and bolts of the therapeutic process.

As Gilroy (1996) writes, the individual process of art therapy is not easily replicated. Also, different professionals, or client and therapist, might draw different conclusions from the same case (McLeod, 1994). While some authors advocate independent raters for objectification or triangulation, Gilroy (1992) suggests that, as art therapists place the patients' understandings of their art work at the centre of their practice, 'perhaps as researchers we should pay attention to the patient's assessment of a successful outcome in art therapy' (237). This conforms to collaborative research models involving client and therapist (Yalom and Elkin, 1974; Mearns and Thorne, 1988; Dryden and Yankura, 1992) and has been demonstrated in art therapy by McClelland's (1993) use of video in her collaborative practice with clients in acute states.

In art therapy, Rebecca had told her story primarily through her sculptures, words following sometimes weeks afterwards. While psychotherapy research is often based on recorded verbal material, Schaverien has pioneered the retrospective analysis of images in art therapy (1993, 1995). She highlights the benefits of this retrospective review:

> Seen in sequence, links may be made between pictures and it is possible to re-evaluate the meanings of particular works in the context of those which both precede and succeed them (...). It may become clear that certain themes, colours, figures or types of marks are repeated in different pictures, these taking on quite different implications from those initially intended. (1992: 75–6).

In the present study, a visual and tactile retrospective display of Rebecca's artwork took the lead in helping me to formulate my ideas whilst my eye-witness records of her art process, together with Rebecca's verbatim commentary, provided a rich context in which to analyze and interpret the visual material.

Rebecca and I had scheduled two retrospective review sessions before she left the institution. We were both curious about the retrospective review but I realised that I could invite her to collaborate in the research through these sessions. Our curiosity seemed a safe enough vehicle for moving from the roles of patient and therapist to those of researcher and co-researcher. Thus the research grew from our intertwined desires for knowledge. For Rebecca, my patient, therapy had arisen from her pressing need to know more about herself; its impending end had generated a wish to make sense of her artwork and of her story from a distance. My interest developed similarly from a need to make sense of our work but there was also a wish to improve my understanding of my practice with other congenitally blind clients.

With Rebecca's consent, I taped and transcribed the two retrospective review sessions. The whole process of these two sessions seemed to be an empowering experience for Rebecca. The transference relationship noticeably dissolved as our initial, general and rather vague curiosity turned into an objectifying, enquiring investigation. Side by side, we explored her sculptures, chronologically arrayed as a tactile panorama some twenty metres in length. I found the metaphor of a panorama helpful in terms of its use as a research approach. For a mountaineer, a panorama facilitates a wide view of the completed route, showing links in a landscape's formations that could not be appreciated at the time of the climb. In Rebecca's panorama, we identified art therapy's peaks and valleys, the significant experiences and interlocking themes which revealed a flow of surprisingly rich, interwoven groups. Our joint feeling about the intensity and importance of a particular sculpture in the therapy and in the review enabled us to pinpoint key sculptures which would best represent a category. These constituted a core for each of the categories we were able to identify and around which the other sculptures clustered.

Rebecca's review session comments became a crucial source of data in this research and assumed a prominent position in all the stages of the subsequent research process. According to McLeod (1994), the analysis of qualitative data is based on five elemental stages: immersion, categorization, phenomenological reduction, triangulation and interpretation. While immersion involves the researcher in an initial internalization of the data in an empathic way, categorization requires the data to be systematically broken down into smaller meaning units. These categories are further scrutinized through a process of phenomenological reduction; this requires the researcher to suspend his or her early assumptions and to identify possible alternative ways of understanding. Through a process of triangulation, central, recurring categories are distinguished from less prominent or false ones; these are finally interpreted against a backdrop of pre-existing theory in order to establish the findings. I incorporated these strategies into seven research stages:

Stage 1. Establishing the background: reviewing the literature on art therapy, body image and psychoanalysis with the blind.

Stage 2. First immersion: photographic documentation of all sculptures; chronological array of photographs.

Stage 3. Second immersion: creation of a tactile panorama of Rebecca's sculptures in preparation for the taped and transcribed retrospective review sessions; collaborative identification of key sculptures and groups by form and content.

Stage 4. Third immersion: looking at the entirety of the visual and text-based data; writing up the case narrative; description of images and sessions in depth.
Stage 5. Further categorization of formal and thematic elements indicating body image representation.
Stage 6. Phenomenological reduction and triangulation using artwork, session notes and review transcripts to identify significant body image categories.
Stage 7. Interpretation of body image categories in relation to psycho-analytic and art therapy theory.

The review tapes and transcripts ensured that Rebecca's voice was with me as I triangulated the session material and artwork with her and my views in stages five and six. This meant constantly shifting back and forth between imagery, case notes and review transcripts to test whether my ideas held true on all levels, if they stayed true to Rebecca's perspective on her work, and to check if there were any contradictions that needed consideration.

Case Narrative

Born three months premature, excess oxygen blinded Rebecca in the incubator. Her father left the family shortly after her birth, supposedly because of her blindness. At age six Rebecca entered our school and its boarding facilities, returning home for weekends. For several years she seemed to have adjusted satisfactorily to her new environment but when she was sixteen Rebecca was referred to art therapy for anxiety attacks, feelings of low self-worth and threats of suicide. For the institution, Rebecca's wellbeing and completion of her training seemed at stake. In art therapy her childhood experience of clay modelling with her grandfather led Rebecca to work enthusiastically and exclusively with clay. Throughout therapy there was a distinct pattern: Rebecca would arrive anxious, crying and confused but would quickly regain her equilibrium when using the clay.

Early Work: Auxiliary Bodies

In the first year, Rebecca created comforting, helping and guarding figures, often compensating for her blindness with imaginary sensory gadgets. Hinting at hidden inner conflict, a few sculptures displayed conflicting good, rescuing and bad, persecutory figures. Rebecca avoided exploring these early sculptures in relation to her self. An example of these auxiliary bodies is Rebecca's work from the second therapy session. Arriving in a desolate state, Rebecca created two objects (Plates 2.1a and 2.1b), one completely closed and one opened up. Absorbed by the clay modelling, Rebecca felt much better as the session ended.

While these objects remained cryptic at the time, the review session revealed the open shape to be a cross section of the closed one, displaying a nourishing interior pipe system. In the review, Rebecca remembered an unspoken fantasy at the time of making: she had imagined these objects as responding to sound and that they, in return, made soothing sounds.

In the review, Rebecca never regarded the group of auxiliary sculptures as representing her self and seldom as the image of another, real, person. For her they were helpful yet mysterious 'other' bodies. In order to understand the supplementary function of these auxiliary bodies I recalled Pankow's (1981) observation that psychotic patients regard their sculptures as unrelated outside objects, that is until their body image had been sufficiently structured. As bodies separate from Rebecca's own body, her sculptures represented a first stage in her body image consolidation. The mere making of these sculptures reduced Rebecca's anxieties but she avoided verbal exploration. At this stage the tactile quality of clay modelling seemed to function as a repressive barrier or filter against her anxieties. I will discuss this in more depth later on.

Changing Bodies

Towards the end of the first year, the auxiliary bodies were replaced by sculptures focusing on change and ageing as a physical and emotional process. Rebecca also began to represent herself. In a series of gyroscope figures, she related the symbol of the gyroscope to safe change. One of them depicts Rebecca as part human, part gyroscope (Plate 2.2). In a play on words she explained that the gyrating figure may turn but that it always ends up in the same place, just as in the change process a person is still – though changed – 'herself' afterwards.

Our physical body is probably the most manifest evidence of our 'self'. However, from the moment of the first mirror-self recognition in early childhood, bodily change poses a conundrum: it must become integrated into our body-self image. The sighted resolve this through constant use of the mirror. Emotional and physical changes may not necessarily be in step but the mirror image may reassure the viewer of their body's permanence in spite of invisible emotional change. As Omwake and Solnit (1961) observed, a blind person may conceive change to be safe only with difficulty. These sculptures functioned as tactile organisers and enabled Rebecca to examine her emotional and physical changes in the absence of vision. Modelling, as a kind of tactile mirror, was vital for Rebecca, who could never rely on the reassurance of a visual mirror image. I will return to this idea at a later point in the chapter.

Passive Victim-Bodies

With the concept of safe change established, more unconscious material was able to emerge in the second year of art therapy and a new category of body image emerged. These sculptures displayed Rebecca's body as a passive object, victimized and possessed by 'others'. Conflict, covertly indicated in the group of auxiliary figures, now became the predominant theme; this continued until therapy ended.

Rebecca produced the initial piece of this group after a teacher had bluntly advised her to separate emotionally from her mother. Rebecca arrived for her session crying and unable to think. Again, modelling restored her composure. The sculpture showed her restrained on a block of stone; two figures, representing mother and teacher, pulled her in opposite directions with chains which were attached to her body, reminiscent of umbilical cords. Between the two opponents, a Solomon-like, fourth figure held a knife which might cut her loose (Plate 2.3).

After modelling, Rebecca described the figure with the knife, who could resolve the struggle, as representing me. However, in the retrospective review she understood the figure more as a representation of her own growing ego or, as Rebecca phrased it, her insight. While the figure representing Rebecca reminded me of a helpless, screaming infant, the umbilical chains indicated that her passive body still belonged to '(m)others'. Laufer (1968) remarked that the derivatives of a failed bodily separation in childhood results in the adolescent's inability to experience the mature body as belonging to him or herself. Rebecca's concept of her passive victim-body indicated an arrested developmental phase, revived when external demands on Rebecca's functioning as an autonomous adult had increased and been crudely expressed. The sculptural representation of her poorly separated body enabled Rebecca to fantasize about the possibility of separation. This produced highly ambivalent feelings which needed to be contained and which gave rise to another group of sculptures.

Container-Bodies

Through her second and third years, Rebecca created a cluster of work exploring her body as either protective or restraining and as a closed or open container. The initial sculpture of this group shows a figure merged with an urn (Plate 2.4). Rebecca titled the sculpture 'Ambivalence' and explained that the vessel contained two opposite things. The figure was to be confronted with the vessel's contents, its hand signalling silence and warning.

Even though Rebecca did not relate the image to the previous theme of conflicting opposites, the warning gesture may have been partly directed at me to not uncover dangerous content. In the review session Rebecca confirmed that, at the time, she could not deal with what the figure on the urn guarded. She clearly perceived the vessel's function as protective, saving her environment and herself from her supposedly dangerous impulses. Their embodiment in a sculpture provided her with tactile confirmation that these feelings were under control. However, as the review sessions showed, with the container tightly closed, both opposites – fantasies of a passive and an aggressive body – were to remain ambivalent until they were explored on a more conscious level.

Halfway through her third year in therapy, Rebecca's container imagery changed from closed to open shapes which displayed detailed interiors. Alongside her continuing clay modelling, memories emerged of traumatic physical and emotional transgressions by educational and hospital staff. Rebecca remembered these as losing control over her body, feeling like a container into which 'everybody can stuff anything, whatever they wish'. As Rebecca worked through these bitter memories sculpturally and verbally, she developed variants of container bodies, ranging from closed to open, from restraining to protective. Finally, she arrived at an open container capable of protecting, holding and ordering its conflicting contents.

As Rebecca conceptualized her body sculptures as containers, she acknowledged the ambivalence inherent to their function. Dalley (2000), referring to Meltzer's (1975) concept of the 'claustrum', points to the art room, the session, and the artwork, as instrumental for expressing, holding and processing conflicting attitudes to containment. Rebecca's container-body variants aided the formation of a concept of the body as 'holding within' and 'keeping without.' As tactile organizers substituting for vision, these container-bodies remedied Rebecca's history of body boundary transgressions and her environment's inability to provide containment.

Aggressive Bodies

Beginning her third year in art therapy, Rebecca conceptualized her body as an aggressive agent in another cluster of sculptures. After an incident of self-harm (in the form of beating herself) for poor school performance, Rebecca created the first piece of this series. This showed a larger figure beating a smaller one (Plate 2.5).

Exploring the sculpture, Rebecca related these figures to three internal self-protagonists and assigned them names. There was victim 'Becky', persecutory 'Rebecca', and a third, nameless and unrepresented figure. The adversaries were united by a reciprocal incompleteness of their bodies: while the aggressive 'Rebecca' had a face but lacked legs, the victim 'Becky' had legs but was faceless. Astonished, Rebecca recognized that they might be part of each other. In the ensuing group of aggressive bodies Rebecca acknowledged her aggressive feelings as belonging to herself and that she had been sculpturally exploring their safe enactment. In the review she realized that both protagonists represented the opposites contained in the urn sculpture.

Until this point in art therapy, Rebecca had shown a marked absence of aggressive feelings towards either staff or her peers at the school. This phenomenon is often observed in the literature on the congenitally blind (Warren, 1984). In the passive body cluster I had first noticed Rebecca's use of flat, stage-like bases on which she set her sculptures. Rebecca's much more emphatic beating of these clay bases indicated their function as a vehicle for aggressive discharge. She was eventually able to confide her apprehension about the potential destructiveness of her anger. Burlingham (1961) and Curson (1979) hypothesize that, in the absence of visual control, the blind individual fantasizes that aggression will cause disaster once unleashed from the body. I suggest that in the self-harm incident, Rebecca had initially used her own body as an accessible and quasi-external object for aggressive discharge. However, in her clay modelling Rebecca could divert her impulses to the material *in lieu* of her physical body, investigating aggression in an increasingly conscious way: first on a sensory level, beating the bases; then as aggressive-body sculptures, which she finally understood to be part of her self.

Integrated Bodies

Initially exploring passive and aggressive body concepts separately, Rebecca integrated both in a new cluster of sculptures. The first piece of this group shows 'Becky' and 'Rebecca' at a negotiating table. A third figure represented a witness-mediator, writing down a peace treaty (Plate 2.6).

In the retrospective review Rebecca linked this mediator to her insightful ego. Unlike the previous, potentially intervening figure with the knife, she described this negotiator as part of her self. A fourth person, sitting at the very edge of the base, represented me, clearly at a distance. This indicated that a remote auxiliary ego was still needed whilst Rebecca increasingly assumed this function for herself.

During Rebecca's third year in therapy the mediating ego figure adopted a powerful role, integrating the conflicting active and passive body concepts on a sculptural and psychic level; no representation of me as an auxiliary ego could be found. In this cluster, three new sculptural elements appeared, enriching Rebecca's symbolic repertoire: a head, as the successor to the mediating figure, represented conscious ego control; a wire-like connection subjected the aggressive protagonists to the controlling ego-head; lastly, a wall structured all the sculptural tableaux. It safeguarded Rebecca's body from being trespassed, controlled excessive aggressive discharge, and kept passive and aggressive inner protagonists at bay.

The review also revealed how the clay bases gradually became more than a vehicle for the discharge of aggression or a technical solution which united different sculptural elements. They represented Rebecca's growing awareness of one unified body-self that reconciled passive and aggressive body-self concepts. Rebecca's increasing sculptural sophistication and ego development were entwined. While the ego-head served as conscious mediator, the walls had the function of assigning distinct areas to Rebecca's sculptural and imaginary protagonists. As both a protection and a boundary, they served as a demarcation of intrapsychic boundaries, separating 'me' from 'not-me' and confirming ownership of her body. During this process our verbal exploration increased, much as Pankow (1981) describes the dynamic structuring of her psychotic patients' body image through modelling preceded verbal psychoanalysis.

Transformed Bodies

Towards the end of her fourth year in therapy, Rebecca's body image was going through further changes. She worked on an enormous sculpture of herself for several months but deserted it halfway through (Plate 2.7).

At this point dreams provided inspiration for new sculptures and brought fresh material to therapy. The prominent theme of the dreams and the sculptures was her development of a new, transformed body which, in human or animal shape, possessed a physical strength fit to defend itself with instinctive force. Rebecca enacted this transformation by disassembling her unfinished self-portrait and reclaiming the material. Soaking the fragments for an entire session she listened to the sounds of the dissolving clay, enthralled by its audible change from hard to soft. For her, this process seemed like alchemy, echoing the theme of change on a more radical, experimental and self-induced level. Again, the art material enabled the safe organisation of internal impulses and acted as a substitute for visual control.

In this cluster, the clay ego-head was absent. The review sessions revealed Rebecca's satisfaction with the ways in which these body sculptures enabled her to enact her aggression without painstaking thought and a disastrous ending. Five years into therapy Rebecca now turned to the last group of body images and perhaps her greatest challenge: her conflicting feelings about her father.

Father Bodies

During our final six months of art therapy Rebecca explored her relationship to her father in a new series of sculptures. She used the reclaimed clay from her unfinished self-portrait for this last group of sculptures, indicating that his and her images, which were physically and emotionally entangled, needed to be reshaped.

Referring derogatorily to her father as her 'genitor', Rebecca planned to rid herself of her hatred towards him by destroying his clay effigy. After several unsuccessful attempts she concluded that never having seen him posed a problem: the ritual was not satisfying without a real likeness. Two previously unconscious beliefs emerged. Rebecca disclosed that her father had insisted on her emergency baptism. This, according to family myth, had delayed her placement in the incubator and caused her blindness. She also remembered two older, stillborn brothers whose death she described as murder because of her father's careless treatment of her pregnant mother. Rebecca felt that her father had attempted to 'kill' her with the baptism, like her brothers before.

Rebecca also acknowledged her long-held belief that her blindness had made her dangerous as it had ousted her father. Following a session that I had cancelled Rebecca once again tried to model her father's face. It turned into a self-portrait which she described as screaming to be accepted and not deserted (Plate 2.8).

It transpired that in the transference thc cancelled session was proof that she had scared me away, as she supposedly had expelled her father. Exploring this belief in therapy enabled Rebecca to explore the story at home; her mother admitted that her husband had left the marriage for another relationship.

Working on the father-bodies Rebecca was able to acknowledge that her family had stressed the physical likeness between father and daughter all her life, infusing Rebecca with a poisonous heritage of a 'bad' father-self image. Rebecca hated the idea of being 'flesh of his flesh'. At this point she recognized her self-beating as a wish to punish and destroy the father inside her own body, and her feelings of worthlessness and suicidal thoughts as an attempt to rid herself from this unwanted physical patrimony and of the 'father within'.

The unconscious idea of carrying her father's body inside her own emerged as a core conflict. Her physical likeness to him had created an ambivalent body-self image: Rebecca as the victim of fatherly aggression and deprivation and Rebecca as the persecutor, giving rise to the split between the bodies of 'Becky' and 'Rebecca.' For Rebecca this recognition was the final cut through a Gordian knot of hatred and guilt which gave way to reconciliation.

Reconciliation

When Rebecca shared her insights at home her shocked mother further mollified her views about Rebecca's father. The myth of the murderous father crumbled. Suggesting that her mother had been struck by her own persecutory reflection, I told Rebecca the myth of Perseus reflecting Medusa's deadly stare in his polished shield. In her last sculpture Rebecca retold the myth. It represents Medusa raising her arms in surrender, Perseus lifting his shield to kill her through her own reflection and a third figure preventing Medusa's destruction (Plate 2.9).

Rebecca now talked about her father's image as something she did not want to lose. In the review sessions, she recognised her two conflicting self-images as derivatives of her two internal father images and described their sculptural exploration as clarifying her own image. Rebecca identified the third figure as her ego, allowing her to settle this conflict and paving the way to reconciliation.

Shortly after, Rebecca, against all expectations, completed her training at the school, left and found a job. From the institution's educational eye this was evidence of art therapy's effectiveness. Invisible to this eye, Rebecca's gain had been much larger. She had survived her urge to kill herself and had resolved her share of unfinished family business, and she had owned her body, reflected in the tangible evidence of her sculptures.

Summary of Findings in Relation to the Research Questions

With regard to the first research question regarding different kinds of body representation in sculptures made by a blind individual, Rebecca and I were able to discern eight groups of body-self representation.

In the first group of auxiliary bodies, modelling established a sensory repressive filter for Rebecca's anxieties, while the second group of changing bodies enabled repressed material to emerge and confirmed change as essentially positive. As a third set of body-self representation, the passive bodies further illuminated this material, Rebecca's ego functions being partly invested in me as auxiliary ego. Through the fourth group of containing bodies Rebecca developed body boundary concepts and became aware of the ambivalence inherent in repression. In the fifth cluster, the aggressive bodies provided Rebecca with a model of aggression as a part of herself which needed organization and integration. The sixth group of integrated bodies merged aggressive and passive body-self fragments into one body concept. Ego functions emerged pictorially and became invested in herself, safeguarding Rebecca's further demarcation of interior and exterior body-self boundaries. The category of transformed bodies, differing from the changing bodies by comprising all previous work, confirmed this integration and prepared the way for an exploration of the father-bodies. In the eighth and final group, the father-bodies, Rebecca was able to differentiate her body from her father's whilst accepting their physical connection. This provided her with a strengthened, unified and individual sense of body-self. Understanding each category as a prerequisite for the subsequent one, this sequence recalls Pankow's (1981) dynamic structuring of body image from isolated fragments.

With regard to my second research question about the links between sculptural body image representations and ego development, these can clearly be seen to have unfolded in a reciprocal relationship. As the ego emerged as a concrete sculptural symbol in Rebecca's artwork, her conscious understanding of her body-self grew. Conversely, Rebecca's increased capacity for thought enhanced her use of artwork.

With regard to my third research question, Rebecca's work demonstrates two factors in art therapy's effectiveness with the blind: the sensory filter and the tactile mirror which I will now discuss.

Modelling as a Sensory Filter

Omwake and Solnit (1961) conclude that blindness interferes with the construction of a repressing filter. In the sighted this filter establishes, through visual selection, a hierarchy of internal and external perceptions, modifying, differentiating and balancing impulses and sensations. For Rebecca the sensory impact of clay modelling acted as a substitute for vision's organising function, creating a perceptual barrier which enabled her to repress her anxieties. Repression was the prerequisite for more conscious work; rather than establish insight these early sculptures helped her to 'forget' or to 'look away'. This explains why Rebecca remembered them in the review sessions as somehow soothing yet unrelated to her.

Omwake and Solnit also stress the need for 'a great deal of compensatory perceptual experience' for such defensive strategies to be developed within the blind individual, emphasizing the importance of the psychoanalyst's lead in play and verbalization in therapy (1961: 399). However, Rebecca's clay work was unsolicited and self-sustained, its tactile qualities particularly suiting her blindness. As Sandler and Wills (1963) observe, the blind child has 'the greatest difficulty in sustaining activities which do not lead to immediate somatic stimulation and discharge' (355). In art therapy and in the retrospective review sessions, Rebecca often mentioned how clay gave her both physical and emotional gratification. Responsive to touch, clay provided an instantaneous, enduring and self-maintained sensory stimulation which helped Rebecca to stay engaged. With this sensory filter successfully repressing her anxieties, the second feature of Rebecca's artwork was able to unfold: the image as a self.

The Tactile Mirror: Sculptures as Lasting Reflections

Adelson and Fraiberg (1973) believed that only sight can transform visual and non-visual perceptions into mental representations of self which unite body parts into an image. However, in the review Rebecca did not explore every part of her sculptures in order to reconstitute the image but instead briefly handled one element and was immediately able to recall the entire sculpture. This showed that Rebecca had formed very precise mental representations of her sculptures which did not rely on vision. The particular nature of the medium explains this phenomenon. Clay invites and retains artistic form. Rebecca used this potential to provide an enduring record of her imagination, exploring and fusing her body-self fragments into a complex but unified concept. Rebecca's sculptures constituted a differentiating and structuring tactile aid with which she was able to develop an increasingly organized body-self image. In a way they were similar to the mirror reflection for the sighted. Schaverien (1997), referring to Lacan's (1949) mirror stage, illuminates this role of the image: 'It is not a mirror but it may have a similar effect. (...) Like the mirror in the mirror-phase, it enables a sense of self as a whole to begin to cohere' (19).

Rebecca's sculptures differed from the specular image in two essential ways. First, they did not reflect objective physicality but instead facilitated Rebecca's developing conceptual ideas about her body-self fragments. Second, unlike the mirror reflection, sculptures persist and store ideas through their form. Rebecca could revisit and examine these complex body-self ideas through touch, like a sighted person returns to the mirror to confirm and examine the self's changing permanence. While clay modelling represented a tactile mirror, the sculptures constituted lasting body-self reflections. My role was to aid Rebecca's awareness of these forms and support her secondary process thinking. Through my descriptions and interpretations I was able to reflect these reflections until Rebecca could understand them as her 'self'.

Evaluation of the Research Process

Evaluating the vast amount of imagery, session notes and review material was laborious but in return it yielded the full picture and depth of the case study approach. While paring down 108 sessions into this brief research report has meant sacrificing much detail, it has also disclosed the essentials of Rebecca's work. The review material proved particularly useful for triangulation, complementing, confirming or challenging my assumptions. Discerning the categories in Rebecca's artwork, it would have been too literal to assume that body-self image was exclusively a representation of a human body. In the review sessions Rebecca and I learned that a broader outlook was necessary in order to capture her imagery's complexity and had to consider that potentially all the elements of a sculpture could represent a body-self. The number of sculptural variants was surprising, as was their developmental order, which showed that our long-term work was crucial for the successful outcome of therapy.

As her sculptures had enhanced Rebecca's capacity for thought in art therapy it also guided our collaborative thinking in our inquiry, revealing a kinship of therapy and research. The tactile panorama of the retrospective review together with my visual array of photographs of Rebecca's sculptures, foregrounded them in the research. These art-based, aesthetic elements of the method suited both Rebecca and me. In retrospect I realized how much this meeting of blind and sighted aesthetics had been intrinsic to the method, revealing the previously unconscious dynamics of our blind-sighted encounter.

From Research into Practice

Completing the investigation felt very much like a spark of ignition. Its findings immediately enhanced my practice with other congenitally blind clients. However, this did not mean that I applied the findings from this research indiscriminately. Rather, I understood Rebecca's successful use of art therapy as evidence of art therapy's effectiveness with one, congenitally blind individual that I began to compare to other cases, discovering similarities, variations and differences. Overall, this research sensitized me to the distinctive nature of visual and tactile aesthetics which, eventually, also influenced my work with the sighted. Tactile and visual panoramic displays in retrospective review sessions have become a standard part of my art therapy practice. In retrospect, this initial study strongly influenced my current research on the gaze in art psychotherapy with congenital blindness. The experience of visually processing and so gaining insight into Rebecca's artwork through the lens of the camera launched the creation of a comprehensive archive and database of artworks, sessions and review notes at the school for the blind at the beginning of my PhD. Since then I have been applying and developing my research methodologies, publishing and contributing to conferences on art and blindness, and working as an art therapy educator (Herrmann, 2006, 2009a, 2009b). Fifteen years after entering the practice-research loop, I cannot conceive practising without it.

HILARY HOSEA

3 The Brush's Footmarks: Researching a Small Community Art Therapy Group

Abstract

This research is essentially a field study bringing an ethnographic and participative approach to exploring a small community art therapy group in which mothers and their young children paint together. It is underpinned by the concepts of parent-infant psychotherapy – the importance of attunement and attachment between infant and caregiver and the intersubjective world of infants – and explores how this is enhanced by the art-making process. Videotapes showing the interaction of six mothers and their infants painting together were reviewed with the participants and their responses recorded and analysed. The research revealed how painting with each other draws mother and child together emotionally and positively affects their relationship and promotes new understandings. Video interaction technique provided a positive reflective space for the mothers and became a sensitive therapeutic tool for the art therapist.

Key Words

infants; parents; painting; video-interaction; mess; chaos; attachment; attunement.

How it all Began: from Practice to Research

The focus of this chapter is the research I did on a small community art therapy group at the heart of which was the activity of painting. The whole purpose of this small group was to strengthen the relationship of parent and infant through mothers and their young children painting together. I had found that this drew together mother and child emotionally, positively affecting their relationship and enhancing attunement. The group was started in 1992 by the health visitor, Ann Pringle and art therapist, Penelope Hall, who were introduced to each other by psychologist, Andy Sluckin. They all shared an enormous enthusiasm for work with babies and their caregivers and were interested in infant psychotherapy and the difficulties that some mothers and babies experience in their early relationship. In 1997, when Penelope left the Child and Family Centre, I took over this part of her work. When I began a research-based MA four years later I chose the painting group as a case study and from this new kind of encounter with the material was able to develop the research question: what happens when parents and young children paint together?

This unusual art therapy group is still running, some seventeen years after it began. It takes place in an NHS baby clinic which is light and spacious with windows on three sides and a brightly painted Wendy House on the fourth. The group is for parents and their pre-nursery school children; a session involves between four and ten children and from three to six families. It is an 'open' group, fluid and homogenous, with a strong community base and, because it is accessible and known, it provides a feeling of safety. The health visitors invite the parents and their young children to the group; they join and leave as they wish, sometimes attending regularly for months, perhaps coming for just a few sessions.

The focus of the group is on the interactions of parents and their children as they are involved together with the art materials, their mutual creativity and the uniqueness of the child being visible for all to see in the paintings. A large sheet of coloured polythene is laid across the whole floor; the art materials comprise a dozen bottles of readymix paint, brushes, palettes, charcoal, pastels, play dough and occasionally clay. Mothers, sometimes fathers and other family members arrive with their offspring and are soon down on the floor painting, finding their own ways of doing things and watching each other. The nursery nurse, the health visitors and I all make paintings on the floor alongside everyone else. We are the holding matrix of the group. Paintings emerge and are laid out to dry and there is respect for the art process and the unconscious themes that arise from the paintings and the verbal exchanges. The group provides a safe, containing environment where emotional understanding of the child is fostered. It is a valuable resource that can help to get parents and their young children off to a good start in the face of environmental difficulties or mental health problems. Work in this small painting group therefore has a preventative function as well as addressing existing difficulties in relationship.

Researching this innovative area of art therapy practice led me into wide-ranging and fascinating areas such as 'the gaze' which included looking through the lens of a video camera and becoming observer and, alongside the mothers, one of the observed. In this chapter I describe the character and history of the group, the literature that I explored, that of art therapy but also on parent-infant psychotherapy and attachment. This includes the ideas of Stern (1985, 1995, 1998) and Trevarthen (1984, 2001, 2002) on vitality and 'vitality effects' and Stern's concept of 'now moments'. I go on to describe my methodology and how I used the video camera, including the background ideas of Video Interaction Guidance (Biemans, 1990). I reflect on this kind of visual research, 'the gaze' and the effect on the participants of being watched, and consider the co-creation of interviews between the parents and myself. Finally I look at the concepts which emerged that focus on how the painting group promotes attunement between parents and their infants and strengthens their attachment.

The Context of the Research

Meyerowitz-Katz (1999) found that there were very few art therapists working with children under five in the UK. The three art therapists who write about this area of work agree that mothers and children using art materials and working together strengthens their relationship and that the process allows a restructuring of that relationship to take place (Hall, 1991, 2008; Meyerowtiz-Katz, 1999; Proulx, 2003). However, the dearth of discipline-specific literature led me to turn to attachment theory, parent-infant psychotherapy and Dissenyake (2000) and Matthews (1989, 1999) on art-making as a vital and innate part of human culture.

Infant Psychotherapy Literature

Freud stated: 'The ego is first and foremost a bodily ego' (1923: 26). In optimum circumstances the mother provides a nurturing environment where sights, smells, touch and mirroring help to bring about a satisfactory, bounded experience of the body and the self with the skin as a primary area of sensitive communication between mother and baby (Anzieu, 1989). Winnicott (1960, 1962, 1971) says that in infants a primary state of non-integration is followed by one of integration: the psyche then installs itself in the soma and this unity is what he refers to as the 'self'. From this position the infant develops a belief in its continued existence, its conscious identity and in the natural functioning of the body. This belief is the basis of the initial pleasure of being alive.

The literature on parent-infant psychotherapy was relevant to my project because it concerns itself with the unconscious mind of both the infant and his or her parents, explaining how anxieties in both child and parent become constellated with the troubling symptoms of infancy: desperate crying, failure to thrive, difficulties in sleeping and eating, and emotional distance. The literature shows how psychotherapeutic understandings can alleviate the distress of the infant and their family, often within a very short time. This kind of sensitive intervention that stresses working with parents and their young children together, focusing on their relationship, can help to prevent later problems and difficulties for the child. The neuroplasticity of the infant brain adds to the importance of intervening early so that the baby's brain, shaped by connection with its carers, has the chance for optimum development (Schore, 2001).

Early experiences have a decisive impact on the architecture of the brain, interactions effecting the neural pathways as they are fired, wired or pruned (Karr-Morse and Wiley, 1997). Bowlby's attachment theory (1969, 1973, 1980) provides a substantial framework for understanding how an environment of emotional safety, together with adequate parenting, are vital to the healthy development of a person and their sense of self throughout the life cycle (Marrone, 1998). Fraiberg's (1980) pioneering work with mothers and their infants helped mothers to 'learn the language' of their babies and removed the 'ghosts in the nursery', preventing them from repeating their own conflicted past with their child.

The research of Trevarthen (1985, 2001, 2002), biologist and developmental psychologist, was a very useful source of understanding parent-infant interaction. He demonstrated the human infant's powerful appetite for companionship and interaction from birth. Mother and baby are active participants, creating a relationship through pre-verbal communications of face, voice and bodily movement. Trevarthen supports the efficacy of therapies that: '... engage and lift the spirit of action and awareness, and that especially support sharing of any vitality' (2001: 118).

The 'Good Grandmother' Transference

While I was doing this research I was fortunate to hear Daniel Stern describe his belief that the therapeutic setting in infant-parent psychotherapy is about the holding which allows mothers to develop their abilities. He believes that the transference from the therapist in infant-parent psychotherapy works best as that of a benign mother/grandmother who holds the new mother positively so that she can find her innate repertoire of mothering techniques. The grandmother transference is appropriate to the motherhood constellation and results in a stronger, more effective therapeutic alliance (1995: 187). Stern claims that the mother, with the birth of her child: '… experiences a profound realignment… her interests and concern now are more with her own mother… more with her mother-as-mother… more with women in general and less with men' (1995: 172). This is not to deny the huge importance of the father who can provide the practical support that protects her in her early relationship with the infant and allows it to be sustained (1995: 189).

Attunement, Vitality Affects and the Art Therapy Process

Stern's (1985) ideas about parental attunement in infant-parent psychotherapy supported my thinking about what happened in the painting group for mothers and children. He writes about the mother's 'primary relatedness', using Winnicott's term, in the infant's first year which includes the attachment between them, security and affection, regulating the baby's rhythms and the pre-verbal induction into human relatedness through the reception of affect and through mutually created reciprocal behaviour. He explains that sensitive mothers modulate their infant's rhythms and patterns of play, stimulating the baby when the level of activity falls and calming them when the baby appears over excited so that equilibrium is restored and the infant's sense of self is built up (142).

Stern's (ibid.) concept of 'vitality affects' was also useful to my understanding of the importance of art materials in motivating liveliness and attunement between mother and child and in their contribution to the child's sense of being alive. Stern describes 'vitality affects' and 'categorical affects' as part of the pre-verbal, perceptual processes that provide the sensory foundations for communication. Vitality affects arise directly from encounters with people and are best captured by kinetic terms such as 'surging', 'fading away', 'bursting' and so on. These qualities of experience are sensible to infants and of great daily and momentary importance (54). They correspond, he believes, to the changes in feeling states which underlie the process of feeling alive. In the group it seemed to me that the art materials helped the parents and children to share 'vitality' as they responded to each other involved in the rhythms, colour sensations, tactility and sensuous flow of painting and mark-making.

'Now Moments'

Stern (1998) also writes about what he calls 'now moments'; these occur in the interactions between parent and child and underlie the process of change in adult psychotherapies. He explains that much of the action of change, of which the developing infant is part, involves the domain of implicit or procedural knowledge and, in particular: '... implicit knowing about what to do, think and feel in a specific relationship context' (302). These 'now moments' are occasions of meeting in which the participants interact in a way that creates a new, implicit, intersubjective understanding of their relationship and permits a new 'way of being-with-the-other' (301). The process requires no interpretation and need not be made verbally explicit. The 'now moment' is a 'hot', present, non-linear moment, charged with emotion. Stern (2002) has said that people are pulled into being present with each other. Things alter between two people – they are 'moments of meeting'. New things emerge between mother and child as they co-create in moments of positive interaction.

Art-making as a Vital and Innate Part of Human Culture

Art historian Dissanayake (1995, 2000) suggests that a 'behaviour of art' (17) exists as an innate part of human nature that 'make(s) special' (182). The 'rhythms and modes' which are used and elaborated through art and are intrinsically non-verbal, are an intermingling of movement and sensory overlapping characteristic of the infant experience of co-ordination and expression with the mother. Patterning and elaborating are innate and occur universally in the productions of young children. This links to literature which argues that our sense of self emerges from our bodies and hence with the importance of art-making involving infants and their carers.

Matthews (1989, 1999) can now be usefully drawn into the debate. He has shown, through his extensive observation and research into young children's drawing and painting, that infants are concerned with their identity. Very young children give both organisation and meaning to their drawings, encoding forms and relations with the environment and conveying emotion. Matthews makes the point that this early symbolisation by infants needs the interpersonal engagement of the caregiver.

Thus I began this research with the question: 'What happens when mothers and young children paint together?' I wanted to examine their activity in a group whose aim was to strengthen the relationship between parents and infants. After absorbing the literature I refined my initial research question into two questions:

1. Does the process of working with the art materials in the community group strengthen the bond between mothers and young children?
2. Does the activity of painting together provide the kind of opportunity that fosters a creative and communicative way of being together?

Method

I chose to investigate these questions through an approach that was both ethnographic and participative. It involved an iterative process of videoing the interactions between parent and child and then showing the videos to the mothers whilst interviewing them about their primary, tactile experience of painting together with their child.

I found Tedlock's (2000) ideas about ethnography useful. He proposes that ethnography '... combines research design, fieldwork, and various methods of enquiry to produce historically, politically and personally situated accounts, descriptions, interpretations and representations of human lives.' (455). It carries the association of depth and detail of description that I wanted to achieve. In McLeod's terms, ethnographic research is 'about spending time with people, listening to them, watching them, taking part in their daily routines as a participant observer.' (McLeod, 2001: 64). I attempted to do this as researcher and art therapist in the painting group but my study was limited in scope and time. I share McLeod's view that this kind of research usefully opens up the 'borderland between therapy and everyday life' and the 'clash of cultures' which exists between clients and therapists (ibid: 69).

I will now turn to the literature on interactive video techniques that enabled me to establish an appropriate way of visually recording what happened in the group when parents painted freely and creatively with their young children.

Video Interaction Guidance

Psychologists, psychotherapists and educationalists have been interested in what actually takes place between parents and infants and have developed models of interaction guidance using video recordings of short episodes of joint play. McDonough (1993) used video to enable mothers to see what they were doing well. A video interaction approach was also developed by Aarts and Biemans (Biemans, 1990) to improve both the communication and the actual quality of the relationship between the child and the carer.This initiative was influenced by the research of Trevarthen into mother-infant communication. The technique involves 'Video Interaction Guidance' where positive moments are selected from a short video of family interaction. Underlying the approach are principles of respect, empowerment and collaboration with families. Sluckin (1999) had adapted this technique to his work with severely, post-natally depressed mothers in a previous art therapy group. His view was that art-making allowed the best in a relationship to be brought out and the resources of the child to be seen.

Grappling with the Ethics Committee

Late on a Friday afternoon, when my research was about to begin, I found myself staggering along a confusion of corridors in the bowels of a hospital with a heavy box of papers. I needed to deliver my answers to the ethics and research governance committees' many questions before their next meeting. I had put aside two or three months before I could begin my study to demonstrate to these committees not only that my research proposal was rigorous and had scientific justification but also that the confidentiality and safety of the participants would be upheld. The group of very young children and their parents was perceived as vulnerable, some were socially isolated or had experienced personal trauma, but they were living and functioning in the community. 'If the study shows that the painting group is effective', I wrote, 'then it will be useful in making this scarce, possibly precious, resource more widely known.' I argued that the 'scientific' credentials were embedded in the study's qualitative approach, pointing out that the background to the research was the increasing recognition of the importance of prioritising infant mental health provision, especially in the light of recent discoveries about the development of the infant brain. I explained that I had chosen a participative approach designed to empower and increase the self-esteem of those taking part (Reason and Rowan, 1991). Thankfully they were persuaded.

Picking up the Camera

Over a ten week period I used a hand-held video camera to record six mothers painting with their child in the group. The next time we met I showed the video to the mother and interviewed her, using an iterative process whereby the footage was a starting point for our discussion which I tape-recorded and later transcribed and analysed.

I picked up the camera when the mother and child were 'settled' and 'at ease' (Brazelton, Koslowski and Main, 1974). I found that the best time was at the beginning of the group when mother and child, with whom I had built up a relationship and rapport, were pleasurably involved in using the art materials together and when Stern's concept of 'now moments' seemed likely to occur. I was looking for short intervals when things were flowing between them.

Although I knew all the people and had their consent to be videoed I was aware that being watched through the eye of a video camera in this particular community could feel like being judged and, for some people, that there might be a disturbing element to being filmed. Some mothers in the group had had involvement with social services and the police, their children had been on the child protection register or they had been victims of domestic violence. The intrusive nature of the camera was in part mediated by the fact that I was not trying to be a fly-on-the-wall; on the contrary I was an active part of the occasion, making my own responses openly as I filmed. It was fascinating and moving, often pleasurable to watch through the eye of the lens the intimate play of mother and child, and I was not afraid to show it.

My research diary revealed, at this point, the conflict of becoming a researcher in the group and no longer just being an art therapist working with my co-facilitators. I was aware I had another agenda and felt I might be preying, raptor-like, on its members as I tried to feed on the meat of their experience. The diary was a sketchbook and encouraged visual recording as well as ideas and observations in words. I wrote down descriptive phrases used by the parents; fleeting perceptions; made splashes of colour reflecting the paintings laid out on the floor; small sketches of parent-child proximity; observations and feelings connected to the group; perhaps a note on boarded-up houses and wrecked cars on the estate as I drove back to base and connected to the pressured lives of the families. As I got deeper into the conversations and began the video-recording the intermingling of my researcher-self and the participating families became stronger.

Gazing Through the Lens

Video, like film or any photographic medium, structures a convincing view of the world of which there can be multiple versions (Pink, 2001). It provides unexpected views and angles and holds something momentary and ephemeral.

I wanted to use the videos to initiate conversation with the mothers about how they saw themselves when engaged in painting with their children and what they thought about the process. However, when I reviewed and then showed the videos to the mothers, I realised that I was using video not only as a way of initiating conversations about how they felt about painting with their child but also as a therapeutic tool. This led me to construct meanings that were influenced by McDonough's (1993) ideas of interaction guidance and those of Video Interaction Guidance (Biemans, 1990). However, my reaction to the recordings was inevitably different from that of the mothers. On the whole they enjoyed seeing themselves doing something together with their child in a way that was not usually possible.

It could be 'a bit weird to start with' but it was 'nice', they derived pleasure from it and felt pride in their child. The distancing effect of the video images seemed to encourage the mothers to voice the abilities and achievements of their child. The story of their relationship was, in a small way, elaborated and built up.

The whole research process developed my 'gaze' and became a tool for therapeutic, as well as research, insights. I think I used several kinds of gaze, including one focused on the interactions and apparent relationship of each dyad. Winnicott (1971) describes the maternal gaze that is part of the mirror-role of the mother which allows the baby to see him or herself when he or she looks at the mother's face. Winnicott relates this kind of seeing of the self to the psychotherapeutic task that reflects what is there in the client, 'giving the patient back what the patient brings' (137). I do not pretend that this benign and creative version of the gaze was how the mothers necessarily experienced the research process but seeing themselves painting with their child was enriching for most of them. Another kind of gaze was the retrospective look. Here I focused on the use of art materials, taking an aesthetic look at the creativity which emerged as mothers and children painted. This included the flow of images – the physical evidence of the connection built up on the paper between the parents and their children.

The making of the videos seemed to be a possible way of drawing out some of the meaning of the 'beyond words' expression of art therapy which is related to the visual, the sensual and the primordial area of experience. Pink, a visual ethnographer, argues that when looking at and interpreting video material one meaning is not replaced by another:

> Rather the images can be thought of as icons in which a range of different meanings may be invested. As such they are used to represent or refer to diverse persons, activities and emotions that may not obviously or directly form part of the visible content of the image. (2001: 100)

I did not want to objectify and categorise the videos in an emphatically objective way, turning the mothers and children into 'the other'. I wanted to be more reflexive and less controlling in my viewing of the material and

I wanted to use the technology to highlight positive aspects of interaction between the mothers and their children which might, in a small way, develop the parents' understanding of their child's behaviour without undermining their role.

Video material from the ethnographic point of view is a form of diary-keeping and note-taking. Pink believes it can record certain processes and activities but these must always be treated as representations, not as visual facts. The analysis of the video material in this research had to take into account the strategies of self-representation and collaboration that were part of its making. I found Christians' (2000) writing on ethics and politics in qualitative research challenging and helpful. He illuminates the radical break which feminist and social ethics have made with ideas of individual autonomy and rationalism. He believes that research should be collaborative in design and participatory in execution, and that social science research should enable people to come to terms with their everyday experience: 'Rather than privileging an abstract rationalism, the moral order is positioned close to the bone, in the creaturely and corporeal rather than the conceptual' (2000: 144).

I was also influenced by the work of Lister and Wells (2000) who provide a useful overview of the voyeuristic and controlling nature of the 'gaze'. This idea of the viewing system became an established one in western art and photography during the twentieth century. Mulvey (1975) used Freud's ideas on scopophilia – the primary instinct to look – and voyeurism – the male desire to exercise a controlling gaze – in her analysis of cinema spectatorship. More recently issues relating to the fluidity of identity as a set of representations has been brought into this debate (Lister and Wells, 2000: 84–5).

Videos and Interviews

I thought the videos would provide the parents and myself with a visual representation of what they did and show how mother and child got involved with the paint together. I examined them to help frame some of the questions for the interviews, e.g. 'What did it feel like seeing the video of you and your child painting together?'; 'I was struck by how relaxed you are in allowing your child to explore the paint; can you talk about that?' Most mothers responded positively to observing themselves and their child and made use of the interview as a space for forming and expressing their own ideas.

The interviews were also conversations; I asked questions and the mothers replied, each submerged in our cultural codes and intuitive interpretations, leaving our mark on the process with slabs of 'the informants' reality' thrown up in the answers to the questions (Gudmunsdottir, 1996). A co-creation emerged between the mothers and me in the exchanges which the six interviews represent. They were subtle and full of imagining, picturing in the mind what the other person may mean. I tried to connect with their sense of meaning and they with mine. On some level we were both engaged with fathoming each other out. Minimal as the conversations were they gave some understanding of the women's beliefs and ideas and the stories they told about their lives.

Coming to an Understanding

I transcribed the tape-recorded interviews and self-reflexively made notes on my thoughts and feelings on reading the transcripts. I colour-coded the transcripts to focus on certain ideas that I felt were embodied in them, laying them out on the fifteen-foot length of a print-down table. I looked for themes, similarities, resonances and categories. I used the ideas of McLeod (2001) and made a preliminary statement of the meaning of the text of each interview and also delved into and opened out small segments of text. I sifted, ordered and identified themes and patterns and made constant comparisons. I looked at the six videotapes. The looking helped me to see more and make connections between the tapes and the interview material. I wrote about the videotapes.

This immersion resulted in several concepts, influenced by the literature that I had read and continued to read throughout in order to see if other people's ideas shed light on my developing conceptual framework. At times I felt as if I was clinging to the sides of a great, slippery broth bowl with ideas and information bubbling and steaming all around me in an overwhelming way. Representing the rich content of the short video of each infant-mother dyad painting and the six subsequent interviews felt like squashing something immense, four-dimensional and dynamic into a flat, verbal space. Nonetheless four main concepts emerged.

First was that painting with each other draws the mother and child together emotionally and positively affects their relationship. Second, that the role of the art therapist and the other facilitators was to contain mess and chaos so that the mothers and infants could get on with exploring the art materials together. Third, that the paintings in the group had symbolic meaning and often embodied the parents' hope for the future happiness of themselves and their children, and for the growth of their relationship. And fourth, that colour, 'something moving and alive in its own right', was an important part of the experience of painting in the group. An unexpected finding was, as previously described, that the research interviews, linked to watching the videos, gave the mothers a reflective space for themselves.

This research demonstrated that working with the art materials in an art therapy group strengthens the bond between parents and their young children, the process of painting enabling moments of connection and understanding. I had wondered if the art materials enabled the mothers and children to share 'vitality' together (Trevarthen, 2001; Stern, 1985): I believe that they do. This affect was visible in the videotapes, the sense of the aliveness of mother and child and the attunement that this promoted being confirmed in the interviews. For example, Susan says that painting affects her relationship with her child, Cabe; it brings them 'close together… because you're actually having to sit down together and you're actually doing something together…' She thinks that you '… express yourself really when you use paint.' June felt that painting in the group was 'time together'. She said, 'We're doing something together... he's wanting me to do it with him...', as if she often feels that her child does not want her closely involved and she feels distanced from him. However she describes painting in the group as 'It's special – something for just me and him.' Thus the mothers recognised that they were brought together with their child in physical proximity and emotional closeness through the co-operative fluency of painting – a place where joy and pleasure could be shared.

What I saw on the videotapes, and what the mothers saw too and alluded to in their interviews, were moments of meeting: hot, present connections which led to new ways of being with each other. Golda for instance felt close to her child when she was painting with him in the group: '... he would join in with my painting and add little bits and talk...' The experience was one of 'warmth'; it was 'relaxed' and 'comfortable'. She felt painting together was '... another form of language... another form of communicating...' which used '... movement and colour in creating something together.' She saw '... how much he expressed himself'. Her partner watched the videotape and described the process of painting between mother and child as 'unconscious communication', something 'symbiotic' and 'flowing'.

Catherine had a reaction of joy to the video images of her and her baby: 'I really like it. I liked the way we were communicating – and to see him enjoying it so much – yeah... so I just like him to have fun'. She imagines herself in the baby's place: '... the texture in your hands and about how it'll squeeze through, and the different feelings and the cold and... it must feel exciting to him...' It seemed from what the interviewees said that, in the act of painting together, the space for growth was created – there was an energy, 'a flow', that provided the space for mother and child to meet and enjoy each other and for 'now moments' to occur (Stern 1998, 2002; Tronnick, 1998).

These moments of connection generate an expanded state of consciousness between parent and infant which lead to changes in their relationship. Winnicott suggests that it is the quality of environmental provision at the early phase of a child's life that is responsible for the feeling throughout a person's existence that life is worth living (1971: 83). This overlaps with Stern's idea of 'vitality affects', attunement and 'now moments' (Stern, 1995,

1998), all of which were clearly evident in the painting group. This leads me to propose that art therapy contributes to the feeling of being alive. It can provide, through the process of parents and children using the art materials together, an experience of attunement and connection that strengthens their attachment and enhances a sense of creative living.

The paintings were always valued in the group but what was unexpected was that, for the parents, they embodied their hopes for the future happiness of mother and child and for the continued growth and aliveness of the relationship that was represented in them as something 'done together'. The affect that the paintings contained was often celebratory, about the expanding skills and personality of the child, confirmed and witnessed by the mother, the facilitators and the other mothers and children in the group. For example Susan thinks that Cabe's paintings are important: 'Yes, they're important... because they're something done together... you got something to show for that.' Golda said of Joe's painting: 'I was amazed that he had done something like that', and Jane, in her damp housing, says of Julian's paintings: 'We're putting them away, we're keeping them for when we get another house.' But then in rebellion at the bleak 'crappy magnolia' walls she suddenly decides to put them up: 'They're going to cheer the colour up of the bloody walls.' Here colour, as the comments of the women participants showed, was engaged with on an elemental and sensuous level, as Tipple (1992) noted. It seemed to provide a form of expression beyond words, both for the mother and for her and her child together. The richness and aliveness of the experience also connects to Stern's 'vitality affects'. As Golda said: 'It was nice to do it with Joe... just to paint for the sake of painting, using colour and exploring it and enjoying it like children do...'

In the group the facilitators provided a metaphorical frame so that parents and children had the freedom to experiment on the edge of mess and create something joyful and meaningful. This strengthened the mother/child relationship without the fear of overwhelming chaos. In this environment children were able to gain a sense of self through the physical, tactile sensations of using the paint and being affirmed, encouraged and kept in balance by their mothers. The 'good grandmother' transference fits well with my and my colleagues' roles which provided the holding that allowed the mothers to find their innate abilities.

The research method also gave the parents a valuable reflective space. The video images seemed to help them recognise and voice the achievements of their child and to see their importance as supporter of them. Art therapy and the technique of video interaction worked well together, providing a useful therapeutic language with which to look at the interactions of parents and young children.

From Research into Practice

The research has informed me in a way that nothing else could have done. It has expanded my range of understandings as an art therapist and broadened my perspectives so that I now see video techniques, for instance, as a valuable therapeutic tool and resource. It launched me into a new relationship with the client group and made me more confident by illuminating what I do. It gave me keener insights into working with children and adolescents and with their parental figures because I am more able to translate the nature of the very early engagement patterns of infants and carers into this arena and to use art materials to promote moments of meeting and new attunements.

Out of this research has come not only this chapter but also a paper (Hosea, 2006), both of which have contributed to the evidence base for art therapists working with parent-infant relationships. I have been able to offer support to other art therapists starting their own innovative work in this field and have given talks within and outside my trust to disseminate the findings. My research has enabled managers and commissioners to understand that the painting groups have a positive, pragmatic, possibly vital function and another painting group within the government's Sure Start scheme has begun. If I had not produced research it is unlikely that I would have been able to continue working in this vital area of practice as a CAMHS art psychotherapist. The inclusion of art therapy in a service for infant mental health has now been established after years of promoting the need.

ELIZABETH STIRLING

4 Collaboration, Education, Frustration: Integrating Art Therapy into the School Setting

Abstract

This chapter describes research which attempted to establish an art therapy service that covered children's transition from nursery to primary education. The aim of the service was to provide early recognition and a supportive intervention to those children who were displaying symptoms which could hinder their intellectual and social development during the transfer period. The research method used was Participative Action Research, an approach which involves collaboration: this was both the method and the key to the establishment of a successful service.

Key Words

collaboration; joint partnership; reflective model; cyclic approach.

How it all Began: From Practice to Research

In 1990 I retired after many years in mainstream and special education of which fifteen years were spent as a head teacher in nursery and primary schools. My teaching career was concerned with providing an inclusive education which supported children learning at their own level and pace. I hoped that, by providing appropriate and interesting learning activities for all, this would eliminate the emotional and behavioural difficulties that hindered their ability to learn. I knew from experience that these problems might persist, or increase, throughout primary school, if they were not addressed. Whilst efforts to improve the learning environment created a more accepting and stimulating atmosphere it seemed to me that a psychotherapeutic intervention might be necessary before some children could cope with the demands of school life. At that time I had no idea what this might be.

On retiring I realized an unfulfilled ambition and became a full-time undergraduate student in Fine Art and experienced first-hand how it felt to be as inexperienced and unskilled as some children surely feel in school classrooms. Edwards' *Drawing on the Artist Within* (1987), especially her discussion of art as a parallel language, offered me the tools of survival in the face of probable failure. Then, with fortunate synchronicity, I learned of the Postgraduate Diploma in Art Psychotherapy and, when I finished my degree, I trained as an art therapist. It appeared to me that the 'parallel language of art' used in art therapy had the potential to support children and staff in mainstream and special schools – as it did me at university.

Although art therapy is practiced successfully in a wide variety of situations my years in teaching and school management led me to believe that it would be especially useful for supporting troubled children in schools. As a result, college placements and subsequent work experience were in special units and schools for five to eleven year olds and in mainstream primary schools with attached nurseries.

In spite of the fact that I had spent a long career working in schools, making the transition from teacher to art therapist involved a major change of attitude and approach. Outwardly there appears to be much in common between the two roles. Acceptance of the child is fundamental to both, rapport and empathy are needed, flexibility is important and both require a safe, secure base for children. A solid background of knowledge and relevant theory and practice is also necessary to both roles and good co-operative relationships with colleagues in schools and multi-disciplinary teams are essential.

Waller (1984) has described the contrasting roles of art therapist and art teacher where the basic difference is one of function. The class teacher's role is to motivate by providing suitable resources and to structure a learning situation that enables successful, identifiable outcomes. The art therapist has to create a safe, confidential space with a variety of resources but awaits the child's actions or reactions. I experienced this as an abrupt change of purpose and direction which required knowledge, patience and self-reflection to make the adjustment satisfactorily. This fundamental difference between teacher and therapist is where the greatest misunderstandings occur when art therapists work with education staff (Wengrower, 2001).

Six years of working as an art therapist in various school environments gave me some experience of the misunderstandings as well as the advantages that other art therapists working in education have encountered. Lack of knowledge about the processes of art therapy and its practical prerequisites seemed to me to be the most common cause of misinterpretation by other professionals. For example, art therapists' need for safe, uninterrupted and boundaried spaces; our minimal involvement in other school activities; the necessity of keeping appointments sacrosanct and not interchangeable; and what may be interpreted in school as a 'laissez-faire' attitude towards 'discipline' – none of these fit readily into the culture of schools. Indeed our prerequisites may even be seen as anti-social, exclusive, undisciplined and unco-operative by a workforce who operate under different professional constraints. For school staff, spaces and times regularly have to be juggled and exchanged, often with little notice; creativity may be subordinated by the strictures of the curriculum or a lack of resources; covering the duties of others is expected and multi-tasking is the norm, all of which makes the art therapist's role seem very enviable to teachers. Another important factor that hinders others' understanding of art therapists' role in education is the paucity of research supporting it as an effective intervention in schools for the increasing number of children who experience emotional and behavioural difficulties.

The problematic nature of these continuing misunderstandings were confirmed by two research projects I undertook prior to the major study described in this chapter. These, together with the literature, formed the background to my research.

The Context of the Research

I will describe the two small research projects that I did before reviewing the literature that informs the research which is the subject of this chapter. The first project (Stirling, 2001) attempted to ascertain the reality of media reports on children's emotional and behavioural problems, to discover how these were being addressed in primary education and to establish what was known about art therapy. This research took place in five primary schools in Scotland. Qualitative and quantitative data was collected from school records and I interviewed the head teachers. The research revealed that these schools were without appropriate interventions for emotional and behavioural difficulties for the 5–18.6 per cent of children who were in need. Further, that although each of the head teachers had evolved coping strategies to manage the children's problems and difficulties in their schools, there was little or no knowledge of art therapy and its potential to support the children and each school's difficulties with them.

My instinct, based on this research and on my years of working life in schools and latterly in art therapy, was that the early identification of children's difficulties in nurseries and the provision of art therapy prior to their transfer to primary school would be invaluable. This could support the needy child through a difficult transition and strengthen the link between both establishments.

I then began the major study which is the focus of this chapter. This involved a search for a nursery and primary school with staff who were willing to collaborate with an art therapist in an action research project that initiated and developed art therapy for children experiencing difficulties in the transition between nursery and primary school. Initially this was unsuccessful. Disheartening though this was I decided it would help to compare my experiences of working as an art therapist in schools with those of other art therapists in the United Kingdom. As a result I embarked on the second of the two small research projects and sent a scoping questionnaire to art therapists who were working in education and who were identified from the register of the British Association of Art Therapists (BAAT). This resulted in a significant response rate: 63 per cent of the one hundred and fifty nine questionnaires were returned. Responses to two particular questions caught my attention. These enquired about the advantages and handicaps experienced by art therapists working in education. Respondents' comments certainly resonated with my experiences, not only about the difficulties but also about the advantages of working as an art therapist in schools.

One of the main problems respondents described was the lack of suitable, safe, private and contained spaces for art therapy. One described '... working in the science lab' and said that 'privacy of space is very difficult to find'. The lack of understanding of the art therapist's role was another difficulty, respondents describing '... a lack of liaison with staff and thus no real understanding of how art therapy works' and '... being last to be told information'. Isolation was another common problem, exacerbated by such factors as time constraints, not feeling part of a team, conflict with school timetables and a lack of opportunities for liaison so that information could be exchanged. One art therapist wrote about '... feeling isolated and not feeling part of the team and occasionally being resented by teachers'.

However art therapists also described real advantages of working in schools. Overwhelmingly the most important was having direct access to children. Attendance was not parent-dependent: '... not having to rely on mum to get them to sessions'. The familiarity of the school environment was also helpful. As respondents said: '... the child remains in a supportive environment, school and home are a joint resource'; '... being in a child's environment where they feel familiar/safe'; '... school is part of children's lives and there is potentially far less stigma attached'. Access to art therapy was easier when it was provided in school, the service seeming to become more inclusive due to labelling and stigmatisation being discouraged in the schools.

For the art therapist there was the feeling of being part of a team and therefore being supported and recognised by the school. Opportunities to liaise with others close to the child were improved by their location on site and morale was boosted by art therapists' autonomy and by their work being appreciated by their colleagues. Respondents said: 'I was able to meet with teachers... who were committed to the welfare of the children and we could share disciplines'. Art therapists worked in 'an appreciative environment that is professional and supportive' and 'I only had one role and it was separate from being a teacher'.

The similarities between these art therapists' positive and negative experiences of working in schools and their resonance with my own encouraged me to persist with the idea of researching the initiation and establishment of a school art therapy service which embraced the positive findings from the survey and attempted to overcome the disadvantages many art therapists seemed to encounter.

Literature

Historically there has been concern about how emotional difficulties experienced by young children impact on their lives behaviourally, socially and intellectually (Wolff, 1969; Rutter, 1975; Winnicott, 1964, 1984; Bowlby, 1969, 1988). Fundamental ideas about what supports or hinders learning now revolves around the concept of the child as a social being, learning being understood as a reciprocal process where both parties influence each other (Coren, 1997).

The UNICEF Report (2007) places Scotland and the rest of the U.K. near the bottom of the league table of children's well-being in numerous categories. There is evidence of children's need for therapeutic intervention in the Office of National Statistics Report on Children's Mental Health (ONS, 2004) and in the ongoing Government statistics on bullying, truancy and violent episodes in schools. According to Pupils in Scotland, Independent Schools Census, ONS (2007), at most 4 per cent of the Scottish school population receive additional support for learning. However, a survey by the charity Mindroom indicates that more than one in six of Scottish school children (17 per cent) are affected by a recognised learning difficulty. This suggests that a significant number of children who urgently require help are not receiving it.

There are many successful examples of therapeutic work in schools. In 1966 students from the Tavistock Clinic worked with children in their primary schools in an inner London borough (Reid, Fry and Rhode, 1977) and in 1996 'The Place to Be', a therapeutic and remedial network, was created to provide a preventative service to schools. Dalley (1990) makes a strong case for school-based art therapy and cites the research reported in *Help Starts Here* (Kolvin, Garside et al., 1982). This project investigated ways of developing mental health services in schools and found that the most successful interventions focused skilled attention on the child and delivered positive effects which lasted beyond the end of therapy. Art therapists have been working in English schools and nurseries with groups and individuals for some time, as the case studies by Case (1990), Dalley (1990), Prokofiev (1998), Boronska (2000), Welsby (2008) and others show. In 2007, a conference organized by BAAT – 'Supporting Learning and Enabling Growth: Art Therapy in Education' – featured five presentations by art therapists and school personnel who had been working collaboratively to provide a service for their schools. However, no record has been found of art therapy services that support younger children in the transition from nursery to primary education, this being the particular focus of my research.

However, I was pleased to discover an interesting research project that explored how the emotional and psychological needs of refugee and asylum-seeking children might be met which helped me think about my research. *Out of the Lion's Mouth* describes research commissioned by the Children's Fund (International New Arrivals Partnership, 2007). This project explored the work of an Emotional and Trauma Support Team which involved a range of therapies: art therapy was one. The research had several aims. The first was to use creative interventions in schools, holistically and without stigma, in order to address the needs of the children referred to the project. The second aim was to change mainstream understanding about children's needs in relation to therapeutic processes. The third was to build partnerships across a wide variety of therapeutic interventions. This research led to the following recommendations:

1. Safe, holding and stable environments are needed in order to work with small children.
2. Still, empathic holding is necessary to address powerful emotions.

3. Policy makers need to ensure that the needs of individual children are addressed by specialist staff who are supported and funded in a well-planned way.

This comprehensive research offers a template for those attempting to support troubled, and troubling, children in schools. As far as my research was concerned it helped me articulate my research questions and formulate a collaborative approach to the project. Thus my research questions were:

1. How can art therapy be successfully integrated into a school setting?
2. How can the cultural gap between therapy and education be bridged?

The main purpose of my research was to use a Participative Action Research approach to facilitate the initiation of an art therapy service which would support children in the critical transition from nursery to primary school. The aims of the research were, first, to demonstrate the collaborative role art therapy might play in the early identification of, and the provision of support for, children needing help in the transition from nursery to primary school. Second, I hoped to develop a reliable means of evaluating the effectiveness of art therapy on individual children's self-confidence, communication and ability to adapt to their new school environment when they transferred. My third and final aim was to develop a replicable protocol or clinical guideline for art therapy services in this area of provision which conformed to professional standards and BAAT's Code of Ethics and which provided the conditions for co-operation, understanding and respect between all the agencies contributing to the provision.

Method

Participative Action Research is a way of investigating professional experience which links practice and its analysis into a single evolving sequence, as described in the work of Ferrance (2000), Zuber-Skerritt (1996) and Coghlan and Brannick (2005). It is a cyclic, reflexive approach to research and was particularly suited to this project because of its potential to empower participants and enable them to collaborate with each other. Collaboration could facilitate learning about each other's profession and lessen the gulf between them which, as my experience, previous research and the literature had all suggested, has hitherto been a stumbling block to best art therapy practice in education. The sharing of information in the collaborative working relationships that the research sought to develop could, I proposed, offer a wider perspective about the children that could lead to positive changes in practice for all involved.

Winter (1996) suggests that there are six principles at the core of the action research process and sums them up thus:

1. Reflexive critique: becoming aware of one's own perceptive ideas.
2. Dialective critique: understanding the various elements which make up the phenomena in the context.
3. Collaboration: where the intention is to consider that everyone's view contributes to understanding the situation.
4. Risking disturbance: a willingness to 'rock the boat' and look critically at one's own processes.
5. Creating plural structures: producing various accounts and structures and not just one authoritative interpretation.
6. Theory and practice/internalised: understanding that theory and practice are interdependent but complementary aspects of change.

In short, Participative Action Research is a fundamental tool of professional development.

I used Coghlan and Brannick's 'Spiral of Action Research Cycles' (2005) to facilitate interaction between all the participants in the research. This is an organic, reflexive model which focuses on working with and for the personnel involved rather than on them. As a consequence the way forward cannot be prescribed as it is dependent on the contribution of all involved. It is a 'bottom-up' approach that links researcher and participants in a joint partnership.

The nursery and school staff collaborating in my project observed and interacted with the children on a daily basis. They also had close contact with the child's home and carers and so potentially a wide background knowledge of the child. The art therapist, on the other hand, had the opportunity to observe and relate to the child in a completely different environment where, in the safety of the therapeutic setting, the inner imaginal life of the child might be revealed. Together they had the potential to create an holistic profile of a child as he or she moved through the transition from nursery to primary school. I hoped that a collaborative approach would enable each practitioner to have greater insight into the purpose and role of the other that would lead, through sharing knowledge and skills, to each having an enhanced understanding of the other and to a growth in the professional expertise of both. My purpose was to improve the delivery of art therapy services in education by studying the processes and outcomes of an attempt to change and influence practice in a particular setting.

Eventually I found a willing collaborator. The head teacher was eager to be engaged in a project which seemed to fill the gaps in the school's support needs. The Head of Schools for the district believed that art therapy had great potential for those children who required extra support and gave formal permission for the research project. She also agreed to pay for an art therapist for one day a week. This action-based part of the research lasted for three years until national educational cutbacks unfortunately led to withdrawal of the art therapist's services.

The research was carried out in a mainstream primary school that stood on an open campus in an ex-mining village which had suffered badly following the closure of the local pit and the redundancy of the miners. The school buildings had recently been refurbished with improved facilities and opportunities for the children. Sharing the campus was a leisure centre with games facilities and a new family centre where the nursery class involved in the project was located. The primary school had approximately two hundred and sixty pupils aged from five to eleven years and the family centre accommodated forty nursery children aged three to five years. The project was planned to begin with the involvement of children in the last year of nursery and the first year of school. The art therapist would work with individuals or groups of children in the nursery and then continue therapy with them on their transfer to the primary school, as illustrated in Figure 4.1.

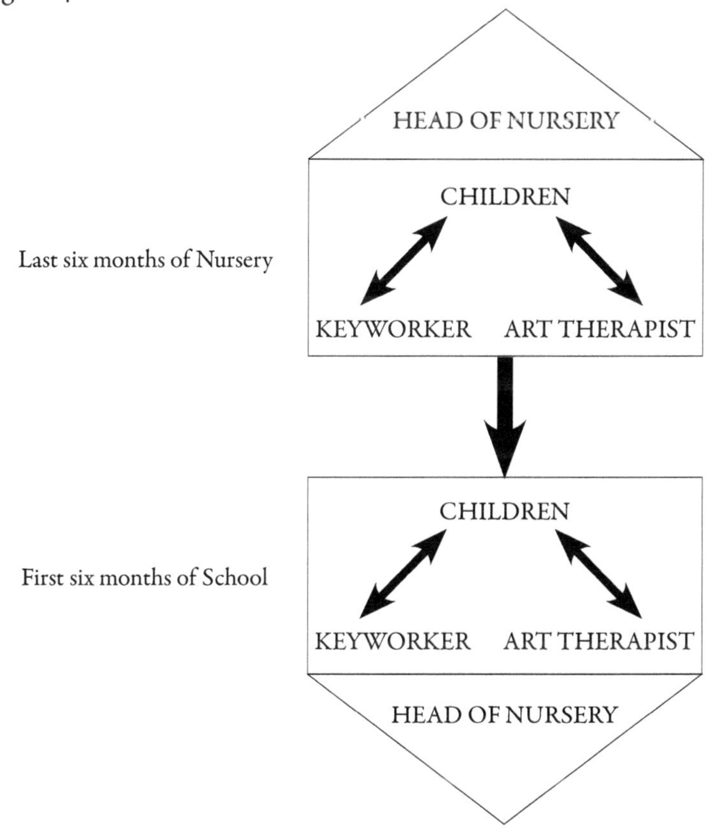

Figure 4.1 Model of Project.

Permission was granted beforehand by the local authority children's services officers and written ethical consent for the project was obtained from all involved parties. This included a letter from the art therapist agreeing to share all aspects of her work with me for the duration of the project. Good liaison practices with visits and meetings were already well-established between the nursery and the school prior to the research. However, in order to explain the nature and purpose of art therapy, and before collaboration could take place, it was necessary for the art therapist and I to provide a variety of explanatory sessions for parents and staff that introduced the project, gave all the necessary information and consolidated everyone's understanding of what both the research and art therapy involved. We also had to set up the necessary protocols for selection and referral, obtain parental permission for the recording and monitoring of art therapy with the children and negotiate suitable accommodation for art therapy and the continuing provision of art materials for the service.

A psychodynamic model of art therapy was used, underpinned by Winnicott's (1964) theories of early relationships and Bowlby's (1988) concepts of attachment, illuminated by Trevarthen's (1989) research on the dyadic interaction between baby and adult. A significant aspect of the psychodynamics of interpersonal relationships is the notion of transference and counter-transference. These embrace the belief that attitudes and feelings from our earliest relationships are re-enacted in the present. I chose this particular approach because it has been recognised that disturbances of thinking in children may be rooted in their earliest troubled relationships and that what happens between the infant and care-giver is vitally important (Hobson, 2002). Indeed Coren (1997) suggests that both teachers and therapists should be aware of the potential for collusion with inappropriate patterns of behaviour which both they and the children have acquired in their early environments.

Familiarisation with the therapeutic approach occurred through group creative art activities with the art therapist and nursery staff; this was for all final year nursery children. Meetings, discussions and awareness-raising presentations were also provided for parents, school and nursery staff. This 'bottom-up' or equal partnership approach (Robson, 2002) introduced art therapy to selected children for their final nursery term and first school term, the purpose being to develop a joint staff support system which responded to these vulnerable children's needs before, during and after their transition from nursery to primary education.

Selection, Referral and Timing

The selection of children for art therapy was based on the keyworker's observation of the children in the art activity groups. Once written parental permission had been received, weekly group (fifty to seventy five minutes) or individual (twenty-five to forty minutes) therapy sessions were offered, according to need. Groups were run by the art therapist and a staff member together in order to ensure adequate containment and support.

The majority of referrals were from nursery staff after the summer holidays, as was originally intended. However, as the project progressed other children's needs became obvious and urgent, both earlier and later than the agreed period. These children were able to be accommodated satisfactorily within the art therapist's schedule, rendering her role more flexible and responsive to the needs of both establishments.

The children referred fell into six categories; emotional difficulties, behavioural problems, social problems, difficulties with cognition, speech and language disorders and behaviours on the Autistic Spectrum (see Figure 4.2). At this stage the referrals for emotional difficulties far exceeded other categories and showed staff's prioritising the support of these particular children in the learning environment.

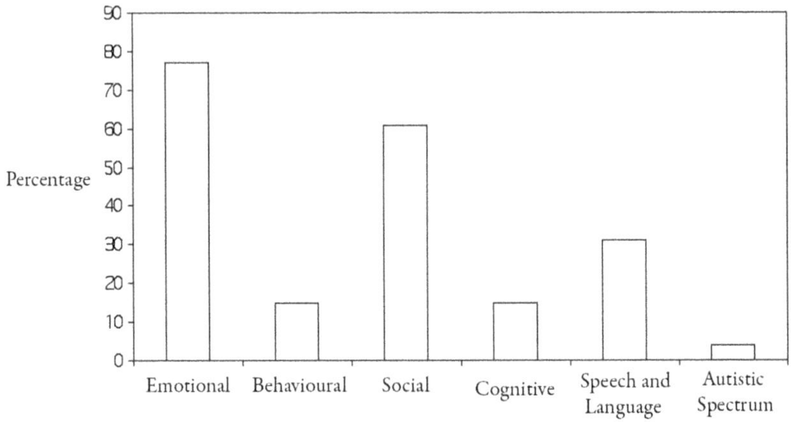

Figure 4.2 Reasons for Referral.

The initial plan was to offer art therapy to those who might benefit most during their last six months in nursery and first six months in Primary One, as can be seen in Table 4.1. This shows the number of children commencing and finishing art therapy in each of the three cohorts across all three years of data collection. However, it can also be seen that in Cohort One, one child required an extra term's support. In Cohort Two, ten children completed a year of art therapy, from January to December 2005, but in August 2005 three Primary One children began art therapy and continued to December 2006. In Cohort Three there was one early nursery art therapy referral as well as referrals for four children in their last six months of nursery. Art therapy, as part of the research, finished for all by December 2006. Decisions about the timing of beginnings and endings of art therapy were made according to the needs of the child and in collaboration with school and nursery staff, the art therapist and myself. Over the three years of the research, twenty seven children received art therapy for varying periods of time. At the end of the project children requiring further support were offered an extension of art therapy.

Cohort One, April–December 2004			Cohort Two, January–December 2005			Cohort Three, January–December 2006	
Apr. 2004	Dec. 2004	Mar. 2005	Jan. 2005		Dec. 2005	Jan. 2006	Dec. 2006
START 7 Nursery	FINISH 6 Primary 1	FINISH 1 Primary 1	START 10 Nursery		FINISH 10 Nursery	START 1 Early Nursery	FINISH 1 Nursery
				Aug. 2005		4 Nursery	4 Primary 1
				START 3 Primary 1	→	→	3 Primary 1
						2 Primary 3	2 Primary 4

Table 4.1 Project Description.

Listening to Staff

Meetings between the heads of departments, the art therapist and myself as the researcher were minuted and displayed for all staff to see and comment upon. I conducted sixteen individual interviews with the nursery and primary school staff at the beginning and end of therapy for the three annual cohorts of children having therapy. This enabled me to ascertain how the project was being received, to identify school and nursery needs, to acknowledge opinions and problems and to adapt the project so that it could meet and accommodate these issues more efficiently. For example, one problem raised by nursery staff concerned the restriction of art therapy to those children who would proceed to the primary school on campus. This was resolved favourably, with permission of the Director of Education at the time, by the inclusion of children for art therapy who were moving on to other local schools, with the promise of a follow-up if necessary. The cyclical model of Participative Action Research enabled such difficulties, as well as bias and differences, to be addressed and changes to be made, thus providing a flexible model of therapy provision and research that was responsive to the needs of the children in both the school and the nursery.

Throughout the study qualitative evaluation took place, in accordance with the cyclical model of action research. This resulted in the ongoing adjustment of procedures, as I have just described. However, to demonstrate more persuasively the fulfilment of the project's aims I also undertook a summative evaluation. This involved nursery and school personnel and the children's parents completing quantitative questionnaires and responding to a series of statements using a five-point Likert Scale.

Findings

A major aspect of the project was to ensure that staff in both establishments had a 'greater understanding of art therapy's role in nursery and school.' Responses from teachers and nursery staff suggested that efforts to achieve this through workshops, presentations and liaison meetings, had a positive effect: 95 per cent of both parties indicated that they either agreed or strongly agreed with this statement (Figure 4.3).

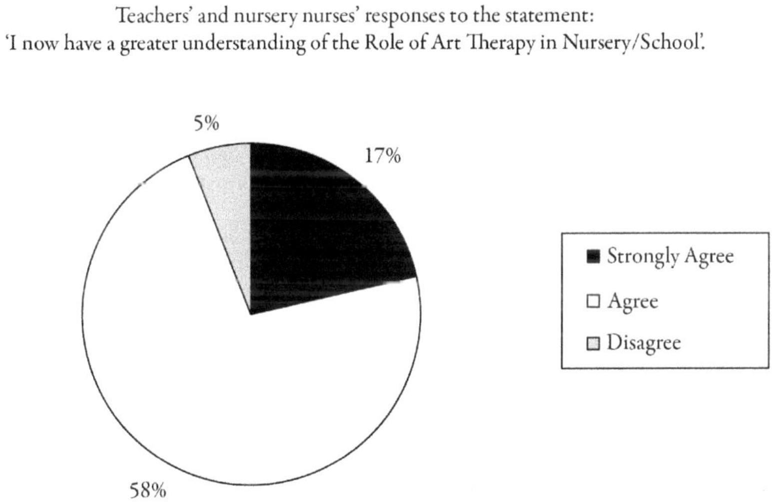

Figure 4.3 Understanding of Art Therapy.

For example, one teacher found the meetings and presentations 'Very clear, straightforward, enjoyable and enlightening – a boost for my Continuing Professional Development.' Another said: 'Communication between class-teacher and art therapist enables both to see a wider picture of the child. Observations from one can support the other.' This was evident in the exchanges between therapist and key-worker which demonstrated the importance of liaison. To the key-worker one little boy was consistently 'very quiet and uncommunicative' in the wider nursery environment. However, and much to the keyworker's surprise, the therapist reported that he was open and talkative in art therapy about his family and their activities. This informal exchange of information was valuable to both and underlines its importance.

However there was a startling difference of opinion between the nursery staff and the teachers about whether or not the art therapist's liaison time had helped them to develop their understanding of a child's behaviour. Only 13 per cent of nursery staff agreed with this statement, the reason being that they felt that they already possessed significant knowledge of children's development and behaviour. This contrasted with the teachers, 71 per cent of whom agreed and 29 per cent strongly agreed that their understanding of children's behaviour had developed as a result of their meetings with the art therapist (Figures 4.4 and 4.5).

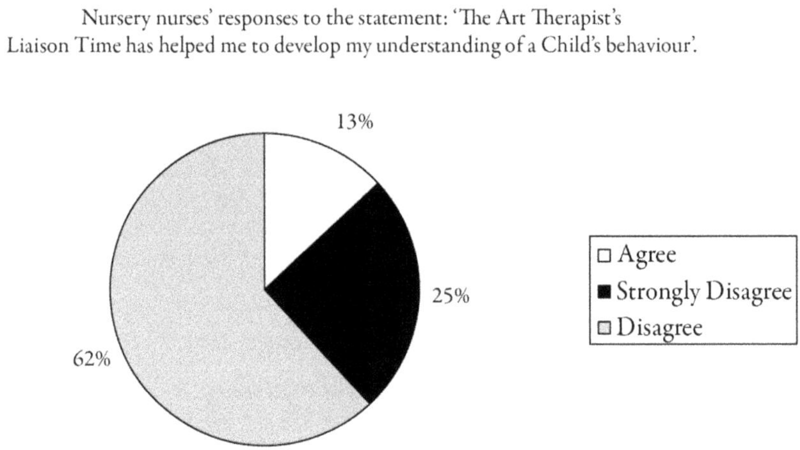

Figure 4.4 Nursery Nurses' Responses to Liaison Time.

There were also some conflicting responses to the statement 'Knowledge of symptoms which might affect children's learning and socialisation are needed for making art therapy referrals.' Although there was general agreement that this was so it was suggested that making referrals helped staff to develop their awareness of children's needs and to understand their behaviors and that this had, in turn, facilitated explanations of these needs to parents.

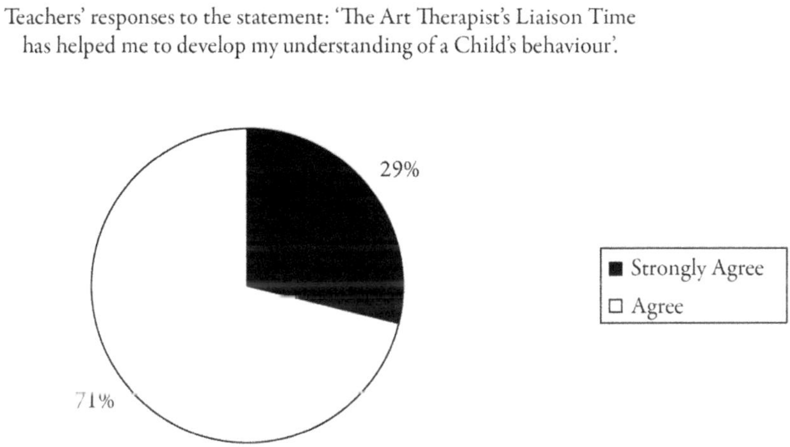

Figure 4.5 Teachers' Responses to Liaison Time.

After three years of developing art therapy in the nursery and in the school it was important to ascertain how all personnel responded to art therapy as an additional psychological service that could assist inclusion and facilitate learning. In spite of previous differences and early resistances, the final response to art therapy was a very positive one from both nursery staff and the primary school teachers: 13 per cent of nursery staff strongly agreed and 87 per cent agreed that children's learning and inclusion was supported; 80 per cent of teachers strongly agreed and 20 per cent agreed (Figures 4.6 and 4.7). Staff in both establishments were therefore in full agreement that art therapy provided a service which enhanced children's inclusion and supported their learning.

Nursery Nurses' responses to the statement: 'Provision of Art Therapy is an important additional Psychological Service to assist in Inclusion and Facilitate Learning'.

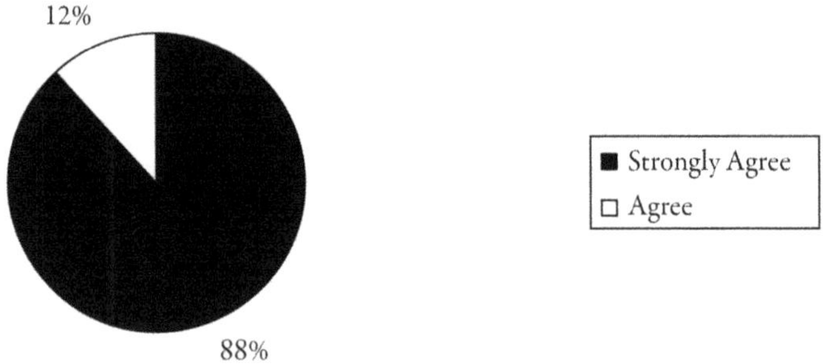

Figure 4.6 Nursery Nurses' Responses to Art Therapy Service.

Teacher's Responses to the statement: 'Provision of Art Therapy is an important additional Psychological Service to assist in Inclusion and Facilitate Learning'.

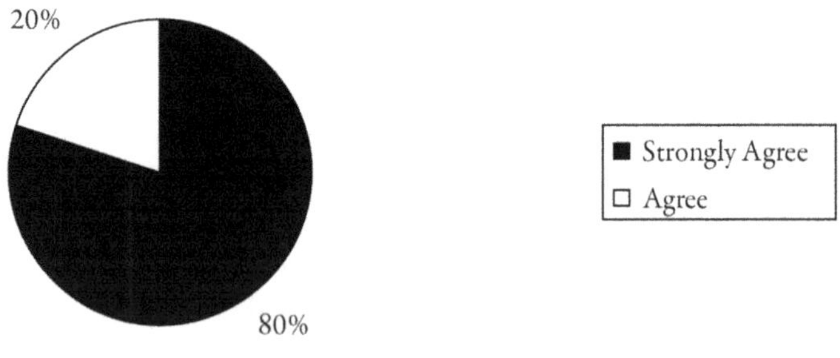

Figure 4.7 Teachers' Responses to Art Therapy Service.

As one respondent said: 'Input to the school was invaluable. Art therapy supports the curriculum for excellence by helping pupils towards being successful learners, confident individuals and effective contributors.'

The main purpose of the parents' evaluation was to elicit parents' and carers' opinions of art therapy at the end of the research. Responses to the statement 'Art therapy in school is a positive way to support children's learning' demonstrated that 40 per cent of parents strongly agreed and 33 per cent agreed (Figure 4.8). However, it seemed to me that parents were more comfortable with responding to the questionnaires than attending relevant school meetings. Sixteen out of twenty-one questionnaires were completed and returned compared with only one parent who attended a final meeting with the art therapist and primary school staff.

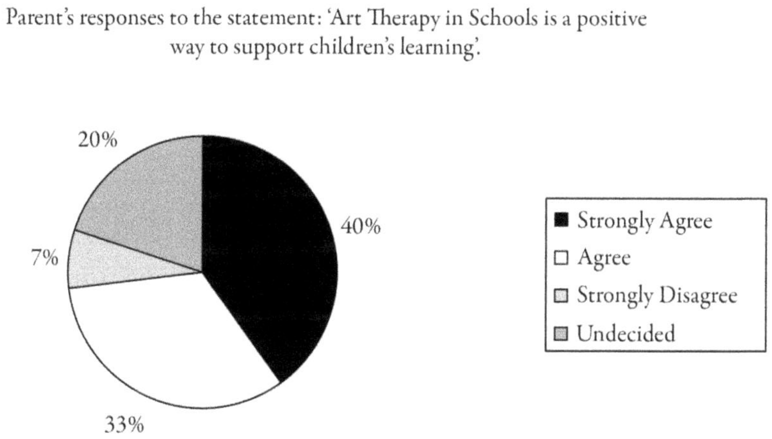

Figure 4.8 Parents' Responses to Art Therapy Service.

The second aim of evaluating the effectiveness of the art therapy sessions was problematic. Permission had been given to use the nursery's official profiles of the children but these were insufficiently focused to be useful for the evaluation of change or progress in the children's learning. Added to this were the nursery staff's strongly held views about inclusion and labelling which made them wary of quantitative evaluation measures. Formal, standardised screening methods were also unacceptable because of language that was perceived as politically incorrect and which used a 'tick box' approach. Discussions about these issues were very lengthy and time-consuming.

The effectiveness of the children's art therapy was therefore assessed (a) by the nature of the art produced, (b) how the child responded to the art-making process and (c) by observation of changes in interpersonal relationships recorded in the art therapist's clinical notes. The table (Table 4.2) gives several excerpts from the children's records which show the relationship between the aims and outcomes of art therapy for some of the children.

	Aims	Outcomes
1	To give meaningful experience re development of expression of feelings and self-confidence	Although very quiet to begin with now interacts and communicates frequently, talking of family
2	To build self-confidence for transfer	From tentative, very quiet and limited to a remarkable development in spontaneous talk and confidence – working enjoyable – tidying up afterwards
3	To support confidence and provide communication oppotunities	From very quiet and almost invisible to more mature than others in the group, communicates easily with art therapist and peers
4	Benefit from small group environment and supportive intervention	

Table 4.2 Aims and Outcomes.

Discussion

Several authors have asserted that art therapy with children is effective. Waller (2006), for example, suggested that those who work psychodynamically with children's problems consider that change may occur because children can channel their negative emotions into art. This makes them accessible and able to be shared and understood – with the art therapist's help – safely, and at one remove. Dalley (1990) stated that: 'The practice of art therapy within a school can run in conjunction with and indeed facilitate the educational process' (167), an assertion supported by Welsby (2008) who argues that art therapy's presence within a school 'raises staff awareness as to the presence of mental health in relation to learning' (213). The positive responses of nursery and school staff to art therapy in this research supports these views.

However, and despite the positive responses to art therapy, there were significant issues surrounding its integration into nursery and primary education. First, a narrow interpretation of 'inclusion', meaning that a child should not be singled out for additional appropriate support, was a considerable handicap which cast a shadow on the art therapist's role in the nursery. Art therapy was accepted later on by the majority of staff, after their experience had led them to consider art therapy to be a suitable intervention for a variety of childhood problems. Perhaps seeing and knowing how the art therapist worked helped key workers to understand that group and individual art therapy supported and enabled a child to fit with school society with greater confidence.

Second, it became clear that the best way to appreciate and support the differing roles of early years' educators and art therapists in constructive ways needs careful consideration. Certainly designated liaison time for the art therapist and staff members is an excellent way to forge professional partnerships and enhance mutual understanding. In too many instances the 'specialist' pays flying visits in and out of school and an appropriate box is ticked. Staff appreciated the 'face-to-face' time with the art therapist, as was demonstrated by comments which said that this had been 'very helpful with all the rest of my work with the child'; 'The art therapist's reports were useful for the children's records and great support at staged intervention meetings'; 'I would have liked longer liaison opportunities.'

Third, it was clear that improving the appreciation of the role of each professional could sharpen the observations of both parties, enabling a more accurate identification of children's difficulties and a more cohesive and collaborative approach to change. This could, in turn, lead to closer correlations between reported symptoms and observed change and provide a more rounded report on children's evolving behaviour.

Finally, the urgent need to recognise and relieve the intense pressure on all staff in both these educational establishments became abundantly clear. The difficulties in adhering to liaison arrangements, in taping interviews and arranging in-service sessions during the three years of the project, offered overwhelming evidence of this. Undertaking a participative action research project means that the process of change and learning cannot be foreseen from the start. This is dependent on the experience, understanding and actions of the participants and their ability to adapt (Dick, date not known). It also depends upon the constraints under which the participants have to practice (Winter and Munn-Giddings, 2001).

As Winter and Munn-Giddings (ibid.) point out, hierarchies of power and status impede and diminish the creation and distribution of knowledge. However, the findings of this research show that, in spite of the inherent difficulties in the situation, considerable progress was made in fulfilling the aims of the project. Good progress was made in the first aim which was to increase knowledge and understanding of art therapy and to create collaborative relationships between art therapists, teachers and keyworkers. The second aim – to develop a reliable means of evaluating the effect of art therapy – did not result in a ready-made solution. All agreed that labeling and standardised tests, couched in what was perceived as politically incorrect language, were unacceptable. Written reports, which linked referral and outcome and indicated change were, everyone agreed, the most satisfactory approach to evaluation. Sadly there was insufficient time in this project to develop a satisfactory system or evaluation tool. Our third aim of producing a replicable model of an art therapy service for nursery and primary schools within an ethical framework was achieved and could be adapted to similar situations.

From Research into Practice

During the three years of this research change was happening as it evolved, with positive and negative experiences shaping the outcomes term by term. If it had been possible to draw on the close relationships between nursery staff and the children's parents and include the art therapist in these at the outset it may have helped to dispel anxiety and increase friendly collaboration between home, nursery and/or school and art therapy. This might, for example, have resulted in better-attended parent meetings. Nonetheless we were able to develop a service which respected regional education policies whilst adhering to the accepted tenets of art therapy. The art therapy service that resulted met the needs of the community but had insufficient time to develop fully. At the end of three years, further collaborative work was required in order to create an agreed means of evaluation that could document and demonstrate the effectiveness of the children's art therapy and capture the changes observed by members of both professional groups.

The research has not created a 'right' way of providing an art therapy service. Instead an agreement was reached between professional colleagues that enabled the development of a service which met the needs of a particular environment. If art therapists have the opportunity to collaborate with others this can only enhance their practice and the profession's reputation. An increased pool of information about the children can enable the creation of a service unique to each situation.

When it is possible to overcome the difficulties observed in groups by Bion (1970), Wengrower (2001) and others when two 'cultures' meet, both can be enriched and strengthened by their combined expertise. As Wengrower says: 'Since both cultures discussed… are focused on the welfare and development of the child/pupil it seems important that the representatives – teacher and therapist – work together to forge a dialogue that will promote their joint objectives.' (ibid. 113).

ANDREA GILROY

Commentary: Art Therapy with Children

Art therapists work with children who have many different kinds of problems and across the sectors that care for and educate them. The chapters in Part One of this book draw on the research of art therapists who, in the main, work in education, albeit within the differing educational systems in England, Germany and Scotland. Nonetheless their research addresses clinical and institutional issues that have a general application to art therapy with children, no matter the sector nor the institution.

The extent of mental health problems in children is well known (Green et al., 2005), as is its impact on children's capacity to learn (Aviles et al., 2006) and the significance of early intervention. Schools therefore have an important role to play in children's development and wellbeing (Pugh and Statham, 2006), especially when NHS CAMHS are frequently oversubscribed and hard to access (CAMHS, 2008); indeed NICE guidelines advocate school-based approaches to children's mental health (2008, 2009). However, there remains little evidence for or against the effectiveness of psychodynamic therapies with children.

Similarly there are many gaps in the evidence base supporting the effectiveness of art therapy with children although the outcome studies there are give rise to optimism (Gilroy, 2006). These show, for example, improvements in children's self-esteem (Onizo and Onizo, 1989) and academic performance (Rosal et al., 1997) as well as reductions in depression and anxiety (Tibbets and Stone, 1990) and problematic behaviours (Rosal, 1993; Saunders and Saunders, 2000). Interestingly, in relation to the three school-based researches described in this book, a number of these research projects took place in schools. These include single case experimental studies (Stanley and Miller, 1993; Pleasant-Metcalf, 1997), RCTs in mainstream education (e.g. Rosal, 1993) and special education (Tibbets and Stone, 1990), and Chin et al.'s controlled outcome study of an art therapy group, also in special education (1980), all of which had positive results.

Other outcome studies have demonstrated art therapy's effectiveness in different kinds of healthcare settings: for example, Kymiss et al's controlled study of art therapy groups in an in-patient facility for adolescents (1996) and Saunders and Saunders's study of an art therapy service within a large, private healthcare facility (2000). More recently Pifalo (2006) followed up and expanded her successful pilot study (2002) of group art therapy combined with cognitive-behavioural therapy for children and adolescents who had been sexually abused. Lyshak-Stelzer et al. (2007) also report positive results of their RCT of group art therapy with adolescents who had Post Traumatic Stress Disorder (PTSD) and Eaton et al.'s meta-analysis of art therapy research shows its effectiveness with traumatised children (2007).

Similar bodies of qualitative research address art therapy with other groups of children with emotional and behavioural problems (Gilroy, 2006). These have demonstrated the effectiveness of structured approaches to art therapy groups in the social functioning of children with Attention Deficit Hyperactivity Disorder (ADHD) (Henley, 1999; Murphy et al., 2004); shown that art therapy can aid the sensory and cognitive development of children on the autistic spectrum (Henley, 2001; Evans and Dubowski, 2001); and indicated the effectiveness of individual (O'Brien, 2003, 2004) and group art therapy (Brown and Latimer, 2001; Buckland and Murphy, 2001) with children who have been sexually abused.

The research described in Part One of this book about art therapy with children supports and develops some of these findings, placing a few more bricks in the evidential wall. Prokofiev, Herrmann, Hosea and Stirling have demonstrated that art therapy leads to improvements in young clients' self-esteem, cognitive abilities and behavioural problems. They have also contributed evidence about the importance of sensory experiences in art therapy in the development of children's liveliness and intersubjectivity in ways that need no interpretation but which require facilitation and containment from the art therapist. These practitioner researchers have shown that the art process in art therapy can move a child towards an understanding of themselves and their experiences through art and put the case for art therapy's role in the repair of developmental deficits.

These themes were developed during conversation between the authors and the editor, especially in relation to the sensory and the aesthetic. How such experience is enabled by the art therapist – through interested, involved modelling and containment that moderates intimacy without impinging on the child – was the subject of much discussion.

The Sensory and the Aesthetic

Prokofiev, Herrmann and Hosea suggest that sensory and aesthetic experiences in art therapy can reconnect children with a sense of self in an elemental, tactile way. We explored how such experiences are not givens for deprived children, due either to an absence of, or insufficient, maternal mirroring, a lack of sensory connection between the child and their primary carer or because children have not been introduced to the pleasure of such experiences by their parents or their schools. We discussed this in relation to Rabiger (1990) who describes the educational aspect of art therapy with children who are multiply affected by deficits and institutionalisation. Contributors felt that some of their interventions and activities in art therapy were 'educational' but all agreed that introducing their young clients to art was an important part of their practice, not via instruction but rather through helping children to discover sensory, tactile experiences.

Hosea's research showed such discovery happening in her painting group for parents and their young children, either through parents painting and playing with their child whilst others watched and then followed suit, or through the art therapist modelling by making art alongside the mothers and babies. She discussed this modelling in relation to a 'good grandmother transference' (Stern, 1995). It emerged in conversation that this linked directly to other contributors' experiences with their clients. Herrmann, for example, described his blind adolescent's attachment to her grandfather who had 'explained the world' to her through tactile models and experiments that involved all the senses; this, Herrmann felt, had enabled her to engage with him and to work with clay. Similarly Prokofiev felt that it was her client's good attachment to his grandmother that had enabled him to make good use of her. In conversation Prokofiev elaborated the modelling aspect of her role as an art therapist and how she was also able to help her client see that order could be achieved in a chaotic world. She described how he would sometimes come to sessions with a bag of junk materials that his mother had collected for art therapy and simply drop it on the floor. Prokofiev would then put the egg boxes together and the yogurt cartons together and so on, helping the child to see that order could be achieved and that there was an aesthetic satisfaction to be had, even with junk. We linked this to Kohut's description of the importance of affirmative, parallel experiences in early life (in Mollon, 2001, who gives the example of a child rolling out pastry beside a grandmother), agreeing that shared experiences and activities in art therapy, coupled with the thoughtful transparency of the therapist, can help to construct an appreciation of sensory and aesthetic experiences which, in effect, help children to develop their art.

Much of our discussion explored the importance of children gaining a sense of aliveness through the art in art therapy. In her chapter Hosea explored the role of art materials in the motivation of aliveness in relation to Stern's (1985) 'now' moments and 'vitality affects'; in discussion she elaborated how 'these have to be triggered in you, there has to be a moment' when an art experience stimulates an enlivened response. This led us to talk about how the babies and toddlers in her research played with the paint, mixing and moving so that they, their mothers, and the therapists were all able to enjoy the sensory, tactile qualities of the art materials. This linked to the experimental mixtures made by Prokofiev's client and the importance of having materials like sand and water in the art therapy room, materials which some might think were rather babyish for older children. This related to our thinking that, at the outset of art therapy, practitioners do not always know what their clients have missed developmentally and that such materials offer a way in to the processes of art-making. In discussion authors gave examples of many children playing with sand or water before they could move on to more durable art materials, Hosea adding that in her experience such play was soothing for many children and a necessary part of the therapeutic process.

We also spoke about Prokofiev's description of a critical moment when she and her client looked at his just finished picture with pleasure and wonder, not quite knowing what it was that he had done but realising its importance. We discussed how this moment was not one where Prokofiev was making an interpretation; rather she had watched a fellow artist create a piece of work that they were both subsequently able to enjoy, realisation of its' meaning and significance emerging later on in the therapy. Contributors agreed that joint appreciation of form, composition and colour (as Isserow, 2008, describes) is an important part of their clinical practice, art therapy being a place where art is made and shape and form are discussed.

Collaboration and Liaison

Collaboration is another theme woven through these research projects. Hosea described how viewing video-recordings of interactions in her painting group became an important therapeutic tool for joint retrospective reflection with her clients and Herrmann collaborated with his client in a retrospective look and co-construction of the meaning of her sculptures. A different kind of collaboration is the subject of Stirling's research which explored the establishment of an art therapy service that aimed to aid children's transition from nursery to primary education. In our discussion Stirling spoke passionately about how practitioners and services are urged to collaborate and how her research had led her to question exactly what this means and to appreciate what is involved in fostering conditions where collaboration is possible. She elaborated on the problem of the differing aims of staff working in schools, including art therapists. She described how her research had led her to believe that these differences need to be acknowledged and continually addressed: we agreed that reciprocity was key to inter-professional understanding and co-operation. The early dissemination of information about art therapy through talks and meetings with all school staff – including support staff – and with parents was pivotal to the establishment of the service in the two schools that Stirling describes. Others' experiences and research (e.g. Essex, Frostig and Hertz, 1996; Moriya, 2006; Nissinmov-Nahum, 2008; Vandgrover, 1998), including research about establishing counselling in schools (Cooper, 2006; Cromarty and Richards, 2009), concur with Stirling's research findings: that when good, effective liaison is established early on and the working practices of all are properly understood, colleagues are usually neither challenged by, nor unappreciative of, a new service like art therapy.

However, Stirling's research also showed that the establishment and ongoing fostering of good inter-professional liaison takes time, as do Cromarty and Richards (ibid.) with reference to counsellors working in secondary schools. Other contributors to Part One of this book agreed and felt that this related to the cross-sectoral work that practitioners are increasingly asked to do (*Every Child Matters*, DfES, 2003; DH, 2004). This led us to think about changes in the philosophies of care in the systems where art therapists work. As three of these four authors work in education our conversation focused on how, when many art therapists started working in schools during the 1980s, their approach matched schools' differentiated, child-centred approach to education. Since then UK government policy had focused on literacy and numeracy skills to the detriment of play in early education but now various initiatives, such as the Extended School (DfES, 2005a) and the Social and Emotional Aspects of Learning (SEAL) programme (DfES, 2005b), promote a more child-centred, whole school approach to children's social and emotional skills, perhaps creating an environment that is once again conducive to art therapy.

We also discussed the different approaches to the ethical approval of research in education and the NHS, recognising that it is essential for the protection of research participants. This arose from Hosea's description of gaining ethical approval. We noted how researcher practitioners working in the NHS have to get ethical approval from their Research and Development Departments of their NHS Trusts and often from the Central Office for Research Ethics Committee (COREC) as well, whereas the contributors working in education had obtained permission for their research from different relevant authorities – Directors of Education, head teachers, Special Educational Needs Co-Ordinators, related social services, parents and

Early Years Local Authority officials. Systems of governance have evolved and become increasingly rigorous in recent years. Ethics applications now entail a long, sometimes overly bureaucratic process, requiring efforts that are not unlike 'trying to crack an enigma code' (Daniel-McKeigue, 2007: 238). Different professions, familiar with different approaches to research and treatment, are likely to vary in their approach to research ethics. Some issue formal guidelines on research ethics but these can only guide researchers and should not be regarded as 'rules' that prescribe how research ethics should be addressed (ibid.). However, the processes of ethical approval can assist the researcher/practitioner in the articulation of their project, especially in terms of speaking to a lay audience.

A Modest Contribution

The evidence offered here is, as Herrmann stated in Chapter Two, 'individualised', and not easy to replicate. Nonetheless consistencies emerged from these projects and from authors' subsequent conversation about them which, we suggest, offers cumulative, inductive evidence about best practice and art therapy's effectiveness with children.

It has been shown that art therapy is a flexible intervention that is particularly good at reaching and repairing early damage. Experimental, sometimes repetitive play with fluid and form-less materials can precede more concrete forms of art-making and introduce children to important sensory and tactile experiences that can restore developmental deficits. Children are able to regress in art therapy and gain a sense of agency through their use of art materials, making developmental advances in manual dexterity, confidence, cognitive abilities and capacity for relationship that transfer to the external world. Clearly the significance of experimental play and art-making with conventional and related materials requires an art environment in which such activities can occur.

It has also been demonstrated that children who have experienced early trauma benefit from slow, non-directive art therapy that avoids early interpretation and proceeds at the child's pace until he or she is able to enter relationship more fully. Further, artworks made early on in art therapy can usefully and appropriately repress painful material whilst enabling it to slowly emerge in a safe form that can later be explored and understood. Art therapy can enable children to integrate a damaged self and, in relation to blind clients' in particular, enables experiences of bodily fragmentation to be constructed into a whole body image. Art therapy enables self-experiences, develops the capacity to symbolise, enhances attunement, strengthens attachment and enables the sharing of 'vitality' and 'now moments' that generate a sense of feeling alive. Thus we can begin to say what works in art therapy with children.

All four projects in Part One of this book have demonstrated the contribution art therapy makes to preventative work with children who, although not necessarily displaying symptoms, were in circumstances where they could develop. Their parents and teachers were able to gain early access to therapeutic care through educational and community-based services, in line with current government policy (DfES, 2003; NICE, 2008). Linking future research about practices and services to policy developments could help secure a sustainable future for art therapy with children within the public services, witness the outcomes of Hosea's research: the development of art therapy services that are addressing gaps in infant mental health care. These four projects have shown the potential contribution that modest, practitioner research can make to art therapy's evidence base.

Plate 1.1 Visual Form of Gesture.

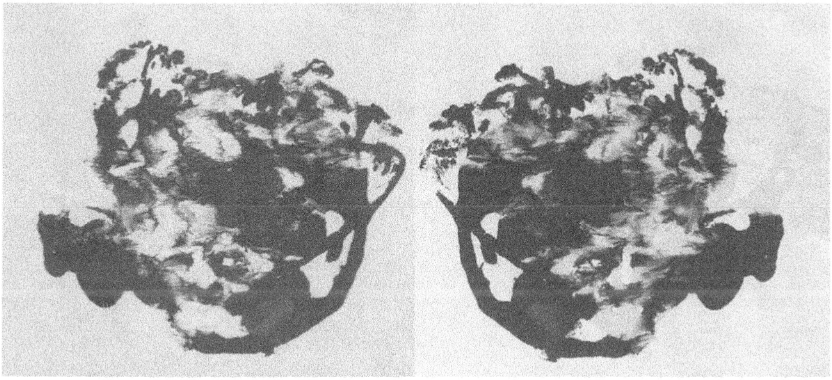

Plate 1.2 Monoprint.

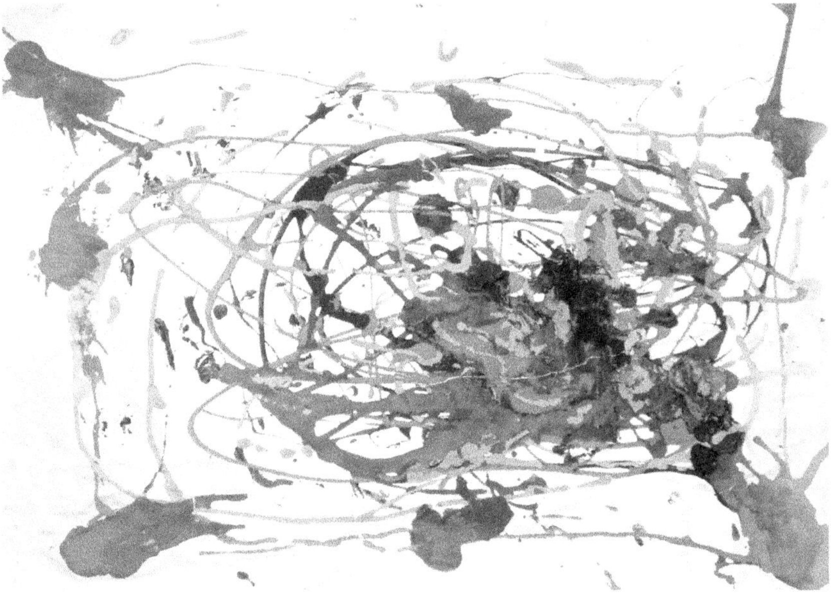

Plate 1.3 Free Action Painting.

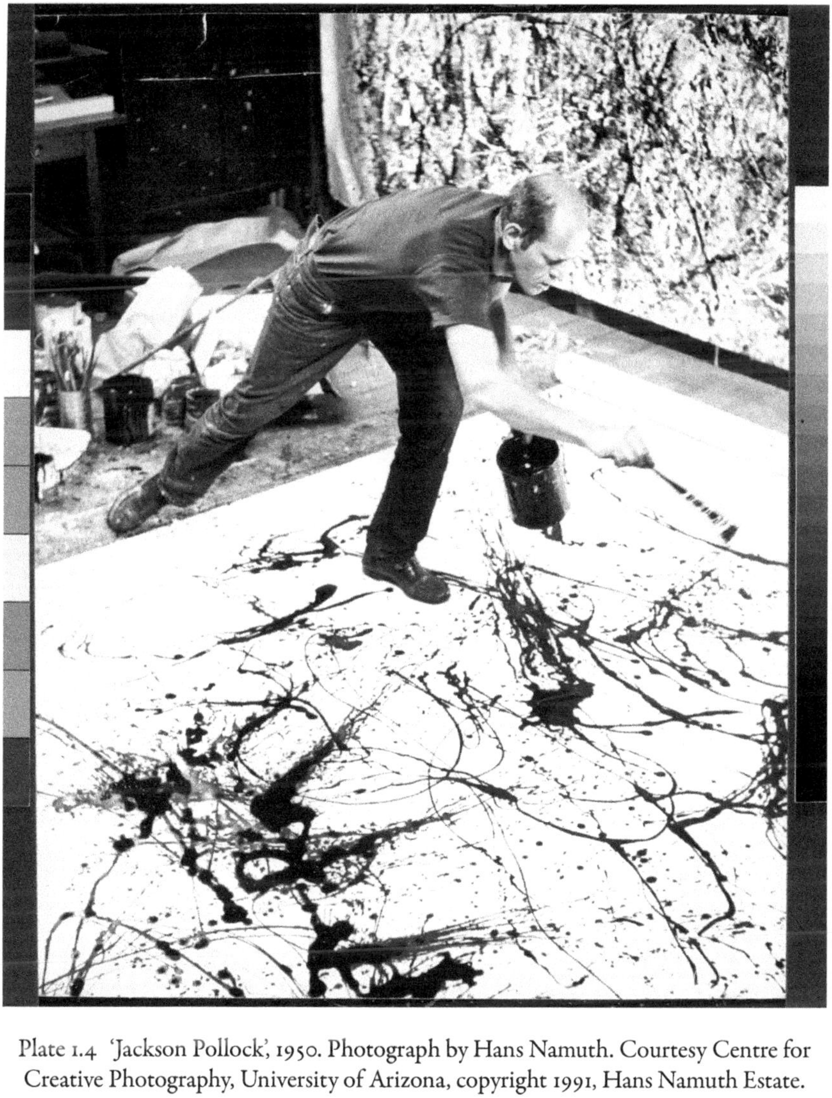

Plate 1.4 'Jackson Pollock', 1950. Photograph by Hans Namuth. Courtesy Centre for Creative Photography, University of Arizona, copyright 1991, Hans Namuth Estate.

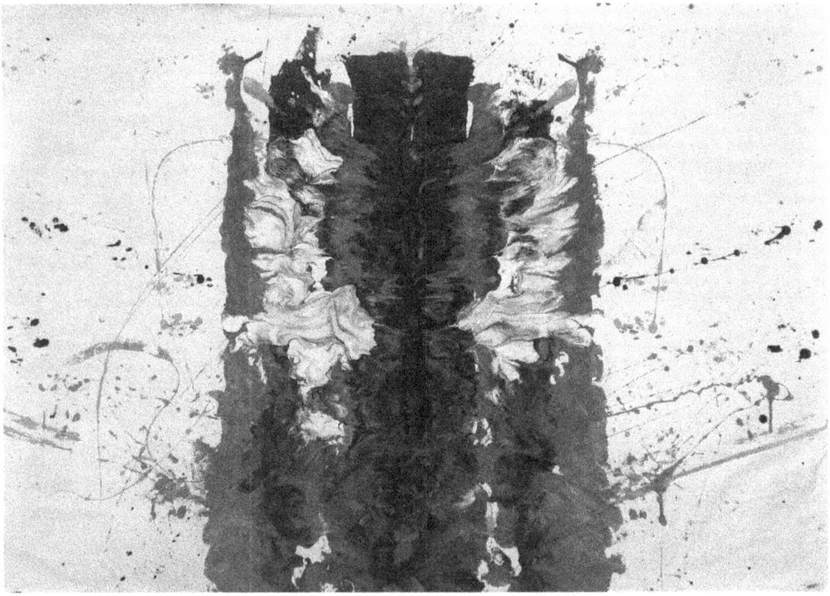

Plate 1.5 Picture-folding (Action Painting).

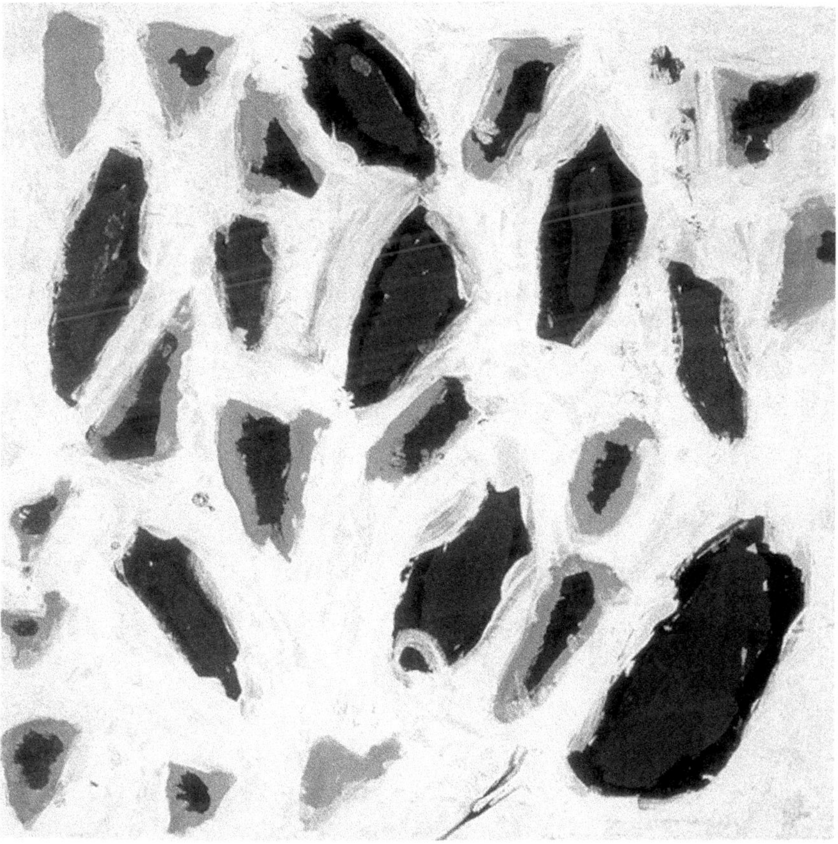

Plate 1.6 Painting in Primary Colours and Black.

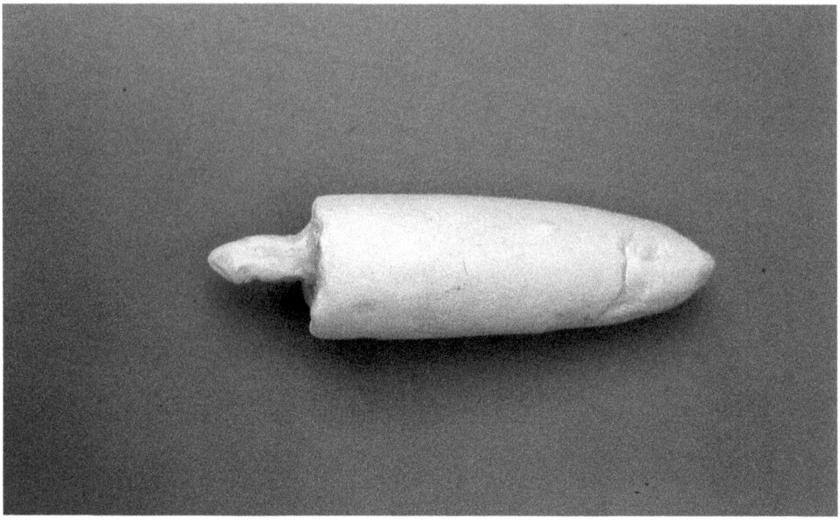

Plate 2.1a The Auxiliary Bodies: 'Helpful Somethings'.

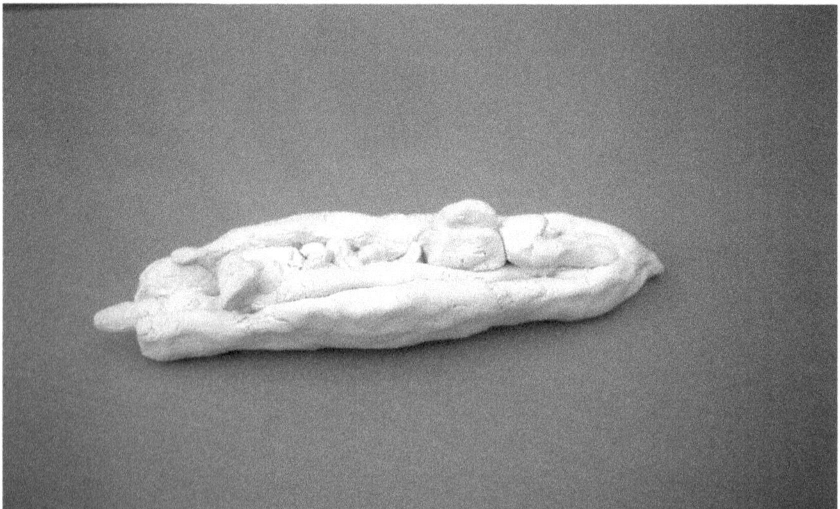

Plate 2.1b The Auxiliary Bodies: 'Helpful Somethings'.

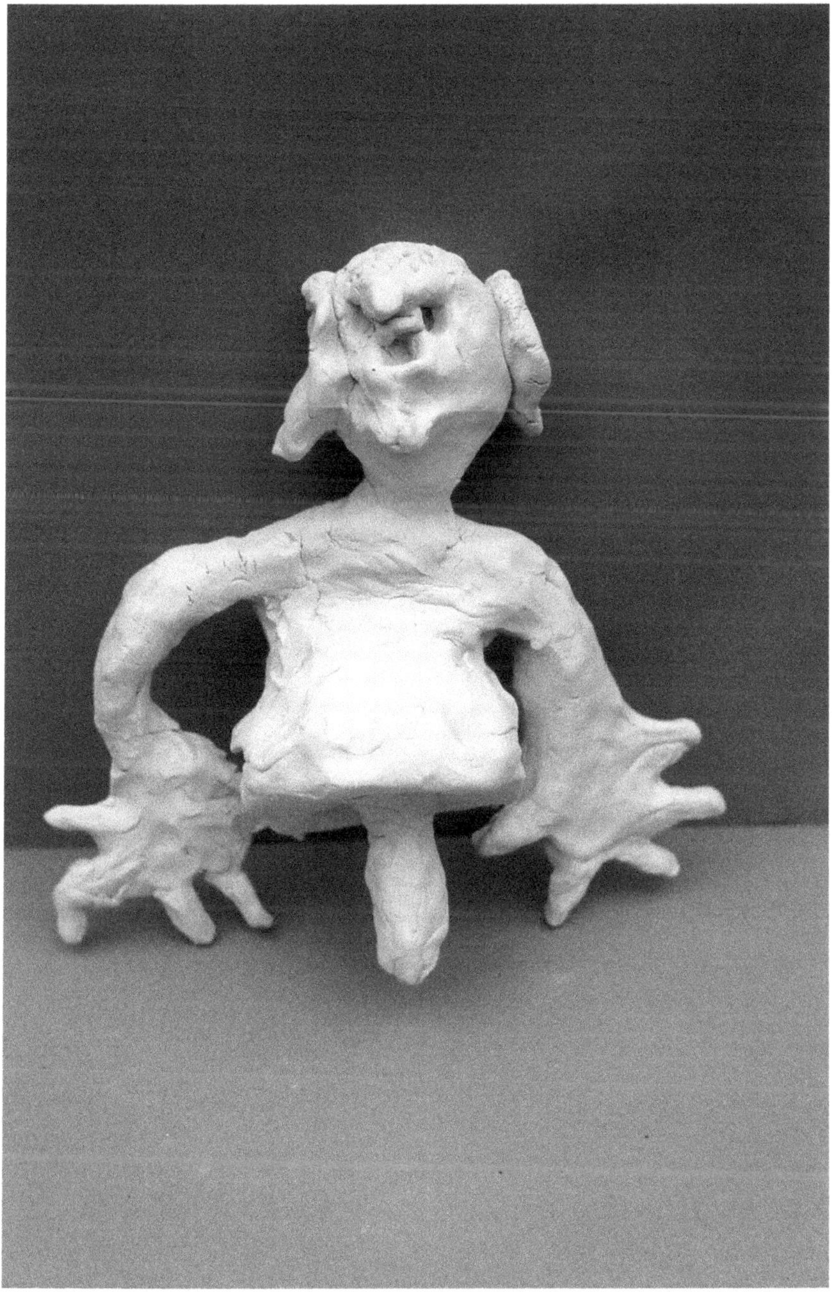

Plate 2.2 Changing Bodies: 'Gyroscopic Self Figure'.

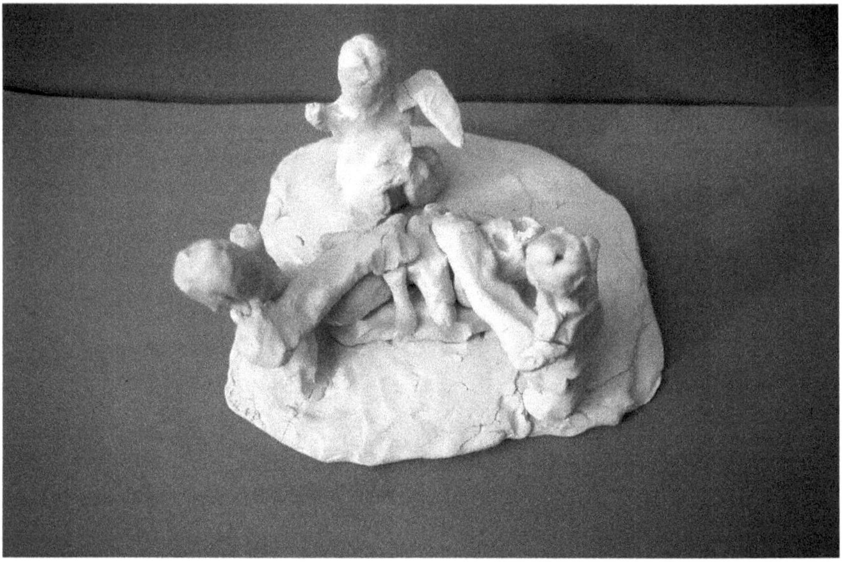

Plate 2.3 Passive Victim Bodies: 'Torn Between Mother and Teacher'.

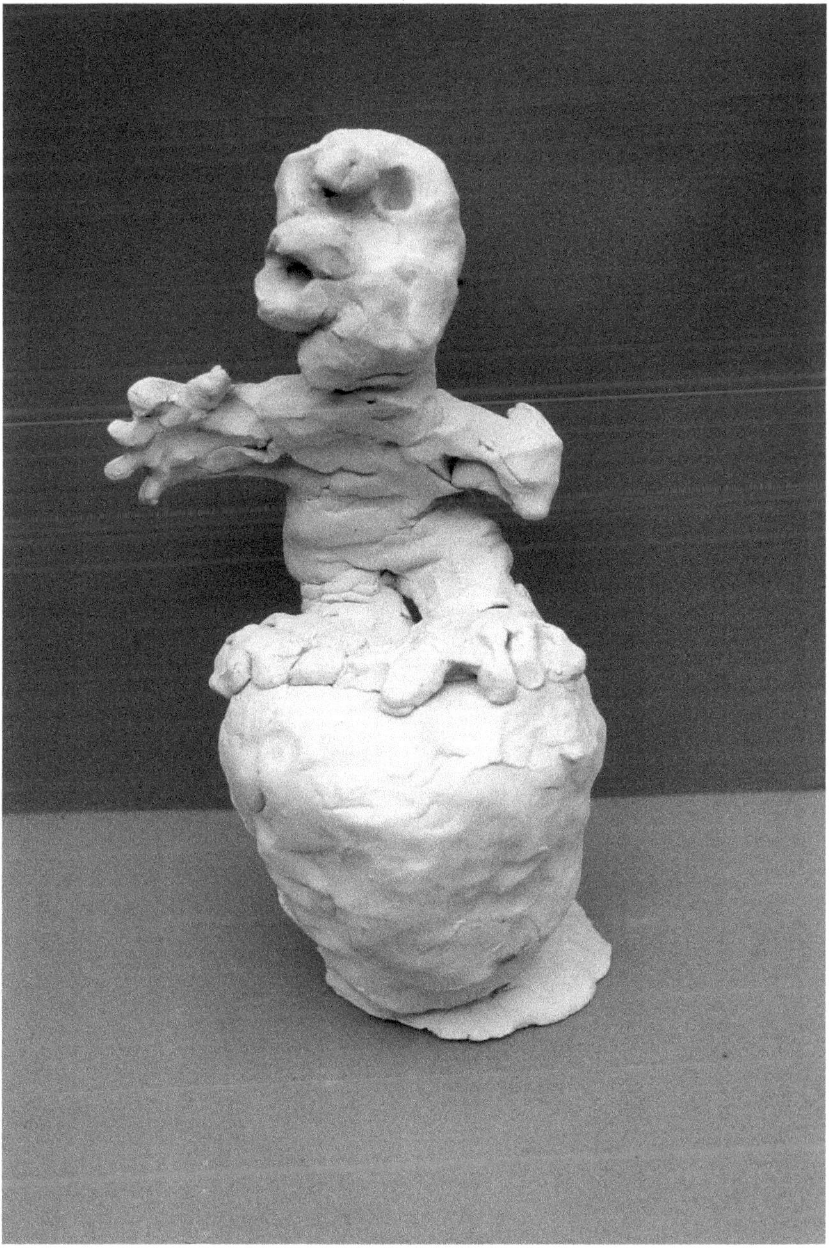

Plate 2.4 Container Bodies: 'Ambivalence'.

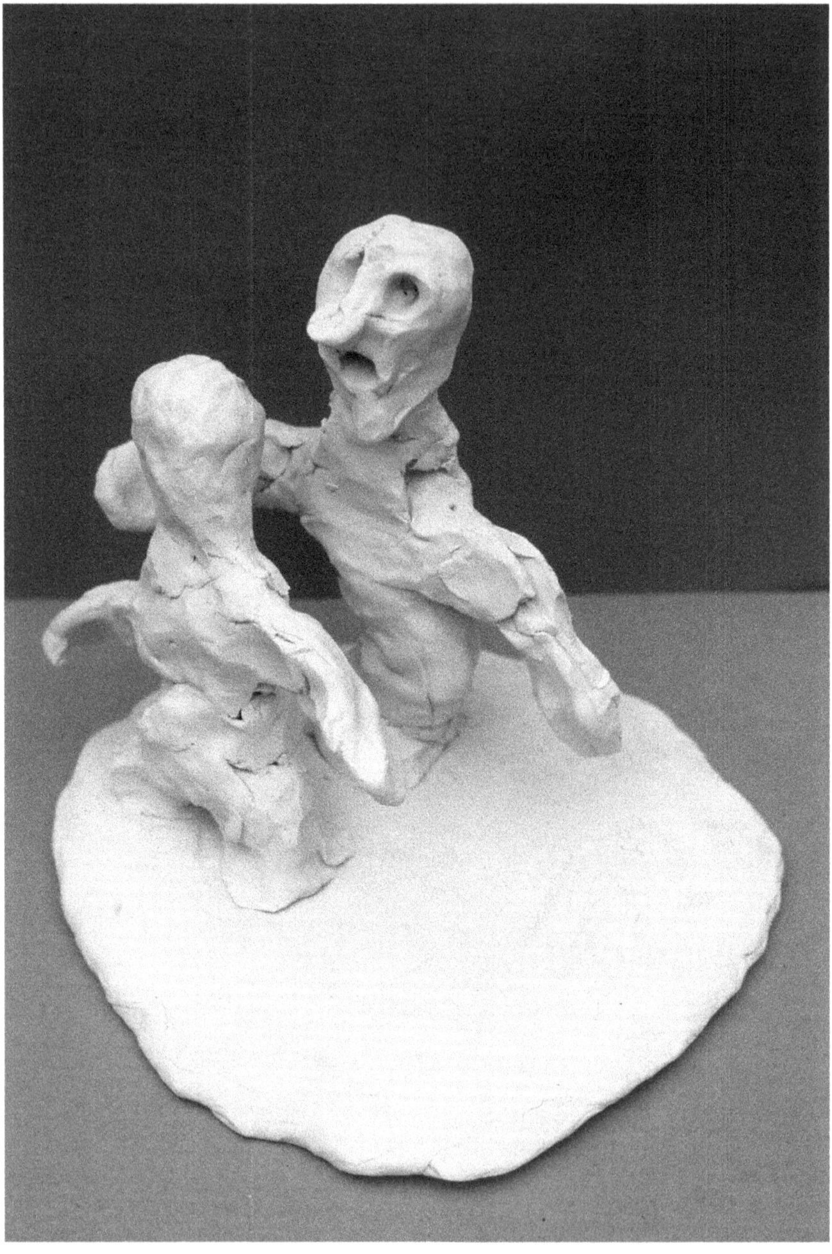

Plate 2.5 Aggressive Bodies: 'Rebecca' Beating 'Becky'.

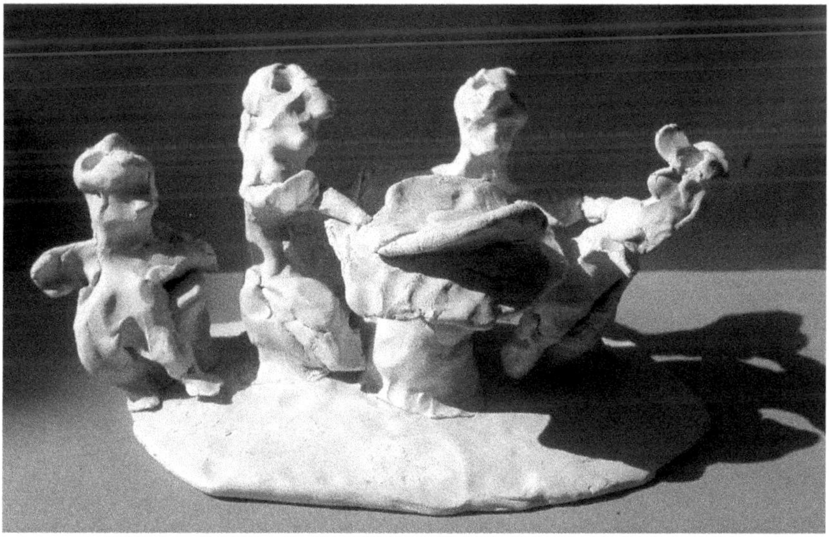

Plate 2.6 Integrated Bodies: 'Negotiation'.

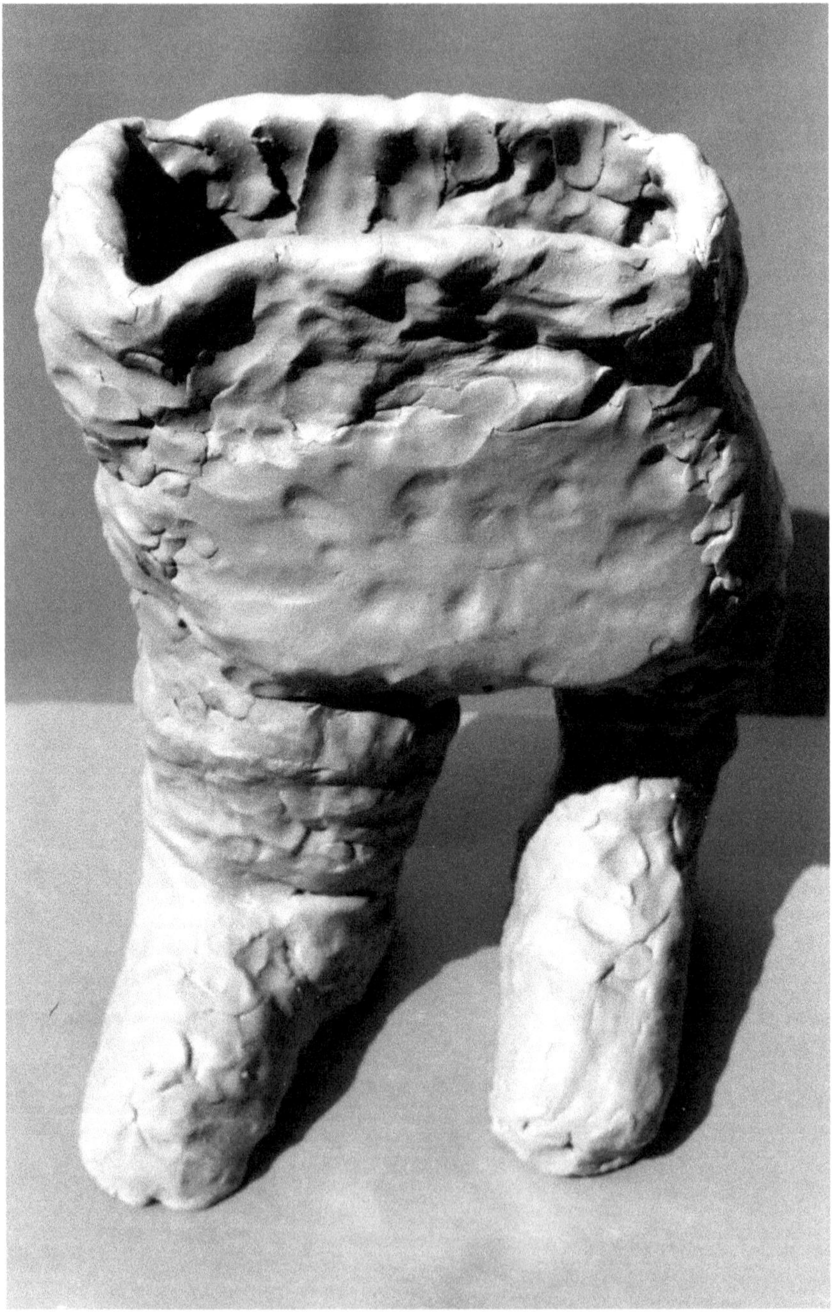

Plate 2.7 Transformed Bodies: 'The Destroyed Body'.

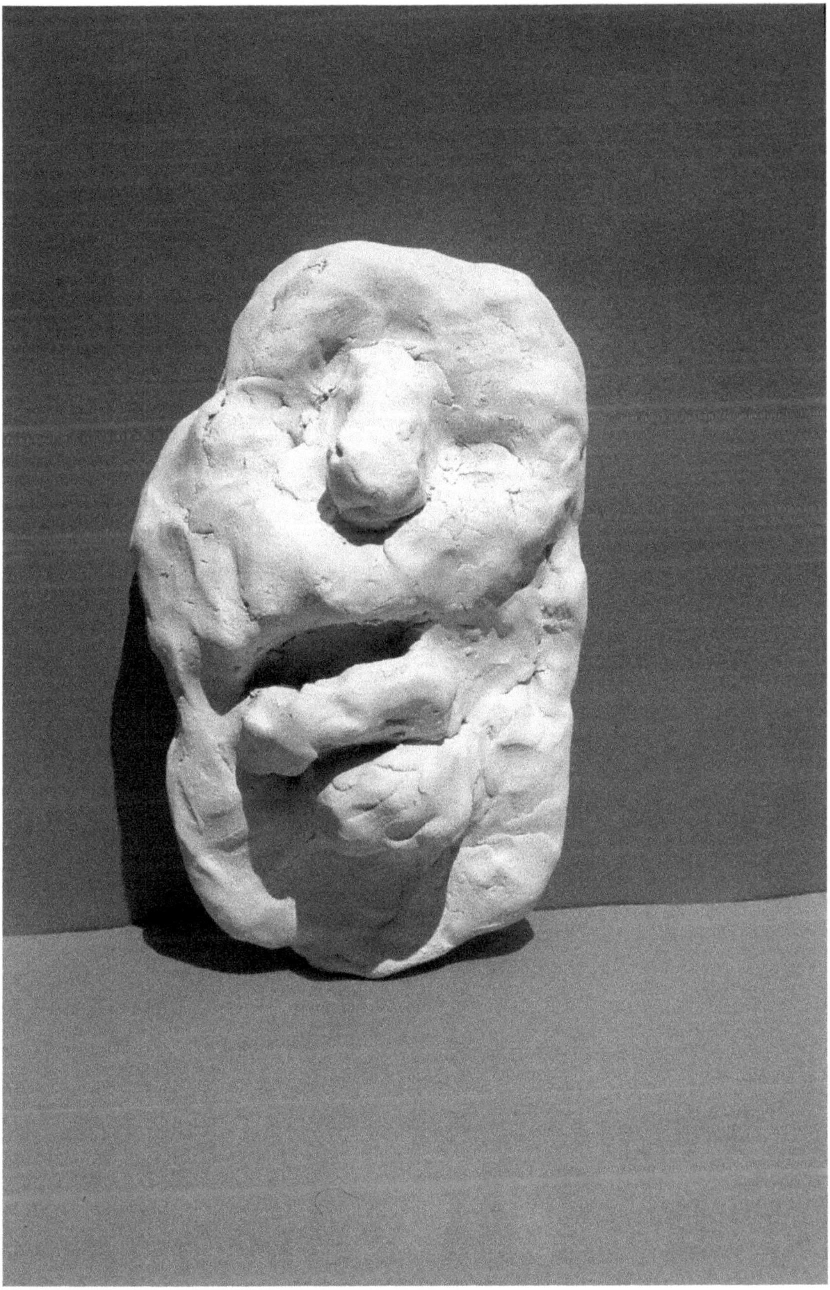

Plate 2.8 Father Bodies: 'Mask Pleading for Acceptance'.

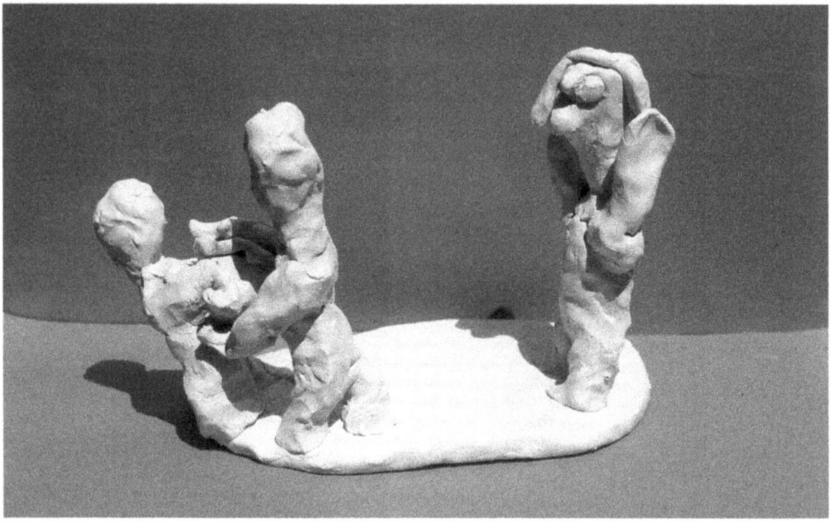

Plate 2.9 Reconciliation: 'Medusa Surrendering'.

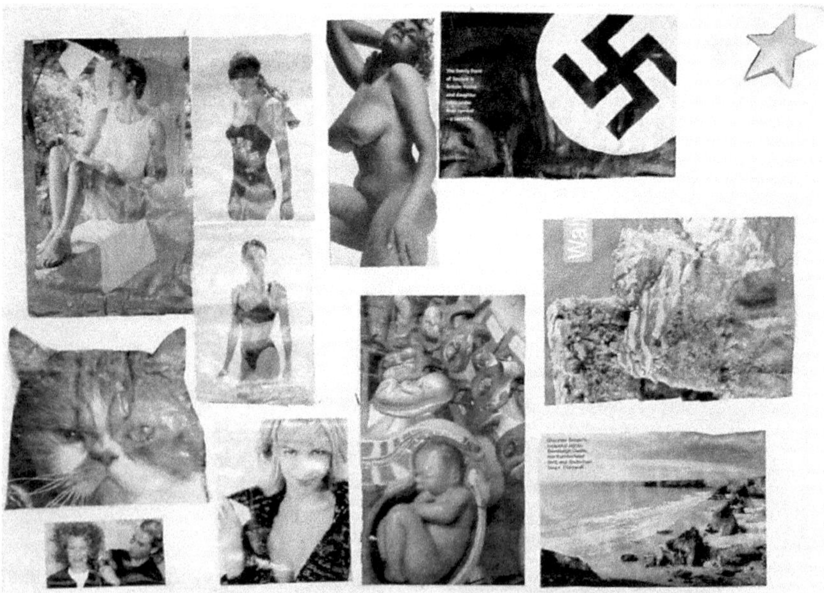

Plate 8.2 Collage.

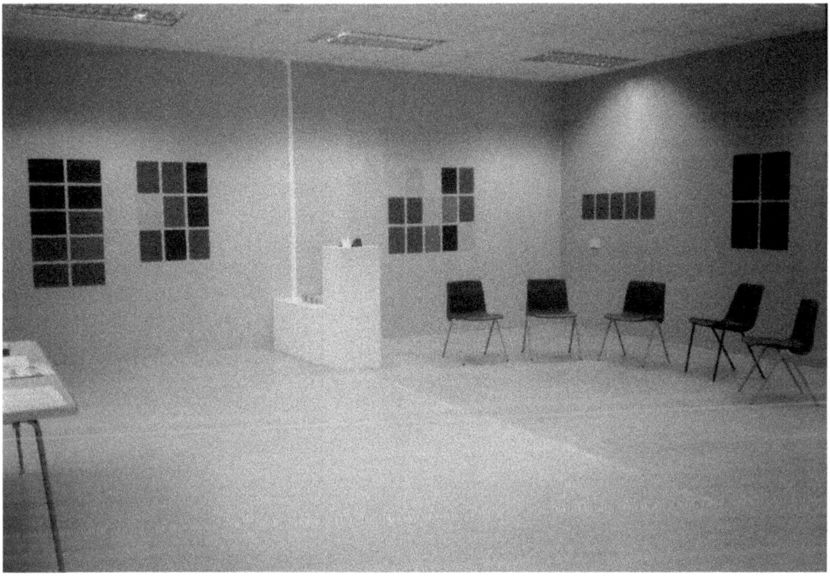

Plate 10.1 Installation View, *Algebra*, Private Exhibition, 2002.

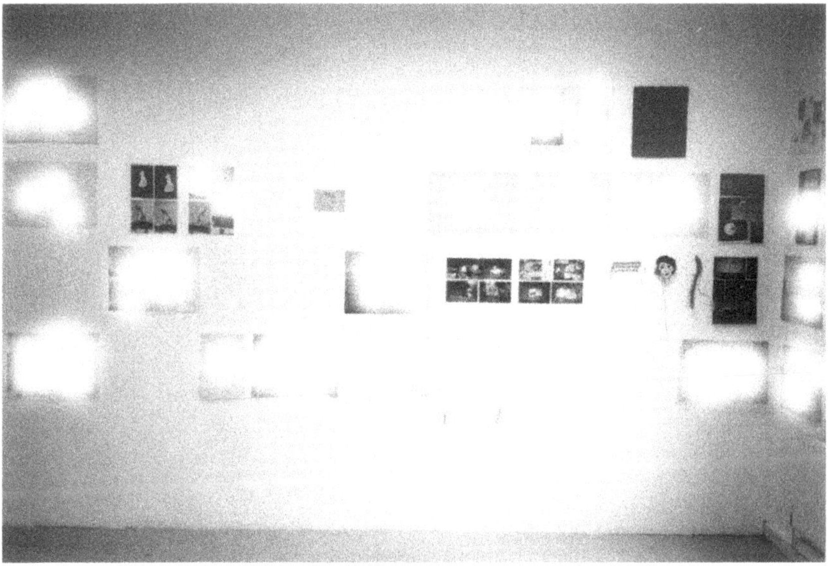

Plate 10.2 Installation View, *Artefacts 1*, Private Exhibition, 2000.

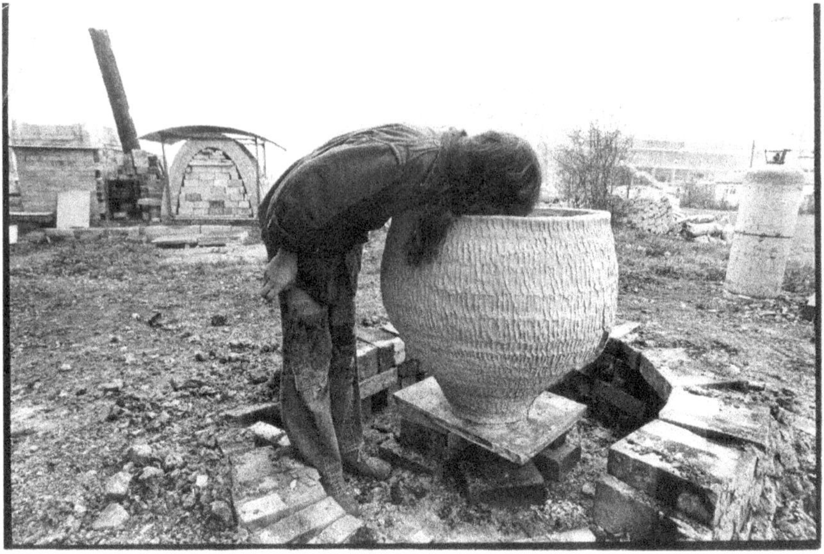

Plate 10.3 Harrow Kiln Site: Jacky Mahony Opening a One-off Kiln, 1972. Photograph by Jay Myrdal.

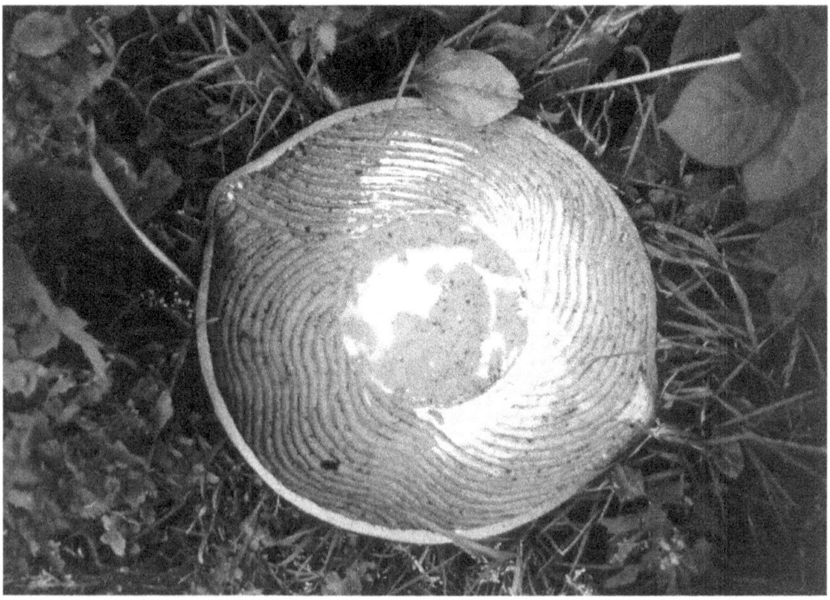

Plate 10.4 Jacky Mahony, *Carved Bowl*, 1972, celadon glaze, 44 cm diameter. Photograph by Jay Myrdal.

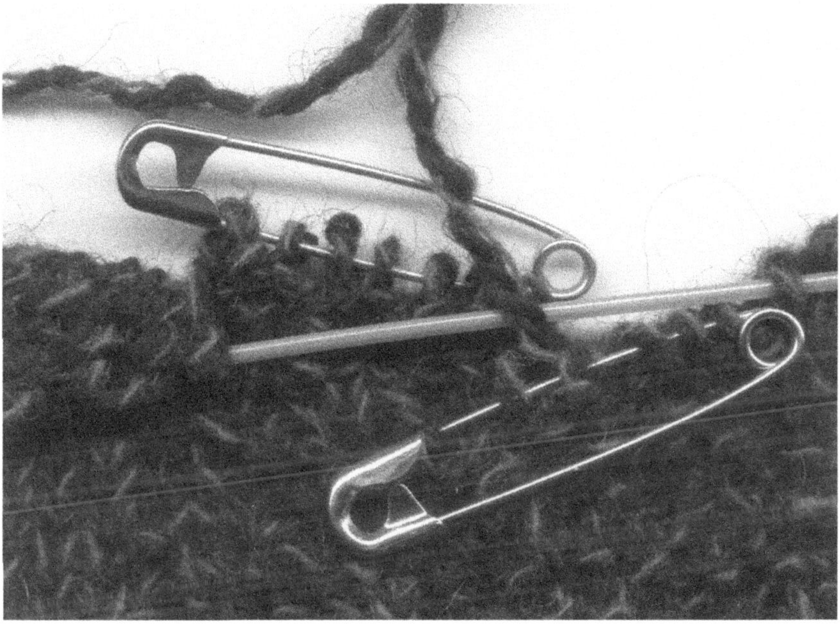

Plate 10.5 *Knitting Grayscale*, handspun Shetland wool, commercial cashmere yarn, knitting needle, safety pins. Photograph by Jay Myrdal.

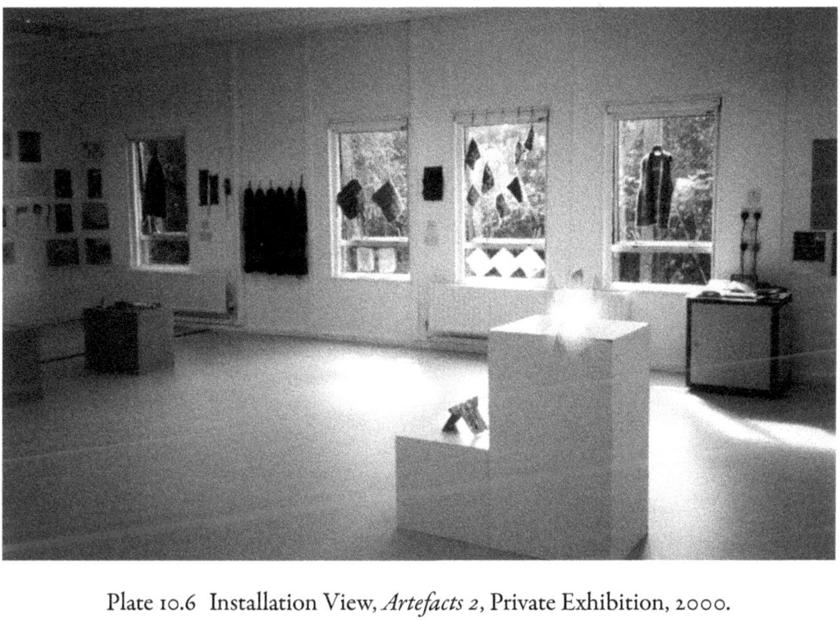

Plate 10.6 Installation View, *Artefacts 2*, Private Exhibition, 2000.

PART TWO

Researching Art Therapy with People who have Learning Disabilities

BARRIE DAMARELL

5 Shaping Thoughts: An Investigation into the Cognitive Significance of Image-Making for People with Learning Disabilities

Abstract

This chapter describes a research process involving people with learning disabilities, their art-making and their self-reported experiences of cognitive enhancement when engaged in such work. The research employs a phenomenological approach to the analysis of video data within an interpretive framework based on the work of Joy Schaverien and Rita Simon. Outcomes suggest unique connections between the subjects' verbalisations and non-making movements during image-making and their capacity to think and link.

Key Words

thinking; cognition; non-marking; utterances; image-making; diagrammati; embodied; learning disability; phenomenological; art therapy; movement; self-talk; gesture; physicality.

How it all Began: from Practice to Research

Reflecting on the process, the birth of the research question emerged rather slowly. More like a gradual dawning than a sudden revelation. I had worked, since qualifying some sixteen years previously, as an art therapist in a community service for people with learning disabilities in the southwest of England. Lying at the core of this work was a regular commitment to a day unit for people with a dual diagnosis of mental health difficulty. There were two main types of common intervention; individual sessions and an ongoing art therapy group. The latter had eight regular members drawn from people attending the unit and a number from 'out-patient' referrals to art therapy from a variety of health professions within the service.

Over my years of practice I had observed, with fascination, moments of cognitive and emotional eloquence that flowed both from group members and individuals that seemed absent in other contexts, away from the art materials. Of course, being an art therapist I was convinced that what I observed had something to do with the creation and presence of artworks in the environment created by the therapeutic relationship. The concrete tangibility of the artwork perhaps functioned as a synapse might in the brain. However, this interest remained merely an informal curiosity until one particular day about a month before the end of an art therapy group. We had been meeting once a week on a Thursday morning for the past eighteen months in a large room within the day unit. The size of the room enabled us to convene in a circle at the outset and move to tables arranged around the walls to concentrate on private art-making when the process led us there, and later, when this phase concluded, back to the circle of chairs to share and reflect upon the work. The co-therapist and I did not take part in the image-making, thereby remaining alert and present for the group.

Of course, the ending of the group was high in the group's consciousness. The end phase characteristically sparked associations with other endings and losses, some of which focused on relationships, frequently care workers, whilst others reached to the core loss of ordinariness in identity and life course. Amongst the reflections two group members, quite independently, appeared to link image-making with cognition. One person, they were both women, put it succinctly by saying that she would miss coming to the group because making pictures had helped her to think. This was important as it brought into correspondence the aforementioned casual observations regarding the thought processes of a group of learning disabled people with the process of image-making within the group environment. It was this fortuitous event that became the catalyst for the research process which will now be shared with the reader.

The Context of the Research

It is important to mention that both the aforementioned group members had, and almost invariably did, produce what Schaverien (1987, 1991) describes as diagrammatic images. It was this that prompted me to associate the diagram with thinking and which led to the first research question: 'What is it about the making of a diagrammatic image that enhances thinking?' I later incorporated two other observations from my work with individuals. These were the prevalence of vocalisation during image-making and the fascinating, non-marking movements with the art media sometimes made during the process of image construction. This extended the research question somewhat to ask: 'Does vocalisation and/or non-marking movement during the process of diagrammatic image production have a link with the cognitive experience of people with learning disabilities?'

To fully understand this web of possible connections it is important to consider the literature on the subject. The obvious place to start is with the work of Joy Schaverien who first applied the term 'diagrammatic' to art therapy imagery. Put simply, Schaverien proposes that the diagram emerges out of the client's conscious intention to give an approximate form to a preconceived mental image (1981: 86). She defines the diagrammatic image as essentially a conduit through which an idea can be conveyed to the therapist (1987: 77). In Schaverien's view this is achieved by the pictorial representation of concrete aspects of the client's outer world. Therefore, the picture appears to operate in a declarative fashion, pointing out, or referring to, material sourced from outside the pictorial boundaries. However, despite the client's hope that the image will communicate there is often recourse to either written or spoken language in order to address the ambiguities of the picture and to explain the intentions that underpin it (1991: 87). This is not to say that the diagram and its maker's emotional life are separate entities. Schaverien makes the point that the drawing is an indication or description of sadness, but importantly it does not, as she puts it, embody that emotion. The viewer understands the reference to sadness but crucially is unlikely to feel that emotion. Schaverien suggests that emotion is more likely to be experienced in relationship to the embodied image which, in her model, is the polar opposite of the diagram. The embodied image appears more connected with the client's unconscious whilst the diagrammatic image seems to have a tighter association with consciousness and, importantly for this chapter, intentionality linked with thought and communication.

There is another art therapist who has proposed an alternative model that also addresses the look and significance of the art object produced in art therapy. I refer to the late Rita Simon who, in her book *The Symbolism of Style* (1992), proposed a more complex classification of eight styles of which four were major and four were transitional. For our purposes the Traditional Linear Style has the closest association with cognition. This pictorial style requires both attention and precision. Planning also tends to predominate. Characteristically, the image-maker is rather restricted in his or her movement (Simon paid attention to the physicality of art-making in all her style-related observations) and might have to use rulers and other drawing aids. Simon says:

> There is little chance of spontaneous artwork under these conditions; fantasy seems totally adopted by conscious intention and manipulated to carry out an anticipated result. The unconscious component of creative initiative lies in abeyance during the work process, although it might be discerned after it has been finished... (ibid. 163)

The reader might recognise a similarity between Simon's description of the traditional linear style and Schaverien's diagrammatic image in that both have an emphasis on a kind of self-consciousness and a need to describe something more premeditated underpinning the representational process.

Other art therapist writers have made similar observations. For instance, Dubowski and James (1998) argue the existence of nondiscursive symbolism in more subjectively-orientated imagery and discursive symbolism in pictures designed to represent. The function of discursive symbolism rests upon the need for a shared language with which to universally decode the descriptive form (55). Interestingly when thinking about the non-marking movement aspect of the research question, the authors trace thinking from kinaesthetic developmental origins and the child's engagement in locomotor activity such as that expressed in early mark-making activity.

Of course, when travelling away from the art therapy literature into the province of psychoanalysis, thinking is frequently found to be conceptually central. From the beginning Freud underlined the importance of thought as an associate of his concept of reality testing. He believed this function enabled the ego to mediate the needs of the id and the constraints of the outer-world. Bion focused more closely on thinking and located the mechanism for thinking in the good-enough relationship between mother and baby. Symington and Symington (1996) describe how Bion theorises a process where the mother converts the indigestible bodily experience of the infant into something more bearable for the baby. One could see this in the feeding relationship, for example. The pain and distress of hunger is relieved through feeding. This led Bion to formulate a structure for thought that begins with a preconception (that a breast might feed) followed by a realisation (either a feed transpires or not) that is followed by a conception (that sometimes the breast is present and one is fed and at other times it is absent and one is not fed). Of course this process repeats and the conceptions become evermore complex and marks the beginnings of thought in the infant. Bion also drew connections between this process and the therapeutic relationship where interpretations are the means by which the unbearably experienced distress is converted into a thought or idea.

Before moving on to consider the research method it is important to acknowledge the work of Vygotsky in relationship to the work of Bion. It is interesting to note the similarities between these seemingly differently orientated thinkers. Vygotsky became a psychologist shortly after the Russian revolution. He believed that dialectical and historical materialisms were valid scientific foundations for his psychological investigations (Cole and Scribner, 1978: 6). Symington and Symington (ibid.) make a connection between the work of Hegel and his concept of the dialectic, whereby a thesis is opposed by antithesis with a resultant synthesis, and Bion's concept of preconception faced with a realisation producing a conception. The Symingtons' conclude that Bion held a constructivist theory of thinking similar to that of Vygotsky (ibid. 75).

Quite apart from this theoretical convergence, Vygotsky independently observed that children employed speech in tandem with visual perception and physical manipulation in order to solve practical problems.

Importantly, Vygotsky also noted the close relationship between thinking and remembering as observable in the very young child (Cole et al., 1978) and recognised that children tended to '… recall concrete instances (of the world)' as they '… do not yet possess the character of an abstraction' (ibid. 50). In relation to this Vygotsky also explores the use of external objects in the service of memory, linked with the development of symbols and their eventual use. From this literature, drawing on thinking from psychoanalysis, art therapy, and social constructivism, it was possible to move to the next stage of my research.

Method

The method chosen for this research was similar to that adopted by Schaverien who investigated the various roles of the image in the art therapy relationship and its influence upon the transference dynamics of the session (ibid.). This research, influenced by the philosopher Cassirer, formed the basis of her first book, *The Revealing Image* (1992).

The rationale for my choice of method can be traced back to the formation of this research and my suspicion that links existed between diagrammatic image-making and an enhanced thinking experience. However it is important to note that there are important differences between this study and Schaverien's methodology. Firstly, Schaverien uses a phenomenological approach within the framework of a single case study, whereas this project, although phenomenological in orientation, involves five, individual, single session case studies. Secondly, this study includes the use of video to collect process data, and lastly, although the research is predominately qualitative in nature, there are certain quantitative elements, for instance the numerical interpretation of non-marking actions.

As is the case with all client-involved research in the NHS, one of my earliest tasks was to apply for ethical approval. This necessitated the development of understandable, consent-related information that would assist the learning disabled participants in deciding whether or not to become involved in the study. I was fortunate in having the support of a speech and language therapist in translating the content of the ethics forms into a symbol-supported format.

Participants were identified using the following criteria. Firstly, it was important that all the participants were familiar with the research space, i.e. the art therapy room, and the experience of making imagery in the company of an art therapist. The intention was to eliminate, as far as possible, the factors that Schaverien (1987, 1991) argued influenced the appearance of diagrammatic imagery, namely newness to therapy, art materials and image-making. Therefore, the selection of participants familiar with picture-making in art therapy would control for these factors. As a consequence, participants were invited from the existing art therapy caseload, with the proviso that involvement was thought unlikely to disturb their therapeutic process. The next selection factor concerned an approximate matching of ability (mild to moderate learning disability), age (between twenty-six and thirty-nine-years) and gender (five men and five women). All were fluent in their use of spoken language. The final criterion sought to address the inclusion of participants likely to make diagrammatic-like pictures. This was achieved through the study of previous work and the estimation of the frequency of diagrammatic work. People who met the research requirements were approached and provided with verbal and visual information and given time with friends and support to consider their involvement.

Setting up the research space ran concurrently with the selection process. A table was set aside in the art therapy room alongside a camera upon a tripod, the visual field of which included the image-making area but not the participant. Art media was restricted to tubs of broad and fine felt pens.

Video would enable the repeated observation of a single event. However, I was aware of some of the difficulties associated with video recording. Renne, Downik and Wasek (1983) point out that the act of video recording itself has an influence on the subject and phenomena being observed. The authors suggest certain routines to reduce the impact of the camera, three of which were used in the project. The first is preparation of the client through conversation and visual information; the second is adaptation, enabled by having the research environment and camera equipment on view for a period of one week before the research sessions; the third is programming, referring to having the tape run for a period before anything happens in the session. Once the participants had acclimatised to the changes in the space and had given their verbal consent to taking part in the project, two days were put aside for the research sessions.

Each session was conducted with exactly the same routine. The participant would be invited into the room and asked to take a seat at the table. The information describing the research was again explained, any questions arising answered, after which the person would be invited to sign the consent form. Once completed there would be a brief run through of the equipment and an explanation of what would happen after the camera was switched on. Once the participant appeared comfortable, the tapes (including an audio back up) would be started, and after a short period of adjustment the person would be invited to draw whatever they wished. This phrase would be repeated exactly for each person. When the drawing was finished the camera would be switched off, the person thanked for their contribution and arrangements made for transport home.

The audiotapes were transcribed and used to cross-reference dialogue and utterances from the video recordings. Repeated visual analysis was used to identify significant events of mark making, vocalisation and non-mark making movements.

The Research Sessions

The anticipated ten individuals over two days were reduced to six as four people failed to attend. This is complex to interpret as the two days were also in the same week as a solar eclipse. Therefore the city was much busier than usual which might have made travel difficult for some. It could also be that the build up to such an event acted as a distraction from routine. Clearly not attending the session could also be understood as a withdrawal of consent, although in learning disability, where people often rely on the cooperation of others, it is never really clear if something is a decision or indicates a lack of reliable and empathic support.

Before moving on to describe an actual session I should add that one person was dropped from the project due to the difficulties he experienced once the session had begun. Even though all had seemed fine during the preamble to the session it soon became apparent that he was becoming anxious due to not being able to think of something to draw. This took on circular quality where anxiety at not having an idea created more anxiety that further widened the gulf. Recognising this I suggested that we stopped and spent time together away from the task in a way that was more familiar to us both.

A Research Session Vignette

This session took place on the second of the two days put aside for the data collection and will give the reader an impression of the process.

Paul is a forty-year-old man with mild learning disabilities. He lives independently in a council flat on the outskirts of the city. Paul has made use of individual art therapy for four years and has, over the past eighteen months, reduced his contact to the occasional visit.

Paul makes a quick and confident start. He takes a black marker and, after some non-marking drawing in the air above the paper surface, begins to form a vertical rock structure within the top right hand quadrant of the paper. He attends to the detail of the rock by adding fissures and some shading. Next, a sketchy line, accompanied by non-marking movements, is used to establish the horizon to the left with some vertical marking to indicate what appear to be clumps of grass. Further sketchy lines are used to build a series of hills and field enclosures.

Paul sits back, apparently admiring his drawing, laughs privately and glances at me, before returning to his picture to add a ruined mine building of the sort found dotted around the Cornish coastline. Window and door apertures are added before more sketchy horizontal lines are placed in the background. Paul sits back again, laughs gently and briefly looks at me before making an 'S' shaped mark in the lower left quadrant. 'You've guessed what it is now, don't you?' breaks the silence that had existed from the start, apart from some inaudible mutterings. Paul follows this by engaging in a guessing game that eventually establishes that the developing picture is a view of Cornwall from the Devon border (at one time Paul had lived upon the moor where this view might have been accessible to him). As he speaks, he looks at the picture and seems to be using it as a conduit in his dialogue with me. Following this, Paul defines two trees on the horizon and works concurrently on in-filling the fields in green and brown. His in-filling activity seems fluent and without the sketchiness observed in association with the drawing of lines. Paul re-establishes the guessing game by adding what appears to be a deliberately surreal drawing of a mug and a doughnut on a plate within a field. His conversation roams over the range of buildings found in Cornwall and the traditional materials used in their construction. He establishes an area of blue sea in the pictorial portion below the land and adds a human figure on an airbed floating in a sheltered cove. He laughs in a way that suggests that this is intended as a visual joke. 'Oh yes, I forgot something else didn't I – where's the black?' heralds the formation of a cluster of rocks on the shoreline. Paul returns to in-filling the sea and then makes a reference to the research process and his awareness that an unknown audience will eventually view his image. A further period of drawing in the air accompanies the addition of cats and birds to his artwork.

The theme of the absent audience re-emerges later when Paul explains that the piece is an 'imaginary picture done out of my brain – so if they ask you what it is – and it looks like mumbo jumbo – it isn't, it's my world'. Paul also occasionally appears to make audible his sub-vocal voice and, in doing so, verbalises his searching for the right colour or his thoughts concerning the construction of his picture.

Paul moves towards completion by drawing an island to which he gives the name of an actual place that would be commonly known to anyone living locally. His final graphic act is the addition of blocks of yellow to represent a beach. Paul concludes by sitting back in his chair and saying: 'I've never seen a picture like this before – all yours!'

This fascinating account of the nineteen minute research session is, of course, rich in psychodynamic material. Paul not only verbally expresses his curiosity about his relationship with me and the fantasies that underpin it but also appears to make visually symbolic reference to it in his picture, for instance the possible dynamic between the cats and the birds. Also woven into the account is a dynamic relationship with the research process itself, characterised, in part, by Paul's thoughts about the imagined others and fantasies regarding their mental processes and judgements. This layer of research process awareness can, I feel, be seen in Paul's giving over of his picture at the conclusion of the session with the words 'all yours!', clearly indicating how the process had created a particular intentionality.

However, it is important to decouple this type of analytical thinking from the process in order to focus on the research question more clearly. Through this lens we can see that Paul produces some of the phenomena mentioned before. He draws in the air before making his marks; makes various sounds; and makes available his sub-vocal dialogue in relation to the construction of the image itself.

Findings

I will now describe what emerged from the analysis of the data collected from all five participant sessions. The initial phase of the analysis concerned the categorisation of the five images made during the research sessions. The first process employed Simon's system which indicated that three participants produced imagery that fell into the 'traditional transitional style'; one made an image that appeared concordant with the 'archaic linear style'; and one produced a landscape drawing fitting the 'traditional massive style'.

When applying Schaverien's model, the analysis became a little less precise. I think this was largely due to the narrower range of categories compared with Simon's eight styles. Of the five images, one appeared to be diagrammatic and four variously were diagrammatic with possible embodied references. This can be represented as in Table 5.1.

	Participant One	Participant Two	Participant Three	Participant Four	Participant Five
Simon	TT	TT	TM	TT	AL
Schaverien	D+E	D	D+E	D+E	D+E
Key: TT = Traditional Transition TM = Traditional Massive AL = Archaic Linear D+E = Diagrammatic with embodied elements D = Diagrammatic					

Table 5.1 Analysis of Image Type

Further video analysis revealed factors that could be interpreted as relating to hesitation or the delay of decision. It was evident that all participants made non-marking movements above the paper surface that was most often, but not always, followed by actual marking. The amount of non-marking activity varied for each participant.

I was also able to observe and categorise four distinct types of non-marking activity:

1. Positional movement: where the marking tool is used to apparently estimate the position of a graphic element.
2. Positional/shaping combination: where the marking tool is used in an often graceful combination to: (a) estimate positioning and: (b) rehearse a shape.
3. Shaping movement: where an apparent rehearsal takes place for a shape that might result in an actual graphic representation.
4. Declarative movement: where the marking tool is used to point out a graphic element in association with speech.

The data for each participant's non-marking activity can be seen in Table 5.2.

Participant One				Participant Two				Participant Three				Participant Four				Participant Five			
P	P + S	S	D	P	P + S	S	D	P	P + S	S	D	P	P + S	S	D	P	P + S	S	D
13	9	5	5	8	0	0	3	19	14	1	3	28	15	5	9	19	11	3	0
Total non-marking 32				Total non-marking 11				Total non-marking 37				Total non-marking 57				Total non-marking 33			
Time taken to make image: 10 minutes				Time taken to make image: 3 minutes				Time taken to make image: 19 minutes				Time taken to make image: 22 minutes				Time taken to make image: 27 minutes			
Key: P = positional P+S = positional/shaping combination S = shaping D = declarative																			

Table 5.2 Participants' Non-Marking Activity

This data shows a correspondence between the scores of Participants One, Three, Four and Five in these areas. However, Participant Two, who made a diagrammatic image, made similar declarative gestures but significantly fewer positional non-marking movements, with no positional/shaping or purely shaping movements whatsoever.

The second outcome from this research was the existence of three categories of vocalisation that were observed to occur during the period of image-making. These are:

1. Utterances such as 'ums' and 'ah's.
2. Inhalations that suggest a moment of thought.
3. Self-talk

The data for each participant can be seen in Table 5.3.

Participant One	Participant Two	Participant Three	Participant Four	Participant Five
2 × utterances 2 × inhalations 8 × self-talk	2 × utterances	2 × utterances 1 × inhalations 15 × self-talk	2 × inhalations	No vocalisations
Total = 12	Total = 2	Total = 18	Total = 2	Total = 0

Table 5.3 Participants' Vocalisations

The data shows that Participants One and Three both engaged in a significant amount of self-talk during the making of their imagery. Correspondingly, Participants Two and Four did not employ self-talk and made similar use of linguistic sounds rather than words.

Discussion

Of course the sample of five people is small but despite this some important possibilities come to light. The fundamental assumption in the research question concerning a link between the diagram and enhanced cognition was not demonstrated. However two important findings emerged. Both concern the identification and classification of process phenomena; the first concentrates upon non-marking activity and the second focuses on the vocal utterances made during image production. Both have potentially important implications for the understanding and practice of art therapy with people with learning disabilities.

Non-Marking Phenomena

Of all four of the non-marking movements the declarative gesture is perhaps the easiest to understand in that it appears to be a direct extension of human pointing behaviour. Butterworth defines pointing as 'the use of an outstretched arm and index finger to denote an object in visual space.' (Butterworth, 1992: 229). In this context there are two forms of pointing. The first, described as proto-imperative, relates to the action of pointing with the intention of gaining an object, for example a drink. The other form, described as proto-declarative, differs in that it is designed to share a perceptual event; in this scenario, for example, the child points to the butterfly in order to share their visual delight with their mother. Therefore, construing a connection with proto-declarative function, it seems possible that the tool-orientated pointing observed during the research sessions is communicatively declarative in nature. In this respect it is therefore significant, that Participants One, Two, Three and Four all employed their marker pens to draw the observer's attention to important material in the makers' imagery. Participant Five, however, and equally significantly, did not verbalise or employ declarative non-marking actions.

Thus, through the actions of the majority of the participants, Schaverien's formulation of the diagrammatic image as a communicator of conscious thought and intention to the therapist/spectator is supported and sustained.

The Positional Gesture

It became apparent that positional movements made above the marking surface have two interrelated functions. The first appears connected to the previously described declarative gesture, except that it is not intended to point something out to the observer. Instead, this gesture appears to be made in relation to the image-maker herself, as if she is pointing something out to herself in her personal dialogue with the art materials. This seems to correspond to Bion's realisation that the capacity for thought is also necessary '... for thinking about the self and one's own thinking processes' (Symington and Symington, 1996: 81).

The second related, and most dominant function, is concerned with the act of composition itself. Kellogg (1970), in her explorations of children's art, identifies the placement pattern and the diagram as important factors in graphic development. A placement pattern is defined as the product of the infant's growing control over her 'scribbles'. Kellogg notes (ibid. 23) that the child might not be contemplating her mark and may be reacting spontaneously to the previous marks she has made. In the case of Kellogg's diagram however, there appears to be far more attention to pre-contemplation which reflects the child's growing competence and capacity to remember (ibid. 45). Working from the basis of Kellogg's thesis, it seems that the positional movements observed during the research sessions are indicative of conscious contemplation and action.

Shaping Movements

Shaping movements were apparent in the artwork of all participants, with the exception of Participant Two who produced a diagrammatic image. This is significant as its absence in diagrammatic production appears to support Schaverien's proposal that the diagram is essentially rooted in the conscious and outer-world concerns of the client (1987: 77). It therefore seems consistent that the appearance of shaping movements might indicate the existence of unconscious and inner-world material, underpinning the actions of the remaining four participants.

I was drawn towards the very physical nature of the shaping movements like Simon (1992, 1997), who had also recognised the importance of the artist's physical posturing during the act of creation. During the research sessions the participants were often graceful and sensual in their execution of shaping movements, and sometimes appeared almost absent-minded in their actuation. Rose notes that: 'Language and thought both develop out of an affective and bodily matrix'. He qualifies this statement in the following passage: 'The first learning concerns itself with bodily things and, as it extends/expands to the world outside, symbolic connections are established between our own body and the external world' (ibid. 159–62).

Rose is not alone in contemplating the body's link with later cognitive ability. For instance, Symington and Symington (ibid.) point out the preponderance of bodily and digestive-related words that have been commandeered to describe the thinking process and provide the following pertinent examples: '... taking material in for thought; chewing over a proposition; swallowing a statement hook, line and sinker; digesting and absorbing an idea; or undigested facts' (88). In a similar vein, Bion's concept of the maternal relationship enabling the conversion of uncomfortable, bodily experienced, beta material of the infant into something more bearable through the mother's alpha capacity, points in a similar direction. Describing the interaction between mother and infant, Britton (1996) states that:

> In this way, something which in the infant was near sensory and somatic was transformed into something more mental by the mother which could be used for thought or stored as memory. The most basic way of thinking these thoughts would be something like having a dream. (105)

Wright (1991: 136–7) usefully provides a bridge between this material and the observed research phenomena in his personal reflections on the nature of thinking. Drawing from his ten-point formulation it is possible to identify the body's relationship to thought in that we sometimes perceive things from a bodily rather than a cerebral orientation. Furthermore the words used to describe the cognitive process have, at times, distinct physical characteristics, for instance in grasping, groping and taking hold of mental material. Seeing, a complex physical activity also finds itself adopted to describe the process of mental introspection. Even the term formulate has at its core a physical and almost sculptural implication. These thoughts from Wright, I think, highlight aspects of the shaping movement phenomena described earlier. The words grasp, groping, take hold of, feel out, looking and formulate all correspond with the participants' shaping actions.

The theoretical material described above appears to support the conclusion that non-marking, shaping movements have a close relationship with the bodily elements of early experience, thought and memory. The occurrence of such shaping phenomena would therefore point to the influence of unconscious material in relation to image-making.

Positioning/Shaping Combination

An interesting development during the research process was the recognition of material that suggested a broadening of Schaverien's definition of the diagrammatic image. It appears that the positioning/shaping combination is an example of a classification within the concept of the diagrammatic. The evidence for this lies in the observation that all but the diagram-making Participant Two made significant actions that combined positioning with shaping. I hypothesised earlier that positioning is predominantly conscious and that shaping appears to have its origins in unconscious function. It is therefore possible to propose that the combination shares something of both and could therefore be described as either post-diagrammatic or pre-embodied, roughly approximating to the concept of the preconscious.

Vocalisations and Verbalisations

The second important area of the research concerned the vocalisations made by the participants during their image-making. Although I had been aware of these during my work I had not recognised their individual character and significance.

I was interested to discover that participants either spoke about their experience or about their knowledge. For example, Participant Two predominately related her experience of shopping before the session in both her imagery and dialogue. With the exception of Participant Two and Participant Four, who did not vocalise, all other participants taking part expressed their knowledge of the world rather than their direct experience of it. For example, Participant Three employed aspects of his dialogue and imagery to illustrate his knowledge of the tin mining industry; Participant One, his knowledge of H.G. Wells' *War of the Worlds*; and Participant Four, a precise description of his knowledge of solar eclipse and planetary systems. For these three participants it is clearly evident that aspects of both their imagery and dialogue were given over to the sharing of knowledge. This is important as it suggests that the production of an image was not some arbitrary add-on but an essential contemplatory and connecting element of the process.

Sinason (1992) makes use of the term 'emotional intelligence', which she defines as the learning disabled person's capacity to '… know and understand what is happening within and around them, no matter their performance intelligence' (214). She provides an account of a changed regime at a residential home whereby residents began to reveal previously unrecognised capacity and awareness. Sinason refers to the physical touch and support needed for the residents to externalise their thoughts and notes that:

> It seems to take two people physically touching before the thoughts can then be expressed by pointing to letters or typing. This takes us again to the psychobiological origins in thinking. It takes the connection of mother and baby with a good-enough relationship for thinking to occur. (ibid. 218)

Although there was no physical assistance during the research sessions it would seem that an art therapy session might have much in common with the above account. For example, the physical experience of marking and non-marking movements and the client's interactions with the art materials seems closely associated with physical touch, particularly as this takes place within the context of a good-enough therapeutic relationship. In other words, the client's connection with the therapist via the image and art materials creates an equivalent condition for thinking to occur.

Utterances, Inhalations and Self-Talk

As with non-marking actions, the observation and categorisation of the vocalisations made by people during picture-making has not, as far as I am aware, been done before. Utterances such as 'um's' and 'ah's' and inhalations seem to indicate a thought process, or a moment of cognition, taking place. These features were observable in all the research sessions, except for Participant Five who did not vocalise at all.

However, the general spread indicated above was not evident when considering the occurrence of self-talk. Cole et al. (1978) refer to children's use of self-talk, or egocentric speech, in their attempts to achieve a goal. Importantly, these authors from a Vygotskian perspective conclude that: '... children solve practical tasks with the help of their speech, as well as their eyes and hands' (ibid. 26).

This description resonates with the self-talk exhibited by Participants One and Three who both engaged in egocentric dialogue about the art materials, the colours used, and the content and construction of their pictures. It is also important to note that Participant Two, who made the diagram, did not engage in self-talk; this seems to be congruent with the diagram's conscious and preconceived nature. From this basis I believe it is possible to argue that self-talk might indicate something of the internal dialogue experienced during the making of less consciously sourced imagery or possibly that it forms part of the transformation process itself. Consequently, self-talk appears linked with non-marking, shaping and positional/shaping actions insofar as they suggest a similar involvement in, or relationship with, pre-conscious and unconscious material and, by extension, pre-embodied and embodied imagery.

It is now possible to argue that instances of self-talk in non-diagrammatic or non-embodied imagery suggest a new classification of the pre-embodied image, whereas the absence of self-talk corresponding with imagery that is neither purely diagrammatic or embodied would attract a new description of post-diagrammatic image.

From Research into Practice

So what difference does this research make to practice and in what direction does it take the art therapist? I began this chapter by describing a particular event where two people with learning disabilities made reference to the influence they believed art-making had on their thinking. That triggered a series of events that returned some quite unexpected results and insights.

A great deal has been written in the art therapy literature about the making, appearance and meaning of art works within the context of the therapeutic relationship. This was my habitual territory and so it was quite a surprise when the research process forced my attention to areas I had not previously privileged, namely non-marking activity and vocalisation. The suggested link that emerged between thinking and these hitherto largely overlooked phenomena is immensely important to the learning disabled person and the perceptive activity of the art therapist in their clinical practice. Being able to observe and identify the four non-marking actions and the two categories of vocalisation and then link them to conscious or unconscious thought processes enables the art therapist to recognise something of the internal dynamics of their client. This has certainly enabled me to expand the perceptual spectrum of my engagement with my clients.

A further, unexpected bonus was the elaboration I propose to Schaverien's model. This is particularly important in learning disability art therapy practice due to the relatively frequent appearance of the diagram. Schaverien's model had, hitherto, appeared a rather limited tool to me in the context of my work with people who have learning disabilities, yet the introduction of two further points on the spectrum (post-diagrammatic and pre-embodied) creates, to my mind, a much-enhanced application of Schaverien's theoretical structure in this area of practice as well as a deepened appreciation of these kinds of art-making.

Finally, and perhaps most importantly, the research underscores the importance of image-making in the thinking experiences of the learning disabled person. For me, a new emphasis has emerged concerning the importance of physicality in relationship to the creative process and the use of the art materials themselves, even before a mark has been made. This begins to open up established art therapy theoretical constructs to take account of these new perceptions.

ROBIN TIPPLE

6 Art Therapy and Diagnostic Assessment

Abstract

This chapter provides an account of some discourse analysis that takes the form of case studies. These explore the use of art therapy in diagnostic assessment. In an attempt to reconcile two different discourses, the neurological and the psychodynamic, the author analysed clinic documents, art production and verbal discourses in order to show how subjects are produced in discourses and how art work emerges in the context of assessment practices. This research emphasises the social aspect of semiosis and shows autistic subjects (children) using cultural practices to shape subjectivity.

Key Words

art therapy assessment; autism; discourses; subjectivity.

How it all Began: from Practice to Research

The research I am about to describe took place in a specialist NHS Paediatric service hereafter referred to as Chestnut House. The service is used by families and referrers who are seeking a second opinion and further help in relation to children who have developmental disorders, mostly where there is a question of autism. In my role as the art therapist in this setting I am employed as a member of the multi-disciplinary team and provide assessments that contribute to diagnostic decisions.

When I began this work at the end of the 1980s it was a challenge. I had previous experience of working with children but had never had to work in an assessment team, nor had I worked with children who had autism. The main surprise was that the work did not involve ongoing art therapy. In this setting the art therapist saw the child for one session and then wrote a report for the team. How was I going to do this? How would I conduct the sessions and what could I say in a report after one hour's work? The members of the team – paediatricians, psychologists, social worker, speech and language therapist, physiotherapist, and music therapist – appeared to be very clear in relation to their role and the processes of assessment. They also seemed to know all about autism: how to identify it, how to talk and write about it, what kind of words to use. The words were alien to me and, since assessments were recorded on video and parents often watched on a monitor, I felt exposed.

Prior to this work I had tried to build on the work of other art therapists and develop a psychodynamic approach to art therapy and learning disabilities (Tipple, 1993, 1994). This contrasted strongly with the model of neuro-developmental disorders that ordered the practices and processes of Chestnut House. Medical and cognitive 'sciences' were stressed in the team. An aetiology that supported the search for genetic, biological and behavioural indices had more validity than the 'psychogenic' accounts of autism that psychoanalysis appeared to favour. Using psychodynamic language or explanation was not encouraged. Formal assessments which measured an individual's performance against a norm were favoured. When informal assessments, such as art or music therapy were used, emphasis was placed upon the disclosure of the phenomena listed in the diagnostic manuals: for example, impaired social interaction, deviant forms of communication, paucity of imagination, obsessional behaviours and sensory sensitivities. Descriptions in reports were obliged to interpret events in the languages of the diagnostic manuals. Only a formal diagnosis supported by the literature of the medical sciences, achieved through practices that clinicians could endorse, would have the necessary authority. Consequently I felt pressured to work quite differently at Chestnut House and was concerned that my other identity, as a psychodynamic therapist, would be split off.

Art therapy and music therapy assessments could be regarded as contrasting with the other assessments undertaken at Chestnut House through their informality. Formal assessments use standardised instruments to obtain measures, measures of development and functioning that can be rendered into a numerical or mathematical form. Informal assessments rely on description and interpretation but they can encourage choice, initiative, social interaction and communications that more directed and structured assessments might restrict or stifle. Experience had shown that some of the children and young people referred to the service found direction difficult and did not like to comply with adult imposed tasks; in contrast, others found the more open-ended and ambiguous situation too anxiety-provoking and could not generate ideas without some prompt or structure.

Therefore I decided to introduce at the beginning of my art therapy assessments a period of choice where direction was at a minimum and initiative was encouraged. This was followed by a period where direction intervened and choice became more limited but still available; in this period interactions were encouraged. I also, on occasions, introduced a period where the task was self-evident and where unambiguous instructions were given by the adult, for instance a drawing task might be given. I reasoned that having this shape to the assessment would allow me to comment on the child's response to different situations.

I often used the squiggle game to encourage interaction and exchange. This is the drawing game invented by Winnicott (1971, 1989). The adult produces a quickly scribbled line, a 'squiggle'; this is passed on to the child for the child to complete or change and produce an image of some kind. The child then produces a squiggle for the adult, and so on. Winnicott used the game in his psychiatric consultations with children. A capacity for play and an ability to respond inventively to visual cues is anticipated. In my use of the game I concentrated on gaining some understanding of the child's motivation and abilities in relation to communicating through imagery and signs, for generating verbal associations, and in relation to turn-taking and shared play.

Thus I had identified, and was trying to reconcile, two kinds of discourses: those that informed my usual, psychodynamic approach to art therapy and the more formal, neuro-developmental discourses that informed the assessments of my colleagues at Chestnut House. A discourse, here, is understood as encompassing a range of objects and activities, speech, written material, visual representations, and social and institutional practices that structure communication and exchanges (Jaworski and Coupland, 1999). This struggle, to understand discourses and their effects, led to the research that this chapter describes.

The Context of the Research

British art therapists' have been reluctant to use art therapy for diagnostic purposes (British Association of Art Therapists, 2009: 4). The 'medical model' has been much criticised and a psychodynamic formulation of a patient's or a child's problems has been favoured (see Edwards, 2004; Dalley, 2000; Case, 2000; Dudley, 2004). In contrast to the British, American art therapists have developed projective tests and incorporated these into their practices in such a way as to legitimate themselves as diagnosticians (Betts, 2006). They have also researched art work in an effort to disclose signs and formal properties regarded as indications of the presence of pathology in, or of, the artist (see Cohen, Hammer and Singer, 1988; Gantt and Tabone, 1998; Gantt, 2004).

In the British literature visual 'style' is sometimes linked to a particular psychological state, disturbance or developmental impasse (Simon, 1992; Maclagan, 1998, 2001), but although interpretations might appear which refer to the presence of pathology in or of the artist, there has been no systematic attempt to establish a language of signs that can be read diagnostically. However, having reviewed the recent British art therapy literature which discusses work with children (e.g. Case, 2000; Dalley, 2000; O'Brien, 2004) and adults (Maclagan, 2005; Schaverien, 2005), I began to realise that although British art therapists wanted to avoid interpretations that lead to pathology, their descriptions of their clients at work and responding to art therapy produced 'subjects'. That is they described and identified others and proposed a relationship between the making, the art product and the individual and his or her problems.

I have now strayed into the subject of 'subjects', not inadvertently, since subjects became central to understanding the discourses that my research attempted to analyse. What became clear from my immersion in the literatures from art therapy and cognitive psychology was that in the interpretations of art works, subjects were constantly in production.

In their discourses practitioners assume subjects who re-present themselves in their art work. The psychology literature which focuses on children's drawings (for example Cox, 1992) describes subjects responding to the problem of describing the world through marks, presenting subjects as essentially rational, autonomous beings. Signifying elements in the drawing are interpreted as the subject's logical response to the problem of depicting objects. In the psychology literature the art product literally re-presents the rationality of the subject, that is the subject's rational endeavour to represent the world he or she encounters. In contrast to cognitive psychologists, art therapists, especially in Britain, describe the child producing art work in the art therapy session as emotionally driven, striving to give expression to phantasy and endeavouring to achieve relief, insight and/or integration through such expression (Case, 2000; Dalley, 2000). Art therapists then interpret the art work as an analogue for phantasy and emotion, rendered present through symbolism. This results in an art work which produces a re-presentation of a subject assumed to be driven by desires in relation to an object, namely the mother, caretaker or some other person.

The literature disclosed what an examination of clinic documents and the study of video material at Chestnut House also demonstrated, namely that discourses were aimed at the production of subjects (Foucault, 1984). Clinicians, including the art therapist, were describing individuals and reaching agreement in relation to the identity of children and their difficulties. This production of subjects constitutes the work of the multidisciplinary team.

Once aware of this relation of the individual subject to the social world, to language and cultural practices and of the subject's relation to discourses, I attempted to focus on human behaviour in its relational aspect, exploring the subject 'as a relational phenomenon, involving the intermingling of bodies and consciousnesses in actions that performatively institute ways of being and doing' (Henriques, Hollway, Urwin, Venn and Walkerdine, 1984: xv). It is this model of the subject that I have worked with, one which is produced by, and immersed in, symbolic or semiotic social practices, subject to others but also resistant, active in producing their own subjectivities, through the use of those powers, those material practices, that are productive of subjects (Althusser, 2001; Butler, 1997).

The recognition that subjects are constituted through discourses and are subject to social practices enabled me to recognise that art production, in the assessment setting, also needed to be related to the larger discourse of which it is part. I needed to understand how the art production emerges in the practices of assessment and how it can be related to subjects who are constituted by this same set of practices. This, I would like to stress, includes the art therapist as well as the child in the assessment.

Method

There were three different discursive materials that I used to construct the case studies in my research: the clinic's documents, the art products produced during the assessments and the videos used for recording the assessments. I named the subjects that I produced through my analysis respectively as 'the documentary subject', 'the ekphrastic subject' and the 'discursive subject'.

The 'documentary subject' describes the broader context of the assessment; it articulates the practices of the clinic through a study of the documents which represent those practices to others. Chestnut House receives documents from referring paediatricians and other local professionals who have been involved with the child and the family. In their turn Chestnut House staff write documents which represent a reply to, and an elaboration of, the referrer's documents and documents supplied by the parents. There is a large range of documents which refer to and produce the subject child: medical reports, the results of psychological tests and language tests, reports from schools and parents and reports from assessments in the clinic. The documents can be regarded as a conversation, a conversation that is held between professionals. Agreement on the conceptual and formal content of reports, if not explicit, is implicit in their production. For example Chestnut House staff would be expected to make use of the diagnostic manuals, DSM IV and ICD 10, when describing developmental difficulties and when producing diagnoses.

The 'ekphrastic subject' represents a description of the art products produced in the assessment, an ekphrasis being a verbal description of a visual experience (Mitchell, 1994). Here I hoped to communicate something of the researcher's experience of looking at the art products produced by the child in the art therapy assessment.

To produce the ekphrastic subject I used an art historical method developed by Baxandall (1985, 1991). Baxandall suggests that, given the nature of language, a description is less a direct representation of the object or picture but more a 'representation of thinking about having seen the picture' (1985: 11). A description does not usually concern objects never having been seen by an audience but is a kind of 'verbal pointing' towards an object or a reproduction. In this research I supplied a reproduction of the children's artworks, aiming to describe the objects in such a way that the description could be endorsed by the reader.

The 'discursive subject' is the subject that arises from my analysis of the videos of the art therapy assessments. Through the creation of transcripts I produced a dramaturgical account of the interactions and exchanges that the video disclosed (Brissett and Edgley, 1990). I wanted a format in my initial transcript that simplified the recording of speech and which allowed me to present alongside the speech brief descriptions of actions. I took the view that 'verbal means are employed conjointly with nonverbal means and together they convey the child's intentions.' (Och, 1999: 172). After producing a full transcript in this manner, I then reduced the manuscript and added interpretative comment. When adding this comment I paid attention to the effects of utterances and considered carefully their consequences and possible intentionality, making use of theories of exchange (Mauss, 1990; Davis, 1992) and social interaction (Charon, 2004; Goffman, 2005), and speech act theory (Austin, 1962).

The research consists of the analysis of four cases. In this chapter I shall present an extract from one of the cases, focussing on three images from a squiggle game. I will begin with an account of the documents which relate to the referral as they show how our subject, Damien, was presented to the multi-disciplinary team and also how the team responded to the referral. I will go on to present extracts from the transcript to show how images emerge in the exchanges between the therapist and the child and I shall present a reproduction of the images accompanied by my description (ekphrasis), or a 'verbal pointing' as Baxandall would describe it (1991 op. cit.).

I aim to show how Damien was shaped as a subject by the assessment process but also how Damien himself shaped this process and contested adult interpretations of the situation.

Case Material

Damien was aged eleven years and five months at assessment. The paediatrician's referral letter indicated that Damien was thought to have an attention deficit and hyperactivity disorder (ADHD) but questions were also raised in relation to autism. Attached to the letter were reports from the school, the results of examinations, reports from the educational psychologist and reports from the speech and language therapist. Reports from another specialist service were also included with the referral, as were reports from his parents.

The parents reported that during conversations Damien watched television but also read a book, and he spoke to others regardless of their activity. He interrupted, then did not stop talking and was literal in his understanding. He did not appear to understand the difference between fact and fantasy. His parents wrote: 'He does not seem to understand our feelings'; 'It is like he is in a bubble and we can't get in'. He was impulsive, his behaviour dangerous; for instance, he insisted on cycling down the middle of the road at speed. The parents apologised and expressed feelings of guilt: 'we know this sounds all so negative'. They also gave some more positive accounts of Damien that stressed his abilities. He was regarded as the 'computer whiz' at school and was loving, 'but his cuddles hurt'.

During the initial appointment at Chestnut House Damien's parents gave an account of his early history. The consultant child and adolescent psychiatrist conducting the interview diagnosed Asperger's Syndrome but said that more assessment was needed.

The documentary subject shows Damien as an individual with whom it was difficult to live. His parents presented him as a subject whose behaviour was in need of correction and themselves as exasperated by his resistances. It had been difficult for others to agree on the nature of the problems;

for instance, Damien was described as socially isolated at home but as a 'delightful boy who is always keen to socialise' at school. He was therefore a subject whose identity was in dispute. However, Chestnut House's production of Damien as a subject with Asperger's Syndrome was endorsed by his parents and appeared to have gained some support from educational authorities since there followed an agreement to begin a formal investigation of Damien's 'educational need' in response to the reports produced from Chestnut House's assessments.

I shall now present some dialogue and social interaction with comment taken from the video analysis. I also include reproductions of three drawings produced in the squiggle game during the assessment, accompanied by my description.

> I explain the squiggle game. I then take up a piece of paper and I draw a wavy line with the red pencil. As I speak I hold the paper with the line out towards Damien.
> RT: You have to see if you can turn that into a picture of some sort/
> RT: You can add anything you like to it.
> DAMIEN: [What] on there/
> RT: Can you do it/
> DAMIEN: Can I have it up that way/
> RT: Yeah you can have it anyway round that you like and you can add what you like/
> Damien begins drawing, adding to my marks. When the drawing is complete to his satisfaction, Damien turns the paper and passes it to me and looks towards me.[1]

1 Key to Transcript:

/ End of utterance. A pause is usually present.
[ ] Simultaneous utterance, brackets begin and end when simultaneous words appear, for example:
Therapist: What is it?/
Child: [its a] man/
? A rising inflection, not necessarily a question.
_ Underlining, indicates emphasis.
* Indicates quieter passage.
. A period indicates a falling tone, not necessarily the end of a sentence.
- An abrupt cut off, halting, a string of dashes in a sentence would indicate a stammer.

Figure 6.1 is the first drawing in the squiggle game. My beginning, a line best described as a rising arabesque, occupies a central position on the page. Damien converts it into a wave, adding broken water to the crest, droplets and lines, suggesting the interior curvature that waves make as they move and curl. Damien also added the sea using a gently swelling horizontal. The wave appears to suddenly erupt. On the top of the wave is a surfer on a surfboard. The board does not actually touch the wave but floats magically just above it. On the surfboard a figure is drawn with outstretched arms, smiling. The hair of the figure is raised, caught by movement and wind maybe. The figure looks free from concern. There is no danger of getting wet. He, or she, is riding the wave with ease and confidence. He, or she, faces the viewer directly, but from a height, the implication being 'I can play this game easily'.

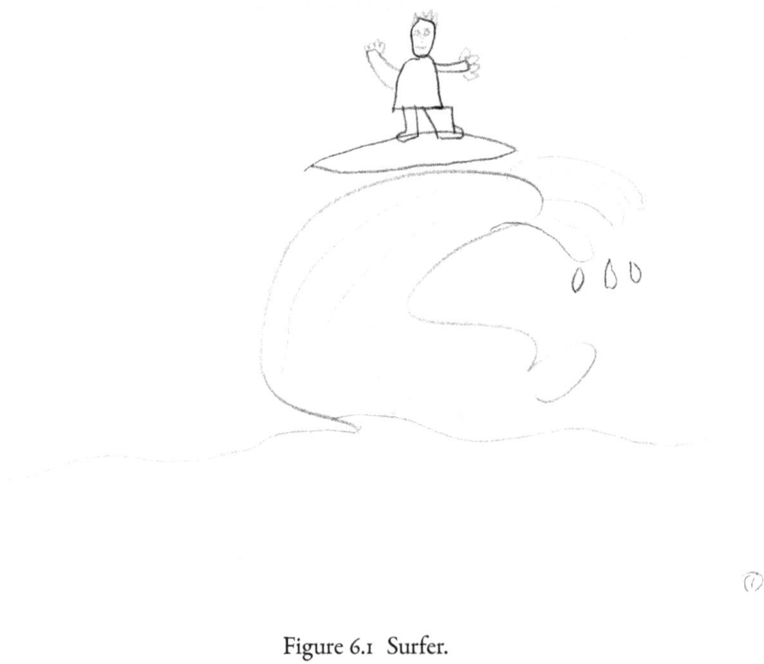

Figure 6.1 Surfer.

RT: Umm/
RT: *Ok*/
RT: He's riding a big wave isn't he/
DAMIEN: [Surf board]/
RT: *Good*/

As can be seen Damien presents his picture to me and awaits comment. Not much has been said about this first image. I draw attention to the size of the wave whereas Damien emphasises the surfboard which enables the figure to ride or to manage the wave. I quietly approve of the start and the game continues.

In the next drawing (Figure 6.2) Damien produced two lines which almost touch. A V shape and an S shape on its back. With my pencil I change these lines into a camel with his head raised in the air, looking proud and content, certainly self-assured and possibly smug. There is a suggestion of a smile on the camel's face. Lines are added to indicate a landscape of some kind. I also produced a short stray mark above the tail, a redundant mark that was probably unintentional. Around this mark Damien added a face and then constructed a body. The arms point downwards but also outward. The face turns towards the left edge of the picture away from the camel. The nose merges into the mouth, with square teeth in the upper part and triangular teeth in the lower jaw. The mouth is open. The mark or short line hangs off the teeth to the right, suggesting a tongue, or blood, or a stray piece of flesh. The spiky hair and spiky eyebrows add to the aggressive, angry looking face whose large, open mouth signals an animal about to bite. There is a discordant relationship between the haughty camel and the angry man. The camel is moving towards the right of the picture frame and the frustrated and angry man is looking in the opposite direction towards the left edge of the picture, as if directing his gaze to someone outside of the frame. Perhaps he has a piece of the camel's flesh in his mouth; if so the camel is not concerned.

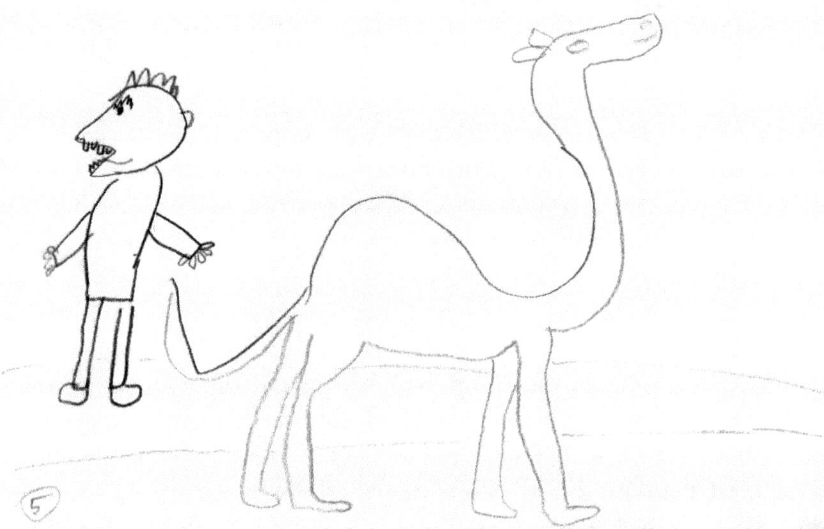

Figure 6.2 The Camel.

DAMIEN: Camel/
RT: Yeah/
I turn the paper and pass it to DAMIEN; he points to the stray mark, to the left of the camel, with my pencil.
RT: *I don't know what this bit could be do you*/
Damien then draws on the picture. He understands the image, its reference, and he converts the redundant mark that I point towards into a signifier.
DAMIEN: *Could be*/
DAMIEN: Sort of a man/
DAMIEN: I don't know what he's supposed/
RT: No/
DAMIEN: To be doing looks like a monkey/
RT: Umm you have given him a mouth here – he has a big nose now/
RT: Giving him some teeth now/
DAMIEN: Looks even worse/
DAMIEN: Looks angry now/
RT: Angry/
DAMIEN: His eyebrows/

The drawing develops and Damien notices that he has produced a 'sort of man' or 'monkey' who 'looks angry'. I am interested in the angry aspect of this figure and a narrative interpretation is suggested to Damien.

> RT: Why do you think he is angry/
> DAMIEN: Don't know/
> RT: Could he be angry with the camel?/
> DAMIEN: *He could be*/
> I point to the man/monkey with my finger.
> RT: What sort of things make you angry do you ever get as angry like that/
> DAMIEN: No not as angry as that/
> RT: Not as angry as that but you do get angry do you?/
> DAMIEN: *Sometimes*/
> RT: *What sort of things would make you angry*/
> DAMIEN: Don't know/

This interrogation is difficult for Damien. Some of his anxiety is betrayed in his motor movements. He moves the pencil up and down his thumb and he also shakes his leg briefly. Damien is not prepared to commit himself on the subject of anger. Instead he moves the game on, re-introducing image-making. He says he is going to make the game 'a bit more obvious' and draws one half of a guitar. I follow Damien's directions and the completed guitar represents agreement and ends the interrogation.

I began the next drawing (Figure 6.3) with three lines. Three joined, semi-circular movements, an extended W, precede a rising line which moves up towards the top right of the paper. Damien used these lines as the basis for a representation of a golf club. The bottom of the golf club is drawn very large and placed in the centre of the paper. A golf ball on a tee is drawn next to the club. The ball has surface markings to indicate the pitted surface and writing, 'top flite 2'. A hand of a figure grasps the golf club. The figure is squeezed into a fairly narrow space on the right of the paper. The left arm of the figure is laid straight against the long trunk. The figure faces the viewer directly although there is a hint in his eyes, a faint indication in the bottom right of his right eye, of a pupil which suggests that he is maybe looking towards the golf ball and the end of the club. The figure is wearing glasses and he has a straight mouth with a row of little, jagged teeth in evidence. His hair, rising vertically, is shown by a zig-zag and he has raised eyebrows. He looks frustrated as if he could be struggling with a club that is too big and clumsy, having been backed into a corner.

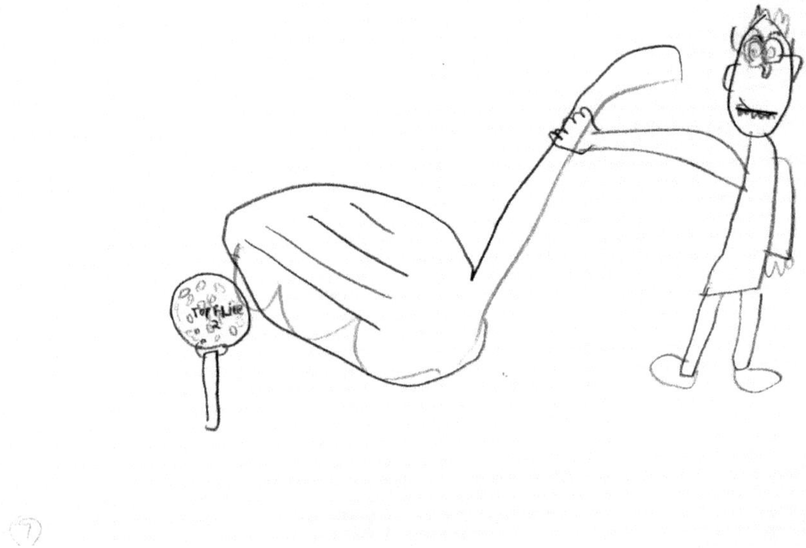

Figure 6.3 The Golf Club.

DAMIEN: *The man's a bit small can't fit him on*/
RT: It's a golf club he's going to have a job swinging that isn't he/
DAMIEN: Bit cross cause he's got a big/
DAMIEN: Got a big golf club – he wanted a small one/
RT: He wanted a small one –so golf club doesn't really suit him does it/
Damien turns the paper so that I can see the drawing. I lean forward to look.
RT: *Oh yeah very good*/
RT: What does this say top?
DAMIEN: Flight two/
RT: Top flight two/
DAMIEN: Yeah *it's the name of the ball*/
RT: Are they the best balls/
DAMIEN: Well no not the best balls/
RT: No they're not/
DAMIEN: What golf/
RT: These are not the best balls./

DAMIEN: Yeah well they are a number two one of the best *weight*/
RT: Huh huh yeah./
RT: He's cross because he's having a job with that golf club/
DAMIEN: A bit too big/

As can be seen, this picture is explored carefully. Damien seems to be still thinking about anger: the man is a 'bit cross'. There is a diversionary discussion about the ball which is an important item in the picture; at least I appear to feel that it is worthy of comment. There is some uncertainty about the meaning of the number two; does it refer to weight, or quality, or both? If it is not the best of balls, it is 'one of the best'. It is the bigness of the golf club that Damien drew attention to in the beginning that appears to interest me and that Damien agrees is 'a bit too big'. Of course the lines, the squiggle, determined the size of the club and, as Damien pointed out, there was not much room for a man. Damien did say that 'he', the player in the picture, 'wanted a small one'. In this sense the picture is one of someone whose needs have not been met as well as a picture of difficulty or 'struggle', the word I use and emphasise.

RT: Looks like he's <u>really struggling</u> are there any times when you have to struggle with things that are too big or are there/
DAMIEN: *Not so much*/
RT: Pardon/
DAMIEN: Not so I mean not so much/

Damien is not willing to disclose difficulties, if he has any.

The squiggle game is returned to after this conversation and Damien makes a suggestion in relation to the next drawing: 'I was thinking what do you call these people that kings have with those funny hats on with balls on it and shoes'. This leads me into drawing a jester and conversation around kings and jesters subsequently develops. Power relations are then explored. Damien would prefer to be a king ''cause you're in charge – 'cause like they use jester as a joke kind thing'. He then talks about Henry the Eighth and in relation to one of his wives he commented: 'one of them wanted to have a sword to have her head cut off with not an axe'. He appears puzzled by this: 'She wanted the er um sword probably 'cause I know they're both painful probably but the heaviness of the axe – probably the sword I don't know really…' Damien then gestures and rehearses beheadings and these provide a dramatic realisation of his imaginary explorations. He tries to understand the victim's choice and this lead him into a recollection of Madame Tussaud's. He describes the guillotine and enjoys the macabre aspects of his recollection, ending the assessment with a harrowing verbal image: 'they had a man in there all rotted and skulls and…'

Findings

As we have seen, Damien is already produced as a subject in the documents before he arrives in person at Chestnut House. In his variable social responses to others he has affected the way in which he is represented by others, to others, and to himself. I, in turn, will be expected to comment on his social interaction in the assessment setting.

When Damien begins the art therapy assessment he has to define the situation for himself and propose an identity for himself in this new situation. He will want support for this identity and he will bring to bear his perspectives, constructed from other experiences of similar assessment settings and from other interactions with adults. He will also use his current view of himself in this process (Goffman, 2005; Charon, 2004).

In the squiggle game, Damien has to use either the pencil or a red crayon. The task, however, allows him to organise a more personal brief; that is he can chose his imagery freely and his drawing style, although he must incorporate the squiggle supplied to him into his work. Rules were given by me to help Damien define the situation: 'You have to see if you can turn it into a picture of some sort', and there is an element of challenge in the situation: 'Can you do it?' I say. Damien asks about the rules and what they allow: 'Can I have it that way up?' If he accepts the definition of the situation that I propose then he is confronted with a question. Can he make use of the cultural tools available and still propose an identity for himself which will gain the support of the adult and confirm his current view of himself?

The first image, Figure 6.1, shows an individual able to ride the big wave, meeting the challenge of a rapidly changing situation. He uses a surf board, signifying cultural equipment of sorts, which enables him to overcome, and enjoy, we might imagine, dynamic situations. This image of an able individual is endorsed and commended, although I stress the wave in my comments on the image, suggesting I have some doubts about this presentation of himself. As the game progresses I introduce verbal association. Here I define my role in the situation, through my practices, as one who encourages and enables disclosure. Insofar as Damien allows the exploration of topics through verbal associations, he supports my role identity and view of the situation.

In the camel and the man/monkey picture, Figure 6.2, there is a contrast between the two protagonists in the scene. The camel's indifferent confidence and haughty demeanour contrasts with the anger of the man/monkey who appears to turn to somebody or something outside of the frame. This looks like a failed social interaction.

I now endeavour to lead the conversation towards a disclosure in relation to anger. How does the anger of the man/monkey relate to Damien's experiences? I am aware of the anger and frustration expressed by Damien's parents in relation to their exchanges with him and hope that I can contribute to the discussion with the parents. Damien, however, does not want to explore his experience of anger; he wants to avoid being identified as an angry individual. He seeks, successfully, to redirect the game, using the imagery, the guitar, to legitimate his intervention. I recognise that Damien needs support in order to avoid loss of face and supply the required half of guitar through my drawing, in this way re-establishing some harmony in our interaction.

In the golf club drawing, Figure 6.3, the figure is shown as frustrated, frustrated with his situation and the club he has to use. Damien's frustration is expressed in part by his comment 'can't fit him on'. Damien points out that the club is 'a bit too big' whereas the paper is too small. The golfer needed a smaller, more manageable club. This image contrasts with the surfer who is able to make good use of his board. Damien is just about willing to concede that he has a relation to the golfer; that he, at times, has to 'struggle' – the word that I introduce. But this admission is diminished with 'not so much I mean not so much', and Damien thereby continues to maintain his 'face', his presentation of himself as an able individual (Goffman, 2005).

My 'face' is dependent, in part, on Damien disclosing some difficulties or at least exploring experiences that might be felt as problematic. In this sense the situation is discordant, since Damien has to find a presentation of himself with which he can feel comfortable, and identifying oneself as an angry individual whose needs have not been met, suffering from difficulties or problems, is uncomfortable if not painful. Adults may, it could be argued, be better at presenting themselves as having difficulties whilst still keeping face intact.

What is important to notice here is that there is an asymmetrical power relation in this situation. It is the adults who have the power to name and identify differences, abnormal and normal behaviour and competencies. Power is direction, acting upon the actions of others, and where there is power, Foucault (1984) suggests, there is always resistance.

Power and resistance are explored at the end of the squiggle game in the conversation about kings and jesters and King Henry's wives. Damien indicates that choice is available, even for victims; one is not obliged to be used as 'a joke kind of thing'. Power he suggests, in his verbal imagery, can be used abusively and when sadistic excitement is indulged we are left with images of death and dissolution. Here Damien is presenting himself as an individual who is not afraid to look upon such things; indeed such imagery may, through identifications, provide the excitement of the possession of power.

From Research into Practice

I have presented the art therapy assessment as a situation which is interpreted by the therapist and by the client/child. This interpretation is continuous and a definition of the situation – a changing role for, and identification of, self, a subjectivity – is proposed by and for the individual during the assessment. The art products and images, visual and verbal, are used in this production of shifting identities and interpretations of the social situation. Affirmation, of interpretation and definition, is sought from the other. Power is contested and loss of face is resisted. This could be reframed as the avoidance of vulnerability. For instance, just as Damien attempts to avoid vulnerability through a refusal to disclose difficulties, I attempt to avoid appearing vulnerable before the parents and the professionals viewing the assessment by maintaining an adult role and pursuing the objects of the assessment. The imaginary is used by both of us to contest the power relationship, to change the direction of the social interaction and to organise the processes of exchange. It is a dynamic process whereby temporary agreements lead to reciprocal exchanges and mutuality but resistance and refusal return.

I would argue that this research has value because it offers an alternative reading of art production in clinical settings. I hope that I have shown that, through the use of a detailed look at discourses (including a detailed and careful look at art products), interpretation can profitably be shifted from a focus on the intra-psychic, whether characterised as cognitive or affective, towards the communication – gestural, verbal and visual – of participants in assessment practices. The emphasis here is on the context of art production and consumption, on the 'participants' in exchanges. Reflection on communicative behaviours, on social role and on identity by the art therapist is essential. Only then can motivation be understood as arising in response to the power relations that the practices of assessment reproduce. Art production in this approach becomes a joint production (not just in the instance of the squiggle game) whose emergence and shape is conditioned by the semiotic environment, that which lies between people and mediates in interactions and exchanges. As Skaife (2001) cogently argues when describing group art therapy, the meaning of the work, process and product, resides in the way it contributes to the intersubjective space.

The kind of approach I am advocating would stress the social aspects of semiosis. The individual sign is not to be read as divorced from the syntagm and from larger texts. That is the mark has to be understood as part of a structured combination of signs such as a picture, and this structured combination (syntagm) is related to a text, the larger organisation of individual messages which might be given in different media, for instance the picture or image and accompanying comments and actions. This smaller text is related to further texts, the text generated before and after the assessment which includes clinical documents and the practices of clinicians. By giving stress to contexts in this way I would argue that the communicative value of art-making is restored.

Social interaction is stressed in this research, as is cultural understanding. This is intentional because the research arose from assessments for autism. Such assessments are situations where subjects who suffer from social impairments are produced, a process in which abnormal social interactions are disclosed. This research gives us an account of how knowledges (discourses in relation to disabilities, for instance) are generated and supported through social practices. For this reason I would hope that the research will be of interest to other professionals who seek an understanding of autism. The research also shows how the autistic subject is able to use cultural practices when engaging in exchanges with others. It also provides evidence which demonstrates how art therapists, when they are prepared to explore the cultural construction of subjectivities, are well positioned to describe and analyse such exchanges.

ELIZABETH ASHBY

7 Resourceful, Skilful and Flexible: Art Therapy with People who have Severe Learning Disabilities and Challenging Behaviour

Abstract

This chapter is an account of a research project that investigated the current practice of art therapy with people with severe learning disabilities and challenging behaviour which came about as a result of the researcher's difficulties in her own practice. The survey-based project investigated the clinical approaches and working conditions of forty art therapists who worked with this client group. It discovered these art therapists to be a skilful and experienced group of clinicians who had developed working practices that were tailored around individual clients' needs, necessitating a highly flexible, sensitive, theoretically eclectic and often collaborative approach. The research also found that, in many cases, art therapists' working environments were not conducive to their work and that this had a detrimental impact on their ability to provide a good service to their clients. Further, that the work had a considerable impact on the therapists themselves.

Key Words

art therapy; severe learning disabilities; challenging behaviour; working methods; working conditions; survey.

How it all Began: From Practice to Research

The focus of this chapter is my research into the practice of art therapy with people who have severe learning disabilities and challenging behaviour. I had been working for some time in a specialist NHS unit for adults from this client population alongside a music therapist and a drama therapist. We had all been finding the work difficult and demanding. We tried new approaches but often felt frustrated, de-skilled and stuck. We also experienced problems with our working environment which affected our ability to provide an effective service to our clients and compounded the impact of the clinical work on us. We lacked the necessary time and resources to identify and explore the literature that might answer many of the questions we needed to ask and wanted to know how other arts therapists approached their work with this client group: whether they had encountered the same difficulties and found similar solutions. My research therefore sought to investigate the working practices that art therapists specialising with this client group had developed and to look at the circumstances in which they worked, believing that practice could not be satisfactorily examined without reference to the context. My research questions were: 'What working practices have been developed by art therapists with people who have severe learning disabilities and challenging behaviour?', 'What working conditions have they experienced?' and 'What factors contribute to or detract from the effectiveness of their interventions?'

The particular client population that I worked with all had severe learning disabilities. There are four levels of learning disability: these are commonly referred to as mild, moderate, severe and profound and are rated in terms of Intelligence Quotient (IQ) scores. A mild learning disability is an IQ between sixty-nine and fifty, moderate forty-nine to thirty-five, severe thirty-four to twenty, and profound below twenty. Hence a person with a severe learning disability has significant problems with thinking, understanding and communication, may not have speech and often experiences features of autistic spectrum disorders. In addition, these clients are also difficult to care for because their behaviour challenges those who care for them. In my workplace the term 'challenging behaviour' was used to refer to all behaviour that presents a challenge to staff, from physical violence (such as hitting, biting and kicking) to silent, withdrawn behaviour and self-injury.

It tends to be easier for people with mild and moderate learning disabilities to access the services they need than it is for people with severe and profound learning disabilities, particularly those who exhibit challenging behaviour. I was therefore pleased to (a) find a number of respondents who did work with this client group and (b) that interesting and apparently effective work was going on, despite the many difficulties practitioners seemed to encounter.

The Context of the Research

Locating the literature to assist my thinking about clinical work was difficult and I was struck by how disparate it was. Art therapists have been working with people who have learning disabilities since the early days of the profession but, surprisingly, the literature is sparse prior to the publication of a book specifically addressing this area of work (Rees, 1998).

In 1984 two conferences took place which advocated a psychotherapeutic approach to work with mentally handicapped clients. Of the papers written at this time, a few are relevant to this client group. Hallam (1984), for example, described his collaborative work with a challenging and destructive client; Dubowski (1984) discussed the stereotyped and repetitive mark-making behaviours of severely mentally handicapped people and their ability to use art therapy; and Lindsay (1984) wrote about transference, although in a restricted sense. Hughes (1988) explored her understanding of her work with three severely learning disabled clients in terms of object relations theory.

Research with this population was conducted by Dubowski (1983) and Rees (1995) who both adopted ethological methodology and investigated mark-making behaviours, Dubowski in relation to strategies employed to maintain desired approaches to image-making and Rees in relation to her subjects' use of physical space. Both concluded that complex coping strategies were employed by their subjects. Dubowski also addressed art therapy with severely mentally handicapped children (1990) and the development of different types of intelligence. In the same year Rabiger (1990) advocated a flexible and responsive approach to each child. Tipple (1992) made an important contribution to the work of art therapists with this client group in his overview of art therapy practice at that time which emphasised the importance of sensory experience. Stack (1996) and Fox (1998) described their work with autistic clients and the theoretical understanding they gained through reading about autism that helped them make sense of their experiences with their clients.

Challenging behaviours were discussed by all these authors who sought to understand what their clients' behaviours meant and to reduce their incidence through therapeutic intervention. Hallam (1984), for example, described tolerating and surviving destructive behaviour until the client was able to tolerate a calmer and more understanding relationship; Tipple (1992) wrote of his difficulties seeing his client in the art therapy department because of his challenging behaviour; and Stack (1996) discussed the reduction of her client's self-harming behaviours during the course of art therapy. Enhanced communication and the development of relationships over time between client and art therapist were fundamental to the changes in behaviour recorded by these authors.

Counter-transference was to some extent addressed by these authors (Rabiger, 1990; Tipple, 1992; Rees, 1995; Stack, 1996). They explain their reactions to their clients' behaviours, expressing feelings such as distress, hopelessness, inertia, and difficulty with thinking. However, they also describe a slow, patient, flexible and tenacious approach that they had found was necessary to the establishment of therapeutic relationships and to the bringing about of change; this included a reduction in violence and/or an ability to tolerate thinking for short periods of time (Rabiger, 1990; Tipple, 1992; Stack, 1996). Despite the difficulties they describe in their clinical work these writers consider psychodynamically-based art therapy useful for people who have severe learning disabilities and challenging behaviours (Dubowski, 1984; Tipple, 1992; Fox, 1998).

These authors provided me with a sense of the development of art therapy with this client population over three decades and addressed many of the issues that I wanted to explore in my research. These included communication and relationship-building, understanding and coping with challenging behaviours, counter-transference, theoretical approaches and the strategies art therapists employed to overcome the difficulties they faced. However, little has been written about art therapists' working conditions and other factors that impact upon the effectiveness of the work which my experience had led me to believe were many, significant and which needed to be addressed.

My research questions arose from my belief in the effectiveness of the clinical work I was doing – from the therapeutic relationships I had been able to develop and the changes I saw taking place – but this was tempered by the emotional impact the work had on me and on my colleagues. Our counter-transference feelings were, on the whole, painful; this seemed to be echoed in the literature. What was not described in the literature was how the negative impact of the clinical work was compounded by factors that went beyond the clients themselves, namely the unsuitability and instability of the working environment and the isolation my colleagues and I felt. I was therefore keen to discover if other art therapists' experiences with this client population and the nature of their working environments were similar to mine. I wanted to know if they had discovered any solutions to their difficulties.

Method

A survey seemed the most appropriate research strategy to gain the data I sought and, following Oppenheim's (1992) advice, I developed a plan. First of all I had to identify those art therapists who were working with clients who had severe learning difficulties and challenging behaviour. I contacted BAAT (British Association of Art Therapists) who informed me that there were, at that time, 304 art therapists working with people who have learning difficulties. A very short questionnaire sent to these art therapists identified sixty who worked with my client group who fitted my criteria, namely (a) a minimum of eighteen months post-qualification experience and (b) had been working with this client group during the last five years and agreed to participate. I designed the questionnaire – which needed to be easy to understand, comprehensive, ask the right questions and not be too long or off-putting – and piloted it with colleagues.

The first series of questions addressed respondents' details and those of their employment; the second investigated their working conditions, for example the therapeutic space, the wider environment in which it was located and issues to do with the multi-disciplinary team; and the third section looked at client details, including their range of difficulties and the extent of the practitioner's clinical experience with them. The fourth section addressed art therapists' working practices, for example details of art therapy sessions and whether they worked collaboratively. The final section addressed the emotional impact of the work on the art therapist and factors they felt influenced the effectiveness of their interventions. Forty art therapists completed the questionnaires. This was a good return and I was excited and encouraged by the responses I received. I used the Statistical Package for Social Sciences (SPSS) (Pallant, 2001) to process the quantitative data and generate descriptive statistics. I also conducted a content analysis (Silverman, 2001) on the qualitative data, categorising, coding and quantifying the material prior to writing up my findings in a thesis (Ashby, 2004).

Findings

This report of the findings is a partial account, limited by the length of this chapter, and focuses on issues to do with service provision, therapeutic factors and working practices that art therapists have developed for clinical work with this particular client group. Other aspects are addressed elsewhere (Ashby, 2004, 2010).

Working Environments and Service Provision

The picture that emerged was of a series of complex organisational issues impacting on the clinical practice of art therapists working with this client group. As can be seen in Table 7.1, a large majority of respondents were employed by the NHS. An additional finding (not represented in Table 7.1) was that 10 per cent of all respondents were neither employed as, nor could practise as, art therapists in their workplaces. This was so across all sectors.

Employer	Art Therapists
NHS	65 %
Sessional art therapists	17.5 %
Education	7.5 %
Social services, charities and private organisations	10 %

Table 7.1 Employers.

Many art therapists worked in physical spaces that were favourable to their clinical practice: 72 per cent had a dedicated studio space that was private, uninterrupted and conducive to therapy. The remainder did not have adequate facilities, particularly those working sessionally. Reports of inadequate physical spaces were due to a lack of resources. However, most art therapy studios were appropriate for the work but many respondents reported that these were located in inappropriate environments. For example, one respondent described therapy rooms that were too close to clients' living areas which led to blurred boundaries; another indicated that the therapeutic space was negatively impacted by the culture of the old style institution in which it was located and a third described the location as a place that was too noisy and smelt of food.

Few clinicians were restricted by their management in determining the length of therapy they could offer (20 per cent) – those who worked in education and forensics or were employed sessionally – but most were restricted to offering one session per week. The majority (72 per cent) worked with both individuals and groups, while 23 per cent indicated they work only individually and 5 per cent only with groups. Their theoretical orientation was predominantly psychodynamic as shown in Table 7.2 while many showed they used more than one theoretical approach.

Theory	Percentage
Psychodynamic	82.5 %
Client-centred	70 %
Eclectic	65 %
Humanistic	42.5 %
Process-orientated	40 %
Analytic	20 %
Behavioural	17.5 %
Systematic	2.5 %

Table 7.2 Theoretical Orientation.

Many respondents commented that they used all or most of these approaches at different times, depending on their clients' needs.

I asked art therapists if they felt they were adequately supported in their workplaces and whether or not their views were valued by their organisations and multi-disciplinary teams. Table 7.3 shows that while supervision was usually adequate support from colleagues was variable and support from management was frequently unreliable.

	Yes	No	Sometimes
Feeling isolated	23 %	15.5 %	61.5 %
Supported by colleagues	40 %	7.5 %	52.5 %
Supported by management	17.5 %	15 %	67.5%
Adequate supervision	60 %	12.5 %	27.5 %
Views valued at work	30 %	10 %	60 %

Table 7.3 Professional Support.

Further, and as can be seen in Table 7.4, practitioners had to contend with significant difficulties that impeded the delivery of efficient art therapy services and effective clinical work. These came from several sources: from inadequate funding; a lack of understanding of art therapy and therefore inappropriate expectations from management, colleagues and allied services; and concerns about their and their clients' personal safety.

People who have severe learning disabilities are dependent on others to meet their needs. They usually live in residential accommodation, receive day care elsewhere, and require constant monitoring if they exhibit challenging behaviour. In order for a client to access art therapy they are dependent on being escorted by a member of staff, having reliable and appropriate transport, feeling well enough to attend and on appropriate support for and understanding of art therapy by their carers. Half the respondents reported significant problems with these aspects of service delivery which further complicated their clinical work. 44 per cent of respondents reported that such issues had a negative impact on the effectiveness of their interventions.

Employer Issues	Insufficient funding; inappropriate rooms or location of rooms; lack of understanding of art therapy; inappropriate referrals; unreasonable expectations; lack of commitment to the work of sessionally employed art therapists.
Allied services	Lack of understanding of art therapy; residential homes' or social care approaches conflicting with those of therapy; lack of support for carers; low staffing levels; staff turnover, attendance; difficulties with appropriate, reliable transport and escorts; problems with timekeeping, consistency and continuity.
Safety	Personal safety; lack of back-up; inappropriate venues; finding the balance between safety, intrusion and privacy.
Therapists' issues	Disruptions; absence of supportive infrastructure; lack of containment; pressure to conform to inappropriate treatment models; feeling de-skilled and disempowered; lack of time for reflection.

Table 7.4 Difficulties with Service Provision.

Thus it can be seen how art therapists have to adapt to their clients' and to their institutions' and other organisations' needs and activities. They therefore have to be extremely flexible in their approach, they have to fight for resources and for professional recognition and support within the multi-disciplinary team.

A considerable body of experience with this client group was represented by the respondents, the average being eleven years. Many had qualifications further to their art therapy training, ranging from post graduate certificates and diplomas to MAs in Art Psychotherapy, but many described feeling de-skilled and in need of yet more training. Their responses suggested that this was influenced by the lack of support, recognition and adequate resources that many experienced in their workplaces but they also revealed the significant difficulties art therapists experienced in their day-to-day clinical work.

Challenges and Strategies

My attempts to categorise and quantify respondents' answers about their practice met with difficulty. I was frustrated by the repeating answer 'it varies from client to client', until I realised that it *was* the answer I was searching for: art therapists had developed an extremely flexible, entirely client-centre therapeutic approach which was tailored to the particular needs, difficulties and challenges presented by each individual.

Respondents reported that problems with language and communication were common to all their clients. Some had no speech at all and others had speech patterns that were difficult to understand. Many difficulties ensued. It was hard to talk about issues because clients' understanding and self-expression was limited; this increased clients' frustration and led to incidents of violence towards others and self-injury. There were also problems establishing relationships, boundary issues were blurred and confused and the pace of therapy was slow. Challenging behaviours were also problematic. These included hitting, biting, shouting, undressing, hair-pulling, smearing faeces, scratching, head-banging, other forms of self injury, throwing objects, kicking, pica, running away, masturbation, drug and alcohol abuse, inappropriate sexual behaviour, elective mutism, swearing, regurgitating, and cutting. Most clients had additional difficulties such as obsessive behaviour, physical impairments and mental health problems as well as difficulties at home, with day care or with medication. Put together this made a grim picture. However, the survey revealed that art therapists had developed various strategies to deal with these and other, service-related, difficulties they encountered.

Working Collaboratively

I discovered that, like me, many art therapists (63 per cent) worked collaboratively with other arts therapists and members of allied health professions (Figure 7.1 shows who they were). This usually involved co-leading different kinds of art/s therapies groups (fifteen respondents), although a few (eight) co-conducted individual therapy with psychologists and occupational therapists.

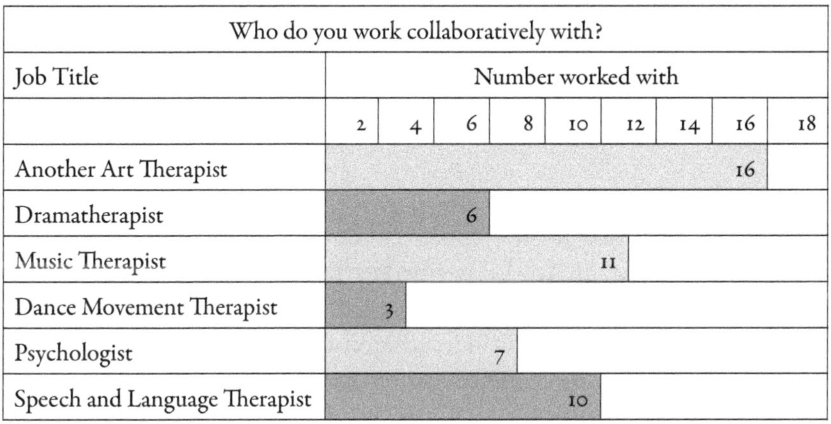

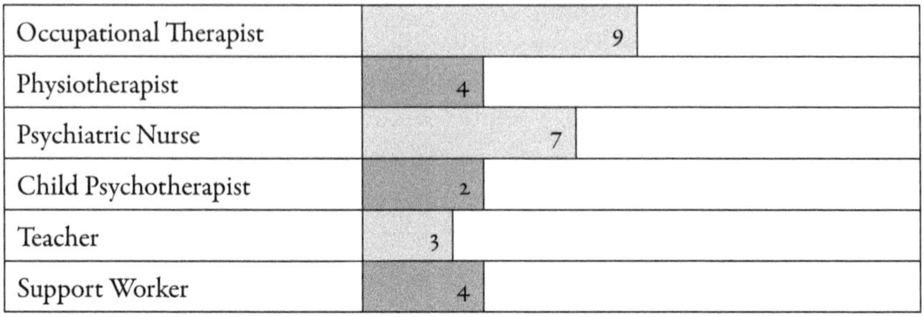

Figure 7.1 Collaborative Work.

Safety was the primary reason for working collaboratively (cited by 65 per cent of respondents), particularly in forensic settings, but respondents reported a number of other benefits that came from collaborative work. It improved the containment of clients, offering them increased attention and additional expertise. It also offered containment for clinicians, principally through mutual support that combated attacks on thinking and ensured a consistent therapeutic approach. Co-working enabled family situations to be mirrored. It also facilitated multi-disciplinary assessments and hence appropriate referrals and so improved the use of available resources. Collaborative work also expanded the potential for creativity through the use of more than one medium. Almost all respondents who worked collaboratively felt it was an effective way of working. As one art therapist said: '... the work wouldn't happen otherwise'.

Communication Strategies

Another strategy that art therapists had developed focused on communication with their clients. I described earlier the serious and profound problems with speech and communication that people with severe learning difficulties face, often resulting in frustration and, consequently, challenging behaviours. Developing communication skills is therefore of paramount importance when working with clients who have such severe communication difficulties. It requires that practitioners listen and observe extremely carefully and become very sensitive to the nuances of their clients' communications, whether they involve speech or not. This survey revealed the range of communication strategies that art therapists utilised in their practice as well as the unique properties of art therapy that enhance the communicative possibilities for clients with language and communication problems. These are in the processes of art-making and in the communication enabled through the language of the image. Together these enhance clients' capacity for self-expression and the communication between client and art therapist.

It was clear in the responses to the questionnaire that practitioners had developed creative ways to communicate with their clients such as using images, symbols, sign languages, object referencing, mime, and play. Examples of difficulties respondents experienced as a result of communication limitations were described. One respondent felt there were problems 'being able to share meanings of certain objects or experiences known only to the client'; a second indicated five difficulties which were 'increased frustration, escalation in noise, escalation in hitting/self-injury, therapist de-skilling and blurred/confused boundary issues'; and a third reported that 'images were more pertinent, more of a focus'. Below is a summary of the strategies employed:

1. Emphasising the language of art and the process of image-making
2. Using symbols and visual communication aids
3. Utilising other creative media such as drama, mime, and sound
4. Heightened sensitivity to mood, body language and gesture
5. Enhanced awareness of vocalisations and possible meanings
6. Drawing on sign languages including Signalong and Makaton
7. Tailoring the approach to individual communication needs
8. Employing interpretation by other members of the multi-disciplinary team
9 Exploring counter-transference responses in supervision

The art-based communicative strategies linked to factors that art therapists considered made their work particularly effective with clients with severe learning difficulties and speech problems.

Therapeutic Factors

This survey did not address client outcomes but focused on art therapists' perceptions of their effectiveness. 37 per cent thought that their interventions were effective and 19 per cent thought their effectiveness varied from client to client. However, 44 per cent indicated that their effectiveness, and indeed the whole therapeutic process, was considerably impeded by the difficulties with service provision previously described and sometimes by clients' physical health (for example, when clients suffered from epilepsy).

The therapeutic factors that respondents identified fell into five categories as follows:

1. Safety and containment
    - Art therapy offers a safe emotional space to express, identify, and contain difficult and disturbing emotions.
    - Making art can contain and embody difficult feelings.
    - Making art provides an outlet for frustration, anger and aggression. without resort to self-injury and violence.
    - Boundaries of expression and behaviour can be internalised.

2. Empowering
    - Clients are treated with respect and a non-judgemental approach.
    - Clients are offered a space to be themselves, are accepted and valued.
    - Clients are encouraged to take control of the art materials but without pressure to make art or to talk.
    - Therapy unfolds at the client's pace.

3. Thinking
   - Clients have a space in which to think, reflect and process.
   - The art therapist's reflections on the art work with clients assists with understanding and the attribution of meaning.

4. Relationship
   - Builds the capacity for meaningful, healthy, trusting and facilitating relationships.
   - Develops a sense of self.
   - Alleviates isolation, builds self-esteem and self-confidence.

5. Communication
   - Art offers a language that enhances understanding and communication between client and therapist.
   - Non-verbal skills are developed that enhance clients' communication. These decrease challenging behaviour which can be transformed, modified or re-directed into more positive outlets or expressions.
   - Making art within a therapeutic relationship develops an emotional literacy and facilitates insight.
   - Making art can communicate and regulate affect. The expression of emotions may be concrete and/or can become symbolic.
   - Artworks can be kept for later reflection and review.

People with severe learning disabilities and challenging behaviours often lack choice and opportunities in their lives. This research demonstrates that art therapy's therapeutic factors offer these clients important opportunities that are often lacking in their everyday experience. It also suggests that careful attendance to their communications, particularly those that are challenging, can assist with understanding behaviours and hence managing them.

Impact on the Therapist

My colleagues and I experienced practice with this client group as demanding and debilitating; this prompted me to ask art therapists about the personal impact of their clinical work. This elicited both positive and negative responses with twice as many negative as positive feelings. Positive feelings included a sense of achievement and satisfaction with the work, feeling interested in their clients and valuing them, but negative feelings included exhaustion and a sense of inertia, feeling disempowered, de-skilled, angry and frustrated, threatened and cognitively impaired. A striking feature was the extremes of emotion expressed – from 'despair' to 'elation' and 'burnt out' to 'exhilarated'. These feelings were directly linked, by 85 per cent of respondents, to a need for further training.

Discussion

For an art therapist to be effective there are basic requirements without which the work is not possible. These include the provision of an adequate room within a suitable environment, sufficient funding, resources and practical and psychological support for client and therapist. This survey showed that art therapists who worked with clients who have severe learning difficulties and challenging behaviour, particularly those who worked sessionally, often struggled to have these basic requirements met. More than half of those surveyed felt that although they had suitable rooms to work in, they were located in environments that were not conducive to therapy. This was my experience too: the room itself was fine but was set within a busy, noisy day centre where few boundaries were recognised. A good room in an unsuitable place becomes an unsuitable therapeutic space.

Foulds (1998) describes a similar situation. She reports that she felt neither heard nor contained by the centre where she was employed, despite repeatedly trying to address problematic issues with her management.

Her sense was that her client's experiences of disempowerment were echoed in her own. The issue of designated art rooms disappearing was considered by Woddis (1992) who questioned whether the result would be an erosion of practice. Sinason (1988) states that therapy can be damaged by changes in the environment: it needs to be supportive. This survey suggests that difficulties with art rooms do impede practice. This needs to be acknowledged and addressed by organisational management.

Relatively few art therapists felt positive about the support they received from their management. This was despite the fact that the provision of supervision was, more often than not, satisfactory, and was considered crucial to respondents' ability to make sense of their work, especially when communication problems were so severe. Stack (1996) considers the importance of good supervision, and emphasises that it was only in hindsight that she could write about the work, once the 'not knowing' had been worked through. However, it is important to note the impact organisational issues and allied services have on the effectiveness of art therapy. The care approach favoured in clients' residential homes and day care provision sometimes seemed, in this research, to often be in conflict with therapy, much as Huet (1997) described. In this survey communication with allied staff such as carers was clearly an issue: art therapy was often misunderstood and under-valued, resulting in events and behaviours that frequently had a negative impact upon clinical work.

The art therapists Huet (ibid.) interviewed (who worked with people who had long-term and severe mental health problems) spoke of conflicts with other mental health workers arising from differences in approach and lack of communication; they found that allied staff tended to take short-term problem-solving approaches (art therapists' work tended to be long-term), the pace of therapy was slow and their client turnover low. Many of the issues raised in this survey were also described by Huet whose audit found that the clients they worked with were also challenging, necessitating a flexible, tenacious and more concrete approach. They too identified feeling de-skilled, depressed and exhausted and yet they were dedicated to their work. Huet's interviewees advocated co-working and identified issues arising from loss of dedicated art studios as a result of the move into community care.

For my respondents, working collaboratively with other members of the multi-disciplinary team clearly had considerable benefits. The synergistic effect of combining expertise enabled therapists to survive the attacks on their thinking processes more effectively and to provide greater containment and attention for clients. It was also necessary for practical reasons. Fox (1998) discussed the increased attention that two group facilitators were able to give to individuals and the likeness to a family situation within the group; Hallam (1984) described a collaborative approach with one client who was very destructive, and the benefits that two therapists brought to that situation. Waller (1993) described nine curative factors of interactive art therapy groups, not all of which would be relevant to this client group as clients are less likely to interact with one another and the verbal aspect of the group would be considerably reduced. However, factors such as the reconstruction of family, catharsis and learning about relationships were noted by the art therapists who responded to my survey. Waller went on to note thirteen curative factors that were particular to art therapy groups, a number of which were very pertinent to this research, namely: the use of art as an alternative to words and as a media for play; the value of creativity per se; the art object being the focus of projection, interaction and a vehicle for the expression of feelings; and images being reminders of sessions. These were also identified by my respondents.

The therapeutic approach adopted by the art therapists in this survey was flexible, client-centred, and individually tailored to each client's needs, much as described by Rabiger (1990). Respondents represented a considerable body of experience, were well-qualified, and had developed particular strategies and skills to manage the difficulties with communication and challenging behaviour that they encountered. This research has demonstrated that these art therapists had learnt not only to fine-tune their observation skills, be aware of body language and use other forms of communication but also to emphasise the role and function of art as the primary language in art therapy, informed and underpinned by a psychodynamic approach.

The therapeutic process with people who have severe learning disabilities tends to be very slow and, as has been described by a number of writers (Rabiger, 1990; Rees, 1995; Stack, 1996; Tipple, 1992), requires patience and tenacity on the part of the therapist. This can result in difficult feelings arising in the therapist in response to their clinical work (op.cit.). The respondents to my survey revealed twice as many negative as positive feelings about their practice. I have mentioned the impact of my clinical practice on me and would say that I too have experienced the range of emotions that respondents identified. In this research these seem to be associated with a lack of clarity and understanding often faced by both therapists and clients, the slow pace of therapy, a near constant threat to personal safety, frustrations consequent upon clients' dependence on others (such as the failure of transport to arrive), the failure of working environments to support therapeutic work and inadequate supportive infrastructures for clinicians. Negative counter-transference feelings tend to result.

Despite being a highly qualified and experienced group of practitioners, a large majority of these respondents felt in need of further training. This seems to me to be the result of several factors: the debilitating nature of the clinical work, the negative countertransference responses that can arise and feelings of being de-skilled and under-valued in the working environment. Cumulatively, these seem to have an impact art therapists' self-esteem which leads them to want further training, i.e. over and above the necessity for continuing professional development. Some have found that conducting research has assisted with these feelings, as described by Rees (1995) and Killick and Greenwood (1995). The impact of mental handicap on therapists and other carers has been documented by Sinason (1992) who wrote of the therapist being handicapped and unable to see what the client is trying to show or say because of the grief and shock they experience. What Sinason described as a handicap in the therapist I have described as an attack on one's thinking processes. However the effect is indeed handicapping.

Art therapists working with other client groups have also described negative counter transference responses such as helplessness, frustration, anger and confusion. Byers (1995), for example, explores feelings of confusion and helplessness aroused by her work with elderly people suffering from severe memory loss; Falk (2002) describes feelings of claustrophobia, frustration, anxiety and difficulties with concentration in his work with young Parkinson's sufferers and the negative impact of running an art therapy group in a physical space and institution that was not entirely containing; and Hardy (2001) discusses the emotional impact of the work on therapists working in palliative care and the importance of addressing transference and countertransference responses. Working with psychotic patients can also attack the therapist's thinking, as described by Killick and Greenwood (1995) who, like Rees, found themselves drawn towards conducting research to help them maintain their thinking processes and make sense of their experiences. And Sheppard et al's (1998) randomised controlled trial demonstrated the negative impact of an unsupportive environment on the effectiveness of art therapy groups with people with dementia (see also Waller, 2002). Clearly supportive organisational structures and working environments enable art therapists to maximise their effectiveness in their practice with many different client groups, especially when working with clients experiencing severe and complex distress and disability.

The dedication of these respondents to their clients, despite the difficulties they faced, was evidenced in their skill, tenacity and resourcefulness. They had developed working practices and strategies that focussed on the particular therapeutic factors that art therapy has to offer to severely learning disabled clients. These enable the containment and expression of feelings, empower clients to make choices and decisions, facilitate communication and thought and the development of meaningful and trusting relationships through the agency of the image and through art therapists' heightened visual and sensory attunement to the nuances of their clients' communications.

From Research into Practice

The therapeutic factors that make art therapy an effective intervention with people who have severe learning disabilities and challenging behaviour have been identified in this research, as well as the complex and multiple difficulties faced by client and therapist that are a direct result of clients' dependence on others to meet their needs. These respondents have been shown to be flexible, client-centred and resourceful in their overall approach and to have developed considerable skill in dealing with communication difficulties and challenging behaviours. Key strategies identified were collaborative work, a necessary attention to the safety and containment of clients and therapists, and a reliance on image-making as the primary language of communication, often in a situation where clients have none. However the emotional impact of the work was, despite art therapists' tolerance and staying power, found to be very draining. Organisational, allied staff and environmental issues compounded the clinical difficulties art therapists faced and had a cumulative negative effect on the effectiveness of art therapists' work with this client population.

The results of this survey shed much light on my own clinical practice and I discovered many parallel experiences in terms of working methods and service provision, as I hoped I would. I felt that my clinical practice had been developing in line with others working with similar clients in parallel contexts across the country. This was both encouraging and affirming. I was critical of the inadequacies in my and my colleagues' working environments and I discovered that I was not alone in this experience either. However, I was, as a direct result of this research, able to make the case for a more conducive working environment to my management that was recognised and addressed. I was also able to make recommendations for changes in service delivery and working conditions, which included restricting the number of hours therapists worked with this client group, recognising the value of a mixed caseload in terms of severity, the need for a working environment that was set apart from day services, enabling it to avoid the chaotic and noisy conditions we had experienced, and greater support for therapists from the department. In addition, management recognized that support staff needed better training, better rates of pay, better support, and that the structure of the day service needed changing. More individual choice was introduced for the clients who, instead of being catered for in teams week by week, spent less time in the centre and were able to follow their interests on a more individual basis. In fact, the changes that took place were far reaching for both clients and staff within the unit.

Art therapists who work with people who have severe learning disabilities and challenging behaviours need their managers to provide adequate physical resources and environments appropriate for the delivery of therapy, together with practical and psychologically supportive infrastructures. These will enable art therapists to deliver effective services and ameliorate the impact of what can be debilitating clinical work. Without adequate understanding of the complex organisational and clinical issues involved in offering art therapy to this particular client population, service providers will continue to under-resource a practice that in some cases, at the moment, is less effective than it could be if the necessary resources were available, to the disservice of the clients.

ANDREA GILROY

Commentary: Art Therapy with People who have Learning Disabilities

Communication is central to art therapy. It takes different forms and occurs in different ways between different participants: through the interpersonal, visual and verbal communication between clients and art therapists; the professional communication between art therapists, their colleagues and the institutions in which they work; and the client's intrapsychic communication, including that with their art work. It is art therapy's major contribution to therapeutic work with people who have learning disabilities.

Communication

Communication emerges as a major theme in Part Two of this book, specifically regarding the minutiae of art-making in relation to cognition, affect and the social construction of the learning disabled individual and their exchanges with the art therapist and others involved in their care. During conversation between these authors and the editor it became clear that communication is both the central task and the main difficulty in art therapy with this client population. This might be when clients' verbal and visual communication is limited or when presenting behaviours are so challenging that they inhibit the art therapist's capacity to think and understand. We agreed that communication is a reciprocal process which involves the art therapist not only in understanding their clients' communications but also in making sure that they are understood by their clients, and by colleagues who might be unfamiliar with art therapy practices.

Our discussion also explored how art is a means of communication and cultural exchange with which members of this client population can engage, not only in art therapy but also through different aspects of popular and material culture such as music, dress and possessions that are valued differently in different cultural domains. Through such engagements people with learning disabilities can, when their disabilities allow, construct themselves. However, no matter how a subject constructs his or her 'self', he or she will be socially constructed by their family and by the services that care for them.

We spent some time discussing the relative paucity of literature and research about art therapy with people who have learning disabilities. Clinical work with these clients has a long and respectable history and a small but useful base of inductive, mostly casework-based literature with adults (e.g. Tipple, 1992; Fox, 1998; Stack, 1998; Kuczaj, 1998) and children (e.g. McGregor, 1990; Kornreich and Schimmel, 1991; Henley, 2001). Research includes the comparative and developmental research by Stott and Males (1984), Dubowski (1984, 1990), Rees (1995), Evans (1998) and Evans and Dubowski (2001); the intersubjective research by Tipple (2003); and the outcome research by Bowen and Rosal (1989) and Mackenzie et al. (2000) which together show that art therapy can address challenging behaviours, develop a capacity for symbol formation and enable the establishment of relationship. More recent research has assessed the difficulties mothers of Downs Syndrome children have with in their relationship with their child (Lev-Weisel and Zeevi, 2007); shown that portrait drawing (Martin, 2008) and visual exchange between client and art therapist (Bragge and Fenner, 2009) offers a means of being in relationship with children and adolescents on the autistic spectrum; and a small scale RCT has demonstrated 'slight' improvements in the social relationships and language comprehension of mild and moderate learning disabled adults following a twelve week, structured 'art facilitation group' in a day centre in Hong Kong (Got and Cheng, 2008). Despite these recent contributions the evidence base about the processes and outcomes of art therapy with this client population remains relatively thin. We noted that NICE has not developed guidelines for work with people with learning disabilities but that guidance for the treatment of those with mental health problems in addition to their disability are included in recommendations for particular diagnoses and services, e.g. forensic services. In the absence of a robust evidence base for art therapy with people who have learning disabilities it was interesting that our conversation then focused on the changing nature of provision and art therapy's place in the care of these clients.

Policy and Provision

Practitioner researchers contributing to this part of the book have all worked in the NHS for some time and have experienced significant change in service provision. We compared the relative paucity of art therapy literature with the significant literature about the social and political empowerment of the learning disabled that relates to the social construction of the person in terms of their disabilities, incapacities and failures and to the 'industrialisation' of their care (e.g. Rapley, 2004). The continuing care of the learning disabled has been the subject of considerable policy development which now focuses on the provision of cross-sectoral services that develop and support social, living and work-based skills and the enhancement of the quality of a community-based life, as described in *Valuing People Now* (DH, 2008). This makes clear the division of responsibility for the care of the learning disabled between social and healthcare services, specialist social care being with local governments and general and specialist health care with Primary Care Trusts (PCTs).

We discussed these practitioner researchers' experiences of services for the learning disabled which, by and large, reflected government policy. They reported that services for children who have learning disabilities are usually addressed by paediatric and educational services and are not considered within a psychiatric remit unless there are clearly defined mental health problems. When such difficulties do occur, links are made to services that assess the child, like the one described by Tipple. However, it was felt that the complexities of perception, diagnosis and care pathways in different parts of the statutory and non-statutory sectors can lead to gaps in provision and care, for example for the learning disabled aged seventy and above. Concern emerged about the sustainability of NHS art therapy practice with this client population as services are commissioned rather than provided and as targets for assessment, treatment and return to employment become key performance indicators, these being measures that do not always fit comfortably with the outcomes of art therapy for the learning disabled.

It was in this context that our discussion explored how referrals to art therapy services for people with learning disabilities have changed over the last ten years: from those who might have general difficulties with communication to a more particular focus on mental health problems. Such is the service provided by Damarell, but this differs from that of Ashby whose service both assesses and works with adults who have severe disabilities and challenging behaviours and develops strategies for clients' future care that enable the person to be better understood and managed by their families and carers.

It was with this mind that we turned to discussion of Ashby's research and what is needed for effective and efficient art therapy services. We agreed that the reality of practitioners' working environments can fall well short of ideal, particularly with regard to designated studio space. Ashby's identification of the importance of appropriate and supportive working environments for practitioners is augmented by her argument (forthcoming, 2010) that designated art therapy space assists the connection of severely disabled clients to their therapist and hence their ability to communicate. Studio space underpins best practice in art therapy (Wood, 2001) but, although desirable, how realistic is this requirement in the current economic climate when space is both expensive and at a premium? The literature suggests that art therapists can work in different places and spaces (e.g. Kalmanowitz and Lloyd, 1997) and are able to make a creative oasis through the presence and use of art materials. We explored how a process occurs through which multipurpose rooms become akin to a theatre: a space that can be transformed and assume a certain character but which returns to a neutral state at the end of the session. However, is this sufficient?

The research described in Part Two of this book demonstrates art therapists' flexibility and creativity and their collaborative approach to working with their clients. It alerts art therapists to client behaviours that surround and accompany art-making which enable thought to occur, extends theorising about the function of diagrammatic images and suggests that artworks are not entirely the product of clients' inner worlds. This research also sensitises practitioners and their employers to the importance of art therapy to the most severely disabled clients and their carers and outlines what is needed to ensure best practice. Viewed collectively, this suggests that a shift away from a focus on the interpretation and analysis of the meaning of these clients' artworks towards a more nuanced microanalysis of the nature and content of different forms of communication in art therapy would be useful, including consideration of how clients, their artworks and their art therapists are 'shaped' by the contexts in which they live and work. But perhaps most significantly, given the concern expressed by these practitioner researchers about the future provision of art therapy services for people who have learning disabilities, these three research projects show that art therapy offers these clients opportunities for communication and thought that could otherwise be absent from their lives. If, as seems clear from the chapters in this part of the book, meaningful communication is art therapy's particular contribution to therapeutic and perhaps other kinds of social and community-based work with people who have learning disabilities then its nature, form and facilitation needs to be a strategic focus in the development of a meaningful evidence base.

PART THREE

Researching Art Therapy with Adults

KEVIN JONES

8 Art 'fer-a-Pee'. An Exploratory Randomised Controlled Trial (RCT) of Group Based Art Therapy as an Adjunctive Treatment for People with a Diagnosis of Schizophrenia

Abstract

This chapter describes the first exploratory Randomized Controlled Trial (RCT) of brief art therapy groups for people with a diagnosis of schizophrenia which took place between 1997 and 2000 in a south London, NHS, mental health trust. The research design, methodology and results are summarized alongside a narrative reflecting my experience as the art therapist who was involved in the RCT as a researcher and the lead clinician. I explore the RCT in its social context, as an object in the transference and through a case example suggest how the interrelationship of these aspects influenced the research process and outcome. The research experience suggests that the RCT is a contradictory phenomenon which art therapists are forced to confront and contest within limited possibilities of action and appropriation.

Key Words

art therapy groups; Randomized Controlled Trial (RCT); the social and the political; transference.

How it all Began: From Practice to Research

The need for research into the effectiveness of art therapy was demonstrated when I, and the whole art therapy department of a major NHS trust, was made redundant. Facing a funding 'shortfall' of £100,000, managers explained that although creativity was highly valued in the NHS, regrettably there was little empirical evidence which could justify continued funding for art therapy. Paradoxically, the same NHS trust then successfully applied to host an exploratory RCT of art therapy. Having been redeployed into a generic mental health worker role I decided, despite having no previous research experience, to apply for the clinician post in the RCT.

The research team comprised the principal researcher who was a psychoanalyst/academic psychologist, an art therapist (myself), a psychiatrist/group analyst and a research assistant. We agreed that the principal researcher and the psychiatrist/group analyst would write up the empirical and statistical 'hard' stuff while I would write up the art therapy 'soft' stuff. I have used this contrast between 'hard' and 'soft' to structure the chapter and convey the different qualities of my research experiences.

The Context of the Research

Writing in 1977 on the subject of 'Measuring changes attributable to art therapy' Holtom concluded with some urgency that 'more needs to be done along these lines. Now' (34–6). Situating the research in a social and political context suggests why, twenty years later, I found myself working as a clinician in an RCT seeking answers to the questions raised by Holtom.

Pringle (1996) described the history and origins of EBP in the 1970s. She argued that the current emphasis on EBP reflected changes in political attitudes to public spending, resulting in changes to social policy agendas which in the NHS included: managing escalating health care costs within limited health care budgets; renegotiating the balance of power in decision making on health care provision between professionals, managers and policy makers; and the creation of an internal market in the NHS. Pringle outlined how the use of empirical methods to compare the effects of different treatments had contributed to the improvement of medical care for clients and challenged vested interests in the public services. Whether or not an evidence-based paradigm derived from general medicine was applicable to art therapy was a question addressed in the art therapy literature from the mid-1970s. Holtom suggested that art therapy might be evaluated in comparison to other treatments as in a trial for a new drug but was aware that art therapists might have a 'healthy unwillingness' to subject their work to 'pseudo medical dissection' (1977: 35). Males (1980) questioned the ethics of providing a treatment without knowledge of a treatment's effectiveness and queried whether the dominant case study approach in art therapy was sufficient for this task. She suggested that controlled experimental investigations might allow for 'an objective statement of fact, rather than a subjective description based on intuition' (13–15). While acknowledging the difficulties of measuring changes in the art therapy process Males suggested that a 'defensive assessment' of the effectiveness of art therapy might persuade other professionals of its usefulness and be an aid to more informed referrals.

In his overview of evaluation in art therapy, Edwards (1987, 1999) stressed the increasing emphasis being placed on the accountability of practitioners and the evaluation of health care provision. He suggested that art therapists might be skeptical about the notion of 'scientific objectivity' argued by Males and have interests in other research paradigms. Arguing that scientific research methods might not be sensitive to communication through art he suggested that there was a gulf between the usefulness of information provided by empirical outcome studies and information derived from case study research. Edwards discussed how a balance might be struck between 'objective' methods of research and subjectively-based therapy.

The first arts therapies conferences in 1989 and 1990 led to two publications (Payne, 1993; Gilroy and Lee, 1995), after which there was a surge of interest in the evaluation of art therapy (Edwards, 1999; Gilroy, 1996;

Jones, 1998; Wood, 1999). This coincides with the emergence of EBP as described by Pringle. It seems that the new political context forced the unresolved questions of Holtom, Males and Edwards once more onto the art therapy agenda.

Method

The formulation of our research question was influenced by two factors. The first was the need for evidence of the effectiveness of art therapy within the EBP framework. The second was that one of the traditional strengths of art therapy is to work with people with diagnoses of severe and enduring mental health problems (Wood, 1997), a priority target group for the provision of services within the NHS. The research team thought that evidence of the effectiveness of art therapy with these people would bring together art therapy and health service strategic agendas. We chose a RCT as the research method because it was, and still is, seen as the 'gold standard' for evidence within the EBP framework, this being 'the method of investigation that can give greatest confidence in hypothesizing a causal association between a treatment and its apparent outcome.' (Richardson et al., 2007; 484: see also Pocock, 1984: 14–18).

A systematic review of the online databases Embase, Medline, Psychinfo and a manual search of all *Inscape*, *Arts in Psychotherapy*, *Journal of the American Art Therapy Association* and the *Canadian Art Therapy Association* journals (all from the beginnings of the volumes to 1997, which was when the research began) was undertaken to find existing evidence for art therapy with adult psychiatric populations. There were a number of single case reports, for example in Waller and Gilroy (1992) and Killick and Schaverien (1997), and some uncontrolled trials of art therapy that reported encouraging outcomes (e.g. Tibbetts and Stone, 1990; Potocky, 1993). There were no examples of controlled trials in the British literature but two were found in North America.

In Borchers' RCT (1985), forty clients on an adult psychiatric rehabilitation ward were randomized to receive either a ten session, one and a half hours per week art therapy group or standard ward care. Outcome measures used included the Progress Evaluation Scale with variables that included attitude toward 'self' and 'getting along with others'. Measures were taken pre-therapy, immediately afterwards and at nine months follow-up. Both these variables showed significant improvement immediately after therapy but not at follow-up. The conclusion from the study was constrained by the small numbers in the trial, the mixed diagnosis of people on the ward and the lack of guidelines on the art therapy intervention.

In Green et al.'s RCT (1987), forty chronic psychiatric outpatients were randomized into either standard treatment for ten sessions, one session every two weeks, or into standard care. They reported significant improvements on a number of self- and therapist-rated indices of self-esteem and 'getting along with others' which lasted at six months follow-up. Each session was preceded by a short relaxation exercise, followed by guided visualization and structured themes. The results of the research were again hard to generalize. Art therapy was one element of a multi-component treatment, small numbers were recruited to the trial and there was no guidance on the intervention. As Gilroy points out, in neither study is the imagery or interaction with the imagery discussed (1996).

Although there were no examples of controlled trials in the British literature we did find attempts to address and develop the question of art therapy outcome measures. Holtom's (1977) survey asked whether expectations of art therapists regarding the outcomes of art therapy matched or mismatched the expectations of other professionals. The survey was circulated mainly to art therapists working in hospitals; only a small proportion of these practitioners replied and no actual figures were reported. However, the replies showed an inconsistency amongst both the art therapists and their professional colleagues as to who would benefit from art therapy and what would count as a beneficial outcome.

Dalley (1980) defined art therapy outcomes more specifically when she used a single case study approach alongside a quantitative method known as a 'time series'. The study showed the progress of one individual through an art therapy open group. After each session the client rated how she felt during the session on a nine point scale along eleven different dimensions of feeling (e.g. not depressed-depressed, creative-not creative). The study also recorded observations of each session by the therapist and the client's comments about her work. Limitations included lack of a control case, no explanation as to how or why the particular dimensions of feeling were selected and no explanation about why this particular client was selected for presentation rather than others who also attended the group. However, the study showed a strong link between the image, the verbal process of a session and client-reported outcome. This study was particularly useful for indicating how a client could get worse in self-report before improving.

Edwards (1987) made the case for demonstrating the effectiveness of art therapy in terms which health service managers and policy makers could understand. He gave two examples of evaluation forms, one designed to systematically gather referral information and provide consistent baseline information on which referrals might be compared, and another to obtain the client's perception of art therapy. Unfortunately there was no indication of whether the questionnaires were used or not.

These early research studies all suffered from a lack of discussion on the construction and validation process for each measure and the small number of clients investigated further limited the possibility for generalization and the validity of the results. Richardson et al concluded that: '... despite its widespread use in mental health services there would appear to be little evidence from within an EBP framework for the efficacy of art therapy with adult psychiatric clients with severe and or complex mental heath problems' (2007: 484).

The primary objective of our RCT was to establish the possible incremental benefit on the quality of care of the clinical outcomes of art therapy plus a standard package of community mental health care, compared to standard care alone. Participants were mental health service users of an inner city London mental health trust which had a high ethnic minority population. All participants signed consent forms for artwork to be used for conferences, publication, research and teaching purposes.

All service users with a diagnosis of schizophrenia (ICD 10) over the previous two years (1995–7) and who were in contact with the trust's Community Mental Health Teams (CMHTs) were invited to participate. Exclusion from the study occurred when a client had an organic illness, a previous referral to art therapy within the last two years, if they were receiving another formal psychological therapy and finally if they were admitted to hospital. Participation followed discussion with the CMHT involved and after obtaining informed written consent from the service user. Service users were then randomly allocated to receive art therapy plus standard care or standard care alone.

Forty three mental health service users were randomized to twelve sessions of one and a half hours per week in an art therapy group. Their clinical outcomes were compared with those of forty-seven other service users who received standard psychiatric care alone. Outcome measures assessed participants' symptoms, their interpersonal functioning and quality of life, and the art therapy process. All participants were assessed at pre- and post-treatment and at six month follow-up (see Figure 8.1). The design used ANCOVA to examine the main effects of treatment using pre-treatment scores as co-variates (Richardson et al., 2007).

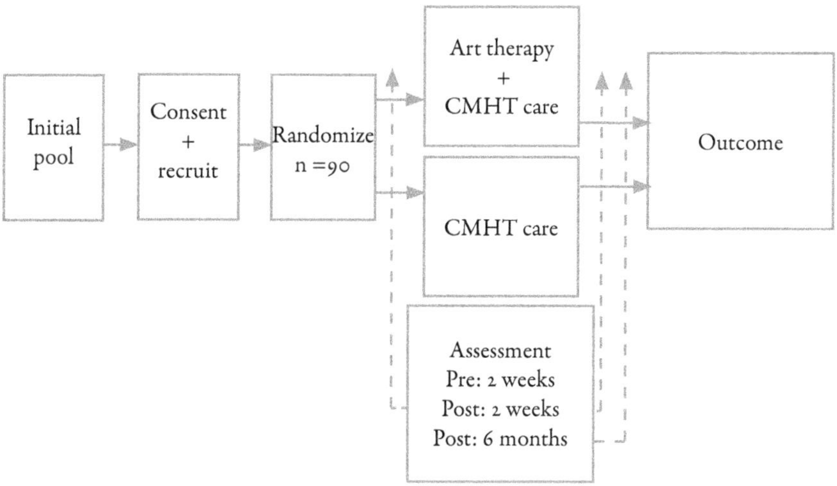

Figure 8.1 Flow Chart of RCT.

The art therapy groups were adapted from the interactive art therapy model described by Waller (1993: 22–34). The main aims of the groups were to facilitate the containment of psychotic anxieties and to provide a space for self-expression and communication. This was to be achieved by focusing on image-making that facilitated interaction between group members and the art therapist, emphasizing the here and now interactions between group members and active management of session boundaries. Particular attention was paid to managing the beginning of sessions, and to addressing the mid-point of therapy and the ending. An art therapist experienced in working with psychosis provided me with clinical supervision for one hour per fortnight.

Richardson et al. designed and piloted two measures that tried to measure aspects of the art therapy process identified as important for the success of the particular art therapy model (Waller, ibid.). Both measures were piloted with clients in an art therapy group with both acute and chronic psychiatric diagnoses. I administered the measures during the RCT at the beginning and at the end of the first, sixth and twelfth session in each group. The completed measures, unseen by me, were put in a sealed envelope and delivered to the principal investigator.

(Hard) Findings

The brief group art therapy was found to have a statistically significant difference on one outcome variable: Schizophrenia and Negative Symptoms (SANS) (Andreason, 1989) which measures clients' negative symptoms. There was little and non-significant impact on other measures.

This research takes a first step towards fulfilling Males' demand for evidence that might convince other professionals of the worth of art therapy (1980). There were however a number of limitations to this research. Funding and recruitment difficulties resulted in the RCT being statistically underpowered and data from the art therapy measures was not used as too few were returned to provide useful information. Further, funding restrictions meant that the therapy was shorter than most art therapists would wish to offer such a client group and it used an art therapy model not usually associated with people with a diagnosis of schizophrenia (see Killick and Schaverien, 1997). Nonetheless symptom reduction after twelve weeks of either group or individual art therapy for members of this client population would not normally be expected.

This is the extent of the 'hard' findings reported within the standard framework of an RCT by Richardson et al. (2007). It was by no means the whole story, as the narrative that follows will show. This draws on case and process notes written at the time. It reflects on the recruitment process and the use of the art therapy outcome measures to explore how the quantitative aspects of the RCT methodology transformed the subjective quality of my experience of transference and counter transference. I use Bion's ideas on containment and the internal object (1990) to conceptualize the RCT as an object in the transference in order to think about its influence on my capacity to provide an art therapy model which focused on the containment of psychotic anxieties. A case example suggests how transference and counter transference to the research process interrelated with the social context during the supervision session of an art therapy group.

(Soft) Findings: from Quantity into Quality

Recruitment merits one sentence in Richardson et al's standard report (op. cit.) although recruitment is a key factor in the success of any RCT (Roth and Fonagy: 1996). Richardson et al reported that four hundred and fifty two service users were identified as potential participants. From this initial pool we identified two hundred and ninety nine clients who could take part. We made between three hundred and fifty and four hundred home visits. Ninety service users were actually recruited.

Recruitment and Randomization

On the first visit the research assistant and I could not get through the entrance doors to the flats where the client lived. A woman shouted down instructions from a first floor window and a small boy let us into a dark kitchen and, to our dismay, locked the door behind. We squeezed through a narrow space between decrepit and filthy worktops, cluttered with unwashed dishes and the torn remains of food packages. As we climbed the stairs a darkened room suddenly opened to the right. A young girl sat in the dark, perched on the end of a bed with her face pressed up close to a screamingly bright television screen with the volume set very high. Disorientated, we were led into the sitting room which was piled with boxes and a rolled-up carpet at one end, giving the feel of a room that was transitory rather than lived in.

Introducing ourselves to the woman who had shouted from the window, we began to explain the research project. An elderly woman now appeared and gradually we realized that she was in fact the client we were looking for and that we had been interviewing her daughter. A bitter argument broke out between mother and daughter. The daughter angrily complained that that she also had problems but it was her mother who always received help. Clearly this argument had taken place many times before. The mother agreed to take part in the research and I took out the laptop to complete the randomization. I put the computer on the table, which suddenly collapsed. Catching the computer just in time, I proceeded to randomize, with the daughter looking over my shoulder, rapidly writing down all the randomization questions.

The sheer quantity of people to be seen and the amount of interviews to complete often felt like a huge dead weight that refused to shift. The research at times was an endless slog of driving round the borough, trying to find entrances to flats, knocking on doors, getting lost in huge housing estates and endlessly repeating to different people the same words of introduction to the project. Disheartened when there was poor take-up we became obsessed with recruitment. Each time we approached the front door of a potential participant we felt the increasing pressure of the same burden: would we recruit, and would the research be a success?

The process came to a head one morning at the Elephant and Castle in the north of the borough. It was cold, with a bleached, white light suffusing an overcast sky. The flats of yet another estate towered above us with huge, white, rectangular slabs that stretched into the distance. There were few people around, increasing the sense of smallness and isolation we felt in the vastness of the estate. We were lost and had been walking back and forth under an overhang which ran the entire length of a tower block and emphasized the huge weight of the flats looming above. A narrow opening led into a gloomy passage, the walls lined with hard brown tiles running with damp. The stink of urine cut through musty odours of rotting litter. At the end of the corridor a dim, yellowish light barely illuminated a dingy room filled with rubbish and old furniture. Sound was muffled, cutting us off from the outside world. We were at the Elephant all right, only we had disappeared up the elephant's arse. Standing in that dank, oppressive space I felt captured inside a huge white elephant, absorbed into the vastness of the research project. We turned, left the gloom and returned into the momentarily blinding light, eventually finding the right door to enter the flats.

The long journey to the top floor led to a windswept balcony with a view across the estate to the loft apartments of expensive riverside developments. The flat was one of many in a long, cold corridor and we stood in the doorway, talking with a desperate and distressed father who explained that his son was not at home because he had just made another of many attempts at suicide. We listened and agreed to inform the community team of his concerns. There were several more clients to find and we needed to recruit. As we left the estate a large, bright yellow sign appealing for witnesses to a murder emphasized a sense of waste, danger and death.

Another day and we had just left a client lying in bed in a darkened room while his mother cried and pleaded with us to get help from the community team. At the next house nobody answered and as we stood at the door two people approached us suspiciously. They were social workers and wanted to know why we were waiting outside their client's house. Identity cards were exchanged, we explained our business and they disappeared inside.

Suddenly the door opened and the sight of an elderly woman astonished us. She had a shock of white hair and her face was entirely ringed in a long, thick, white beard whose splendid aura was emphasized by her bright blue jumper. Despite ourselves we looked her up and down, marvelling. Completely laddered, her flesh colored tights imperceptibly blended with the bruised and mottled colour of her skin with the stocking feet torn and rent by her gnarled toenails. Inside, her flat had bare floorboards covered in thick rolls of dust, an unintentional parody of the minimalist loft apartments we had seen days earlier from the top floors of the Elephant and Castle flats. In the front room the curtains were drawn and the light was grey. Instead of a carpet cigarette ash, dust and a jumble of litter covered the floor. A small light brown teddy bear sat in a red and white-stripped plastic bag, propped on a chair facing another chair, as if a conversation had recently ended. The woman was very friendly and as we clicked into our routine explanations all we really wanted to do was ask about that beard but as good professionals, we didn't. She seemed very interested in what we had to say and I wondered how she would fit into a group. I felt a guilty sense of relief when she declined to take part in the research.

A short walk took us two roads away into a very busy, very noisy shopping street. The research assistant talked about being unable to switch off when she got home. Her previous experience in mental health was in a very white, middle class, suburban setting and although she had worked with a similar client group she had been able to leave work behind at the end of the day.

The Administration of Measures

The second quantitative aspect of the RCT methodology which shaped my experience of transference and counter transference was the administration of the art therapy measures. I was disappointed that many of the art therapy measures were not completed and wondered what might be represented by this acting out. Those people who did complete the art therapy measures did so without comment. It was rare to have a direct discussion about their experience of completing the forms. One person said she found the forms hard work and hated filling them in as they reminded her of job application forms. In a different group, another person said with real feeling and interest that he wished he could be there when 'the psychiatrist' analysed the pictures. In a longer-term therapy with this group of client, or with other kinds of client, exploration of these dynamics might be more possible. Gilroy (1995), for example, describes how the questionnaires in her research about experiential art therapy groups with postgraduate trainees became a hook for projection of anger and a defense against the transference. She describes how it took her some time to feel confident enough to be able to work openly in the groups with the art therapy students about both their, and her, feelings about the research.

The measures completed by the research assistants and those that I introduced into the art therapy sessions became objects into which I would project anxieties, hopes and fears. My relation with this 'research object' affected the quality of my transference and countertransference within the art therapy groups. Given the close relationship between EBP, research and political agendas connected to the control of public expenditure, the administration of these measures felt like the naked presence of the government in the groups. I often felt like a tiny finger on a hand at the end of an arm of a fantastic body politic that stretched all the way up to the state. Giving out the measure, I was the direct reflex of government policies, introducing material into the session that would not normally have been there. The hand would then take the information out of the session to be analyzed to make a judgment about art therapy, using a scientific methodology and a political agenda under whose dispassionate gaze I felt exposed and alienated. The traumatic memory of redundancy haunted my knowledge of how the state would implement its decisions. Handing out the measures punctuated and structured the twelve weeks of the art therapy groups, the presence of the state providing a heavy, rhythmic counterpoint to the sharp alternation of paranoid and depressive anxieties I experienced during the sessions.

Recruitment and Ethnicity

Richardson et al. reported that 47 per cent of clients in this RCT recorded their ethnicity as Afro-Caribbean, African and Black British. As previously described, I had worked as an art therapist in the same geographical areas and community teams as those from which the RCT recruited. The figure for black and ethnic minority clients on my caseload prior to the RCT had been about 20 per cent. Although these figures are anecdotal, the RCT recruited approximately 27 per cent more black and ethnic minority clients to the art therapy service than was the case for routine clinical practice. Disappearing up the elephant's arse had, after all, been worth it.

Case Example

This example is taken from the fifth of eight groups that I ran as part of the RCT. The core group consisted of two women: Mary, black British of Afro-Caribbean origin and Alice, black British, of African origin. There were three men: two black British, Dave and John (who was unable to attend the group under discussion), both of Afro-Caribbean origin, and Jim, white British. Their age range was between thirty and mid-forties. One white British woman and one woman of Philippine origin had been randomized to the group but never attended. I am a white, British male.

Each group began with the clients deciding what they would like to do. If a client seemed particularly anxious or stuck I would acknowledge this; if they remained stuck I would acknowledge this again and remind them that they could paint or draw anything that came to mind. If this continued I would suggest that they could focus on something that had happened to them recently which they thought was important. At approximately ten minutes towards the end of the group I would suggest that people show each other their work and say something about it, if they wanted to.

The supervision session after the first group focused on a painting by Jim. The image was of a yacht on water with white clouds, birds and sun in the sky. It had provoked no particular associations for him. I found him quite likeable and was struck by the sense of peacefulness he described in his image. A silence descended and I began to feel a sense of depression connected to the pressures of the research, linked to my desire for its success. I began to feel guilty about the process of randomization. This group was taking place in an area of South London that was notorious for the presence of political parties such as the British National Party and the National Front. I suddenly thought: what are we doing randomly allocating black people into groups in an area which is highly likely to contain white racists?

I thought about Jim. He was a tall, shaven-haired, white man who in my mind now became a potential fascist skinhead. I joked about this with the supervisor and wondered if I was projecting something of my own internal fascism and racism. Far from the peacefulness Jim had evoked in relation to his image, fascism brought up ideas of authoritarianism and control and the violent abolition and negation of difference through extermination. Authoritarianism and control linked for me with certain aspects of the research process, particularly its relation to political power and the imposition of a particular kind of research in an art therapy context. I returned to the innocuous looking image, feeling ashamed of my unscientific train of thought. I was not looking forward to the next group.

The same people attended the second group. Twenty minutes passed in silence as people concentrated on their images. I then saw that Jim's had used an image of a swastika in his collage (Plate 8.2).

I felt an immediate sense of relief, then amazement and dismay that the image had appeared after my speculations in supervision. I was now faced with the dilemma of how to handle this potentially difficult material in the group.

Jim was the last to show his painting. Alice remarked that Jim's picture was 'nice'. I asked Jim if he could say a little more about why he had chosen those photographs for his picture. Jim replied that he had chosen the women because they were pretty and added rhetorically that 'Women are like cats, aren't they?' Mary immediately snorted and shouted 'Cheek!' Alice asked if the woman was naked. Jim said 'Yes' and Alice replied: 'I like your picture very much.' Jim went to put picture away. I asked about other images on his picture. Jim said 'Cake, beaches, nice places' and again went to put picture away. I felt a strong urge to just let Jim put the picture away so that we did not have to discuss the swastika. 'And the swastika?' I asked. 'I thought it looked good' Jim replied, again starting to put the image down. Persisting, I asked, 'In what way?' 'Like a parent and a child under the banner, know what I mean?' answered Jim, still holding the image up. 'I'm not sure, what do you mean?' 'I could have used a Union Jack', smiled Jim, and again he went to put the image down. I asked the group what they thought of the swastika. Mary very quickly said: 'It's the Germans'. Everybody laughed. 'Nobody likes the Germans', smiled Jim. It was time to stop the group.

Jim's image seemed to resonate with tensions in the group around ethnicity, gender and sexuality. I was surprised by Alice's positive reactions to the image and wondered if she felt she needed to placate a possible threat. Mary gave a confident and strong response to Jim's link between women and cats. Dave had remained silent. I had felt a temptation to manage their, and my, anxiety and contain potential group conflict by ignoring the swastika. This was linked to my desire to see the research succeed, which conflicted with my desire to remain as a therapist and stay with the group process.

When Jim talked about 'a parent and child under the banner' and asked if I knew what he meant, I felt he was potentially making identification between the two white males in the group. I was mindful of the uncomfortable feelings that I had projected onto Jim in supervision and aware that the meaning of our both being white might have resonance for the group. I decided not to focus on the identification at this moment as the important issue seemed to be the swastika.

In the supervision session following the group, the supervisor remarked on the star shape in the swastika painting and its resemblance to the Star of David and the sun in the first image. He associated the medical models of babies in the womb to experiments in Nazi camps. Preoccupied with the group process, I had overlooked these aspects of the image which amplified the themes of the session.

Discussion

Pringle described the sea-change in social and political relations which lead to the adoption of a new agenda of EBP in the NHS (1996). This change forced the questions raised by Holtom in 1977 to the top of the art therapy research agenda. These changes in turn led to my engagement with the RCT, a research methodology based on theoretical assumptions and practices very different to those of mainstream art therapy.

Despite these differences, this RCT provided tentative support for short-term, group interactive art therapy but the limitations of the RCT make it difficult to generalize the results to routine clinical practice. In this respect it meets Males' criteria for art therapy evidence based upon the 'hard stuff' of empirical investigation and for defensive practice that might communicate the effectiveness of art therapy to other professionals.

In relation to the 'soft stuff', like Freud in *Studies in Hysteria*, the temptation is to apologize that '... much of what I have written bears the stamp of a short story rather than serious science'. (Freud and Breuer, 1991: 231). Grubrich-Simitis suggested that both Breuer and Freud struggled to find a way of reporting adequate to their new way of listening and that this led both to describe their therapy in minute verbal description and to evoke scenes 'in the manner of a painter' (1997: 35). Interestingly, when presenting the RCT in lectures or seminars several people have remarked that in my attempt to describe the new experience of working with the RCT, I also describe scenes like a painter. Similarly in the case and recruitment vignettes here, I attempt to bring the objective and the subjective aspects of art therapy research together as described by Edwards and, through attention to group process and imagery, address Gilroy's critique (1996) of the RCT's by Borchers (1985) and Green et al. (1987). However, the examples I give are highly selective and no attempt is made to systematically compare and explore the interactions in the different art therapy groups and the imagery created in each group context. To misquote Freud, however: 'I must console myself with the reflection that the nature of this particular RCT is evidently responsible for this, rather than any preference of my own' (Freud and Breuer, 1991: 231).

The hard, 'objective' statistical analysis of the data was carried out by the principal researcher and the psychiatrist/group analyst. The 'hard' and 'soft' signify hierarchies of professional and political power that frame the RCT, privileging the legitimacy and ownership of particular kinds of scientific knowledge. The metaphor evokes the unconscious sexual fantasy integral to all social relations and which have effects in terms of access to funding, legitimacy, status and power within the NHS. However, taking part in the RCT was collaborative rather than alienating and I feel a tremendous debt for what my colleagues taught me and for their friendliness, humour and for the quality of their thinking. Alliances with sympathetic professionals with research skills are essential for art therapists who have no experience of working with quantitative methodologies. However, while goodwill and collaboration with other professionals can be essential and empowering, political and social power mark an inevitable alienation in these relationships.

Hierarchies of power structured client participation in the research. Clients were able to make an informed choice about participation in the research but we, working within the context of government policy, determined choices about research methodology. There was no formal collaboration with client user groups in the research design and limited feedback to clients at the end of the research.

One unexpected, if anecdotal 'soft' finding was that although this RCT was not designed to investigate ethnicity it suggested that this RCT improved access to art therapy for service users from black and ethnic minorities. This suggests that the open invitation sent to all clients eligible for participation in the RCT and followed by home visits was more accessible than the assessment procedures in the art therapy department and CMHTs. A similarly 'assertive art therapy outreach' policy toward service users might increase the ethnic diversity of clients participating in the routine clinical practice of art therapy services.

Recruitment was a journey through a multitude of diverse and often deprived social spaces, a sometimes mind-numbing repetition punctuated by fantastic encounters with psychosis and mistaken identity, the inside of an elephant, suicide and a bearded lady. Images of an ambiguous female body, waste, engulfment, murder and death still linger as unprocessed afterimages from the dark heart of the RCT, where the encounter with psychotic excess threatened to lay bare a symbolic wasteland embodying the end of hope.

Containing psychotic anxieties in routine clinical practice is difficult and in this RCT the sheer volume of groups being seen, and the quantity of projections to which I was exposed, amplified the difficulties. My key anxiety related to the success or failure of the research and the remorseless momentum, the elephantine weight and the dispassionate gaze of the RCT often threatened to crush the reparative hopes which made research and therapy possible. Thinking about the RCT as an object into which I projected anxieties, hopes and fears was essential in helping to contain and work with depressive and persecutory anxieties in the art therapy groups and in maintaining a positive attitude to its final outcome.

This RCT led to an encounter with unconscious psychotic processes and highlighted the social world of people living with a diagnosis of schizophrenia and the realities of deprivation, health and dis-ease in a manner quite unlike routine art therapy clinical practice. This was perfectly illustrated in the case example where the image of the swastika provided a dense condensation of images related to personal history, family identifications, class, ethnicity and gender. The image resonated deeply with the group dynamics and swept beyond the confines of the room, linking personal and local history to conflict and trauma on a world historical scale. Understanding the interrelationships between unconscious process and social context was a key factor in providing an art therapy model for the containment of psychotic anxieties and contributed to the positive outcomes in the research.

From Research into Practice

Over coffee during one of the routine research meetings, the principal investigator described the research as a 'bog standard' RCT. At the time he had not seen the image in Figure 8.3, drawn by a participant in the very first of the art therapy groups. Bringing the 'hard' and the 'soft' together would need an RCT that is more than bog standard.

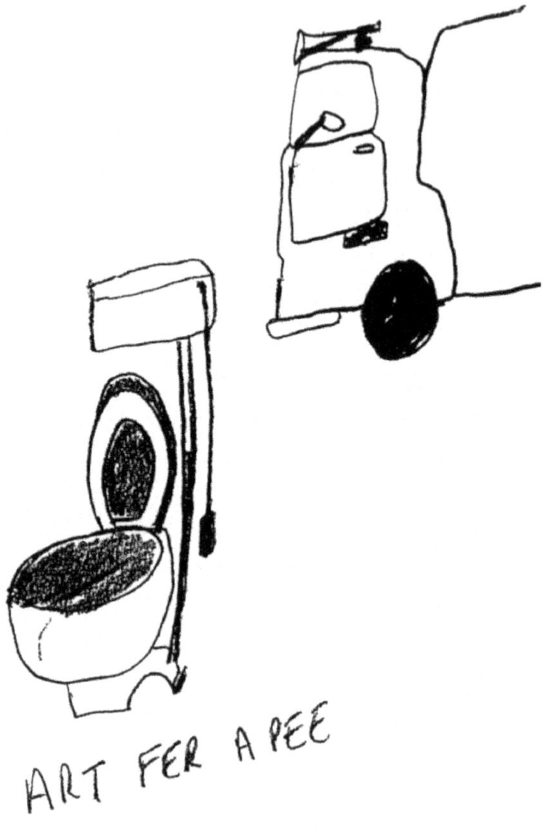

Figure 8.3 Art fer a Pee.

The disjunction between 'hard' and 'soft' suggests the space in which a future RCT of art therapy might need to work and include as part of its design: a longer period of art therapy; the measurement of relapse rates (i.e. containment) after art therapy had ended as well as symptom change; the inclusion of a cost-benefit analysis using health economic and service utilization measures; multi-site trials to improve recruitment; collaboration with other professionals; active user participation in developing the research design and more structured user feedback; and finally qualitative exploration of the art therapy process, the image and social context.

Eleven years after the redundancy and nine years after the research was completed, the results of this RCT were one of the two RCT's of art therapy with people diagnosed as schizophrenic cited by the National Institute of Health and Clinical Excellence (NICE, 2009) in its recent guideline of the treatment of these clients. The anecdotal evidence for increased participation by black and ethnic minorities in this RCT also supports the conclusions reached by Hussain-Gamble et al. in their paper for NICE, 'Involving South Asian Patients in Clinical Trials' (2004). They suggest that organizations undertaking clinical trials for this client group should be organized to a level of 'cultural competence' that reflects the diverse cultural backgrounds of their clients, including staff development in this area.

I presented results from this RCT at the Theoretical Advances in Art Therapy (TAAT) conference (2002) and at a number of others, including the Royal College of Psychiatrists 'Mind Odyssey' (2001) and the American Association of Art Therapists' Conference (2008). Echoing Holtom (1977) and Edwards (1987, 1999), at the TAAT conference I argued that the political context demanded that art therapists challenge the NHS research agenda in two ways: first, through the British Association of Art Therapists and trade unions, which they have successfully done and continue to do; second, by undertaking research based in other research paradigms, as others have also suggested (e.g. Edwards, 1999; Gilroy, 2006; Wood, 1999). Art therapists should be clear that this RCT, like others, is significant because of its link to public funding within a particular social context. The methodological, financial and logistical difficulties imposed definite limits to the expropriation and contestation of the RCT by art therapy. This remains the case when an RCT occurs in the context of a narrow, empirical interpretation of EBP that is legitimated by political power and especially when it is backed by continuing threats of cuts and redundancies.

This chapter is dedicated to the memory of Phil Richardson, who sadly died on 4 December 2007.

CHRIS WOOD

9 The Evolution of Art Therapy in Relation to Psychosis and Poverty

Abstract

In this chapter historical research is discussed as a method for investigating the development of art therapy in relation to psychosis and poverty. The links between general approaches to psychosis and those used during periods in the history of art therapy are considered. The research points to the ways theories and research about improvements in mental health are influenced by the circumstances of the historical period.

Key Words

historical method; psychosis; poverty; art therapy; effectiveness.

How it all Began: From Practice to Research

Throughout many years I have continued to work with people who have a history of psychosis. I feel privileged to continue with clinical practice whilst also working with students. When I registered my research, I wanted to develop my practice and understanding. I was and I continue to be motivated by the desire to respond well to those forms of experience shared with me by clients who are either in the midst of psychotic episode or those who are trying to live in the aftermath of a breakdown.

Context of the Research

The original research took place between 1994 and 2000 and aspects of it have been developed in the following decade. In 1994, during a period of right wing politics, people everywhere were still watching the impact of the special relationship between Thatcher and Reagan on the world stage. Then, during the following period in Britain, the New Labour government continued much of what had gone before with an increasingly regulated culture in health, education, and public life, and deregulation in some parts of employment law (Bunting, 2004). Stringent accountability has existed alongside removal of some safeguards. This has had an impact on both research and practice. Although the political ideology of the historical period may not seem relevant to an understanding of the details of psychotic terror, it has influenced the shape of therapy and its study. The research reviews literature that examines the internal psychological experience of psychosis and that which situates mental health practice in relation to what is going on in society – for example in politics, culture and television. It also examines art therapy practice in the light of themes within the literature, including a caseload census.

Method

Kuhn's *History of Scientific Revolutions* (1962) is a landmark text which shows the use of a historical method and a dialectical approach to identify paradigms. This fitted my research because it parallels the ways art therapists work with clients, moving attention backwards and forwards to consider the client's history, living circumstances and current experience from different vantage points. Kuhn's work made me look for paradigms in the history of art therapy. This meant tracing the history to find discontinuities and sharp changes in direction that showed how new forms of practice have developed.

Initially I researched the general history of psychosis and its treatment, I then used the themes identified to research the history of art therapy. I read widely about the history of madness (considering primary and secondary material in the field). I was looking for relationships between the history and the contemporary that would help me understand current and developing forms of practice. After reviewing this literature, I focussed upon works that offered explanations of how the circumstances of a period influence the forms of treatment that emerge. I found different but powerful explanations of historical forces influencing treatment, in works like that of Doerner (1969) and Warner (1985).

Then, using different vantage points (the backwards and forwards dialectical method), I explored the history of art therapy in Britain with people experiencing psychosis. Primary source material drew on conversations, some contemporary and some remembered. These included clients of the pioneer art therapist, Edward Adamson, who had worked in the twenty years following the Second World War, and art therapists who were working during the 1960s and 1970s, for example, Patsy Nowell-Hall, Michael Edwards, John Henzell and Peter Byrne. I also drew on my own primary experience of practice documented in publications, notes and artworks during seventeen years at that point.

Since the Second World War documentary evidence providing secondary source material about the discipline has greatly increased. I was therefore also able to draw on books, professional journals, newsletters, conference papers, films, client artwork and many unpublished case studies in my search for relationships between the past and the present.

A dialectical framing of the history of the profession helped me understand how instances from my therapeutic practice had arisen from their societal context (Wood, 1997a). In science (Kuhn, 1962), sociology (Weber, 1904) and aesthetic criticism (Eagleton, 1990) historical methods with a dialectical pattern have been used in ways that are relevant to art therapy. Such studies go to the heart of interconnections between personal experience and political life and they point to many ways in which culture and the media affect lives. This became part of my research.

I identified a number of historical themes which I then used repeatedly to interrogate what I had found in relation to contemporary practice and to examples from my own practice. I was helped in this by the rigorous questioning of two academic and one clinical supervisor.

Historical Themes in the Treatment of Madness

During the last four centuries the social realities of *poverty*, the philosophy of *mind-body dualism* and *moral treatment* have influenced the treatment of madness. These three, interwoven themes are part of a history of mental health care that clearly predate the emergence of art therapy. They are nevertheless, relevant to the way the discipline emerged and the scepticism with which it has sometimes been received (Wood, 2000).

Throughout the seventeenth, eighteenth and nineteenth centuries madness was associated with poverty and disgrace. Many in the seventeenth century equated madness with bestiality; this meant that those who went mad were thought to be beyond the reach of reason and insensitive to hard physical circumstances. The 'accommodation' for the majority in the old asylums was therefore cold and dirty and often worse than sheds for farm animals (Porter, 1987). Gradually, during the late eighteenth and the nineteenth centuries, reforms in the treatment of madness developed; fundamentally these grew out of the French Revolution and the Industrial Revolution (Doerner, 1969; Foucault, 1967). Although after these upheavals the philosophical proposition of a split between mind and body continued to be influential, the physical care of the 'insane paupers' improved and moral treatment philosophies meant that their minds were newly thought to be subject to reason (Pinel, 1801; Tuke, 1813).

Pinel's removal of the chains from people incarcerated in Parisian Asylums is associated with the optimism born of the French Revolution. Pinel's *Traitement Morale* (1801) is often mistranslated as implying a moralistic approach, when in fact he proposed a system of treatment based on the emotions and on genuine concern for those who were ill. His revolutionary ideas were powerfully influential at the time for the Quaker family named Tuke in England. They elaborated a moral treatment approach based on respect for the person deemed 'insane' at the 'Retreat' near York. My understanding of the work of Pinel, the Tuke family and of moral treatment philosophy is that it was pivotal and positive in the history of mental health (Wood, 2000): this is different to the account offered by Hogan (2001).

Social psychiatry, an international psychiatric movement that developed from optimism following the Second World War, had much in common with the earlier, moral treatment approach. This was based on the idea that taking account of the context of a client's life reduces the danger of pathologising the individual. Both moral treatment philosophy and social psychiatry were demonstrably effective for the treatment of people with serious mental disorders. This can be seen in Ray's (1879) discussion of the successful levels of discharge from nineteenth-century institutions that adopted the moral treatment approach in America and Britain (cited in Warner, 1985; 125). They are also seen in Warner's meta-analysis of the international indications of the benefits of social psychiatry (109–27). Nevertheless, both treatment philosophies were subject to changing economic forces and suffered an increasingly sceptical response, both going into decline fifty to sixty years after their inception.

The Influence of Poverty and Class on Treatment Philosophies

A variety of factors can influence the political will about whether or not to support work with those people deemed to be mad. Fluctuations in the circumstances of a historical period influence which treatment philosophies survive.

The 1834 Poor Law sent people too poor to support themselves to the workhouse. It was out of these much-feared institutions that the first Victorian mental hospitals were created at the height of the Industrial Revolution. The Poor Law in Britain reiterated legislation passed centuries earlier in its provision for the 'deserving' and the 'undeserving poor'. It is my contention

(Wood, 2000) that this distinction passed generally into provisions for the mentally ill. This is because there are examples of subsequent legislation and practice which seem to be predicated on some of the mentally ill being 'undeserving'. Throughout the history of psychiatry in the twentieth century there were times when moralistic judgements about psychiatric patients continued from previous centuries. This happened even though the treatment of madness came to be seen as a branch of medicine.

The material poverty behind many general health problems and much psychosis has sometimes been hidden by the success of medical techniques. One example is the way the conquest of the disease Rickets was popularly attributed to the introduction of vitamin D alone, without initially understanding the need to remove Industrial Revolution smog in order that the children of factory workers would have enough sunlight (see National Academy of Science, 2000). Another example is seen in the 'open door' policy in psychiatry. This is popularly attributed to the introduction of major-tranquilisers alone without acknowledgement of the preceding improvement in treatments for the majority of psychiatric patients, not only for those who could pay. This meant that hospital doors did not always need to be locked and indeed had started being unlocked before the advent of tranquilisers in the 1950s (Warner, 1985).

Two issues that were, and are still, regularly overlooked are, first, that if the poverty of a person's living circumstances can be improved there is a strong chance that their mental and physical health will improve too. This certainly seemed to be the response of people given improved life circumstances by nineteenth century moral treatment and twentieth century social psychiatry. Second, there is an increased likelihood of people receiving a more serious psychiatric diagnosis when they are materially disadvantaged (Brown and Harris, 1978; Harrison et al., 1988). This, and the anti-psychiatry concern with diagnostic labelling, is now much less dominant in multidisciplinary discussion, although increasingly it is spoken about in user movements (e.g. in the Voices movement and within MIND).

Numerous research studies point to a correlation between all forms of ill health and poverty (e.g., WHO, 1985; Commission for Social Justice, 1994). How poverty is significant to mental health is not easy to articulate, yet international evidence has repeatedly shown that the incidence of psychosis increases in relation to poverty. This is seen in World Health Organisation studies with evidence from many countries. Warner's research (1985) showed how a range of social and economic factors influence the course and appearance of schizophrenia. This included a meta-analysis of sixty-eight follow-up studies of recovery from schizophrenia, conducted in Europe and North America since the beginning of the 1900s until the 1980s (61–72). A clear example of the influence of poverty and the stresses of lower class life was the finding that recovery rates were significantly lower during the Great Depression of the 1920s and 1930s in America, Europe and Scandinavia (73, 77, 79; see Table 9.1).

Admission period	Complete recovery	Social recovery	US Unemployment	UK Unemployment
1901–20	20 %	41 %	4.7 %	3.5 %
1921–40	12 %	29 %	11.9 %	14.0 %
1941–55	23 %	44 %	4.1 %	1.5 %
1956–85	22 %	45 %	5.4 %	2.7 %

Table 9.1 Correlation of Recovery Rates from Schizophrenia with Average Unemployment Rates in the USA and UK during Four Periods of the Twentieth Century (adapted from Warner, 1985: 72).

These examples of the impact of poverty and repeated failures to find solutions suggest that the political will to support and sustain effective treatments and improvements in health have been negatively influenced by those forms of class prejudice which place less value on the lives of the majority.

Central to an experience of psychosis there is often (but not always) a terrifying sense of being psychologically out of control (Wood, 1997b). Poverty also places serious material limits on personal control (Wood, 1999b). Consequently therapeutic relationships with people with serious mental disorders can be complicated by the client's actual poverty and deprivation, as well as by their fear of repeated breakdown (Wood, 2000). Other complications can arise as a result of limited resources available to the psychiatric services.

Historical Periods of an Art Therapy Response to Psychosis

Having discovered many examples in my research of how historical and economic circumstances influence changes in general treatment philosophy, I looked for examples of where this can be seen in the history of art therapy (Wood, 1997a, 1999a, 1999b, 2000).

Between the late 1930s and the end of the 1950s, the first ideas about using art as a therapy in hospital settings began to emerge, although these were not recorded until later (Lydiatt, 1972; Adamson, 1984; Waller, 1991). The relief at the ending of the Second World War and the excitement of art movements like Surrealism, contributed to this first period of art therapy being one concerned with the *healing power of expression.*

The second period, between the early 1960s and the late 1970s, saw the creation of the British Association of Art Therapists. During this time many art therapists allied themselves to the anti-psychiatry movement, influenced by R.D. Laing (1959). Interestingly this was a movement greatly supported by *social psychiatry* teams (Elliot, 1978). Therapists working in such teams were encouraged to understand the links between the social and the emotional worlds of their clients. A sense of legitimacy for making appropriate links between inner psychological experience and the outer world was therefore a part of this period and taken much more for granted. Art therapy did well and grew during these times (Waller, 1991). Sadly, the economic upheavals associated with the OPEC crisis of 1973–4 led to the gradual demise of social psychiatry in mainstream British psychiatry. This meant that the hospital closure programme and moves by psychiatry into community provision (starting in the early 1980s) were governed by economic strictures and did not achieve their progressive aims (Barham, 1992).

Towards the end of the twentieth century in Britain, and in the wake of the economic decline of the late 1970s and the 1980s, there was a shift towards greater psychotherapeutic clarity in a third period of art therapy. This shift in approach included work with people with serious mental disorders. Yet even as *psychotherapeutic understanding* was being developed, in practice art therapists continued to use aspects of late 1700s and early

1800s moral treatment as well as mid-1900s social psychiatry, both of which hold respect for the client to be fundamental. This can be seen in such texts as *Art Therapy in Practice* (Liebmann, 1990) and *Art Therapy Race and Culture* (Campbell et al., 1999) where many of the edited chapters adopt humanistic, client-centred or social psychiatry approaches.

This third period of art therapy history had its beginnings in the early 1980s and continued throughout the 1990s, a time when art therapists lived through many changes in public sector provision. These historical circumstances also influenced practice, for example the organisation of the profession (Waller, 1991) and a more obvious linking of practice to models from analytic psychology (Schaverien, 1991) and group analytic processes (McNeilly, 1984; Waller, 1993; Skaife and Huet, 1998). Also, judging from what happened to art therapists near to where I worked, practitioners were often working in community settings, away from team bases, a situation that seemed to provide the impulse to refine and develop *psychotherapeutic understanding* (e.g. Greenwood and Layton, 1987).

Throughout the 1980s and the 1990s the accounts of art therapy with people with serious mental disorders increased (e.g., Molloy, 1984; Greenwood and Layton, 1987; Liebmann, 1990; Greenwood, 1994, 1997; Killick and Greenwood, 1995; Killick and Schaverien, 1997; Huet, 1997; Wood, 1997a, 1997b; Deco, 1998; Saotome, 1998; Sarra, 1998). A range of psychotherapeutic approaches were being used but analytic concepts predominated; these concepts led to a greater understanding of the experience of psychosis although they were necessarily used with adaptations to the circumstances of the public sector. The continuing commitment of art therapists to using a range of therapeutic models for these clients (Killick and Schaverien, 1997) seems to me to have grown out of its roots in social psychiatry.

Although we are in the midst of a fourth contemporary period (literally halfway through the first twenty years of the twenty first century) it is possible to speculate about the ongoing art therapy response to psychosis. In the context of much NHS work the movement for psychosocial intervention has filled a vacuum created for long-term clients with the loss of prominence of social psychiatry and psychoanalysis in the public sector (Williams, 1999). Psychosocial intervention has been more visible than art therapy because it is has produced some evidence of the effectiveness of its outcome (Williams, 1999; Brooker et al., 1994). It seems now to have merged with the cognitive behavioural therapies and an assertive outreach approach and although it is too early to see what historical impact this merging will have, these services have improved the level of attention given to clients.

Art therapy, when acknowledging its roots in social psychiatry, has much in common with psychosocial interventions. However, art therapy is different because it acknowledges unconscious processes (Wood, 1997b). These processes are not used in cognitive work and yet they can be valuable for clients who, as a result of psychosis, are trying to find ways of managing mental upheavals. It is interesting that NICE cites arts therapy approaches which have 'predominantly emphasised expression, communication, social connection and self-awareness through supportive and interactive experiences, with less emphasis on the use of 'uncovering' psychoanalytic approaches' (NICE, 2009: 201). In my experience an 'uncovering' approach would be unusual. Art therapists would be more likely to try to help clients contain strange or frightening mental processes. The art-making within the therapy can be of particular value in helping clients find the agency with which to compose themselves (Wood, 2000).

Within recent art therapy literature there is a renewed focus on art-making and its materiality; there is also excitement about the impact of the art world and mass media for clients (Aldridge, 1998; Wood, 1997a, 2001; Mahony, 2001; Gilroy; 2008; Springham, 2008). Art therapists are increasingly responsive to clients who make reference to popular culture and contemporary art and such connections (even at a symbolic level) can be empowering to those living at the margins of society.

Mass culture includes myriad references to all aspects of human experience, often referring directly to the different kinds of deprivation that clients face. Of course it can inoculate against thinking and feeling, but it can also provide modelling and ways of resolving the problems of living.

Many themes in contemporary art reflect social change. Others seem to be a part of a therapeutic repertoire: self-disclosure, confession, bodily functions, sex and food, family and death, all figure largely. During the last twenty years many of those artists celebrated and collected in Britain originated more from lower class backgrounds than has previously been the case (e.g. the 'Young British Artists,' associated with Damien Hirst and Tracey Emin). This does not automatically widen access nor increase the understanding of art, but it has provoked a different kind of interest.

In this fourth, contemporary period of art therapy it seems there is another strange marriage or 'uneasy relationship' (Champernowne, 1971: 1), this time between *evidence and adaptation*, and *popular culture and the materiality of art.*

Quantitative Findings

Despite the fact that since the Second World War art therapists in Britain have been working with people who experience psychotic episodes, for much of the late twentieth century practitioners encountered scepticism about offering psychotherapy to people with serious mental disorders. For example, a comment in Parry and Richardson's *NHS Psychotherapy Services in England: Review of Strategic Policy in England* (1996) reads as follows: 'Art therapists work with some patients other psychotherapists would not consider taking on' (107). This could imply something about the folly of art therapists in making psychotherapeutic relationships with seriously mentally disordered clients. Similarly, the limited amount of outcome research for art therapy with people who have serious mental disorders led Roth and Fonagy (1996) to make no mention of the work of art therapists. In part this was because much of the profession's energy during the latter part of the twentieth century went into developing its psychotherapeutic credentials in both group and individual work. Consequently practitioners did not focus on outcome research and, until relatively recently, there has a preference amongst art therapists in Britain for qualitative research (Gilroy and Lee, 1995; Edwards, 1996; Gilroy, 2006). However, there are outcome studies in the field of general psychotherapy which, I have argued, could supplement art therapy evidence (Wood, 1999a). A small number of practitioners with psychotherapy credentials have continued working in the public sector with people who experience serious internal attacks on their capacity to think. Examples are seen in work at the Tavistock Clinic; in the work of a range of professions aligned with the newly named Bowlby Centre; and in that of disciplines (including cognitive psychotherapists) linked in the UK to the International Society for the Psychological Treatment of Schizophrenia. Although such work in the UK is not widespread it has international links. My view is that this theory, practice and research can supplement the work of art therapists with public sector clients who experience psychosis.

Nevertheless, during the 1990s scepticism was often levied generally at psychotherapeutic work which was said to be for the 'worried-well', the implication being that psychotherapy was not effective in the field of 'real' mental illness. This impressed me with the need to provide information about the clients art therapists actually worked with and so I did a census of the caseloads of practitioners in my area in the North of England (Wood, 2000).

The census demonstrated the poverty and difficult living circumstances of most art therapy clients. It showed high levels of unemployment, with 82 per cent of art therapy clients being unemployed at a time when the national average for unemployment was at 6 per cent. Also 69 per cent of art therapy clients were disadvantaged in terms of their accommodation (either renting or living in hostel or hospital accommodation), and many were either living alone (32 per cent) or had no main relationship (72 per cent being separated, widowed or divorced). This indicated that in terms of poverty, accommodation and loneliness, art therapy clients (certainly in Sheffield, but also I suspect nationally) experience high levels of deprivation and alienation (Wood, 2000).

The task remains of making art therapy more visible, not only in terms of demonstrating the nature of our client caseloads, but also in terms of outcome research with the seriously mentally disordered. The National Institute of Clinical Health and Excellence (NICE) cites the history of arts therapies in psychiatry (201: Bunt, 1994; Wood, 1997). However, NICE focusses upon the small amount of outcome research in art therapy (Green, 1987; Richardson et al., 2007), and the other arts therapies to recommend their use in its updated Schizophrenia Guidelines (2009). Whilst acknowledging the limited range of evidence from RCTs it nonetheless asserted that: 'Despite this small but emerging evidence base, the Guideline Development Group recognise that at present, arts therapies are the only interventions, both psychological and pharmacological, to demonstrate consistent efficacy in the reduction of negative symptoms' (ibid. 205).

These recommendations make it possible to hope that the knowledge born out of the discipline's historical commitment to these clients will not be lost. Art therapists working in the public sector have been told by managers and hard-pressed finance officers that the favourable recommendations by NICE have given arts therapists a toe-hold in the public sector from which they can continue to work and research. I have heard this reported by senior NHS managers; art therapists at local and national BAAT meetings in England and Scotland; and by placement supervisors during 2009. This is a heavy underlining of the need for more systematic research.

Qualitative Findings and Effective Strategies

The range of experience accumulated by the art therapy profession with this client group since the Second World War means that the most effective strategies for art therapy with people with serious mental disorders are likely to involve adaptations of the different forms of attention developed during three periods of the profession's history and a fourth, developing contemporary period (Wood, 1997a, 1997b, 1999b, 2000, 2010).

For particularly vulnerable clients, often living in very difficult circumstances, their state of mind and their art-making processes seem to benefit from a safe physical location in the form of a studio (Killick 1991, 1993, 2000; Wood, 2001). Giving careful attention to art-making is a strong legacy of the first period which focused on the *healing power of expression.* Some art therapy literature suggests that best practice with these clients includes a supportive psychotherapeutic approach (Greenwood, 1997) that acknowledges the impact of their material circumstances (Wood, 1997a). Both these elements have roots in the *social psychiatry* ethos of the second period but they are also branches of the third period which saw the development of greater *psychotherapeutic understanding*. This involved benign but clear management of the therapeutic frame (Killick and Schaverien, 1997) and an understanding of the attacks on thinking that might be experienced in the midst of a psychotic episode (Killick and Greenwood, 1995). During the late 1980s and throughout the 1990s this approach of combining knowledge from the profession's history was being developed and, to some extent, it reflects the approach seen in the Clinical Guideline produced by Brooker et al. (2007).

In much psychoanalytic thinking the tendency to not consider the external is particularly strong, perhaps in part because recent history has placed its practice mainly outside the public sector and away from many of the most seriously disturbed clients. Nevertheless, unlike other psychological approaches, psychoanalytic theories provide useful ways of thinking about the upheavals of unconscious material with which people in the midst of psychosis are trying to contend.

In a collection of papers edited by Ellwood (1995) authors explore ideas related to the concept of 'symbolic equation' (Segal, 1955). They offer sensitively drawn images of those occasions when their clients have, in the very midst of psychosis, been unable to distinguish between concrete and symbolic aspects of the world. For example, Jackson (1995) describes a person in the midst of an episode who: 'attending for twice-weekly psychotherapy, enters the room, and remarks that when he comes in a bird lands on his head and when he leaves it flies away' (10). As the therapy proceeded it seemed that gradually the meaning of the bird became clear. The bird was no longer mentioned but a 'heavy feeling' took its place. A little later the same patient brought a cartoon of a patient with a cloud over his head; his therapist was unravelling the cloud by a thread and putting the unravelled thread in his pocket as the cloud grew smaller. Jackson suggests that the patient was acknowledging that his work with the therapist brought him relief. This patient came to recognise the symbolic significance of the bird whereas originally it had seemed concrete with a delusional quality.

There are examples of such work within art therapy (Killick and Greenwood, 1995; Wood, 1997b; Killick and Schaverien, 1997). This literature suggests that the first focus of therapeutic work with a client who is experiencing 'attacks on linking' (Bion, 1967) is containment and not interpretation (or uncovering). Killick (1993) describes the evolution of her approach and shows that the journey from concrete to symbolic thinking for someone in the midst of psychosis is often painstakingly slow, suggesting that only when the symbolising function has been restored can therapeutic work focused upon the relationship begin.

This suggests a sharply different understanding of the content of a client's words and art objects to that proposed by R.D. Laing. He invited us to view the content of what was being shared by people in the midst of psychosis as being immediately symbolic. This was the approach taken by most art therapists during the second period of professional history (Elliot, 1978). Post-Laing, and during the third period of art therapy's practice with these clients, the literature has been informed by psychoanalysis. However, although my research has given me a greater understanding of the value of general analytic theory in response to psychosis, it has also led me to the conclusion that its main frame of reference is insufficient. Also although it is extremely helpful to understand how psychosis attacks thinking and symbolising functions, it is important not to generalise from this and assume that once someone has experienced psychosis their thinking will always be disordered and under attack. This could come perilously close to the prejudice of several centuries about the invalidity of 'mad' thought (once mad you are always mad and little credence can be given to what you say). Laingian ideas remain a helpful check against the dangers of pathologising.

Case Vignette

A collage has stayed in my mind as evidence of the importance of paying attention to the impact of a client's life circumstances, even when I may suspect that some aspects of their thinking are under 'attack'. I will call the young client Delia. She had a diagnosis of manic-depressive psychosis and was in the midst of an episode when working on the collage. She excitedly made a collection of things she found all over the hospital and used them as the raw material for her artwork. I would hear her singing loudly as she approached the studio with whatever she had found for her artwork.

While making she was often humorous. It was clear that the image concerned painful feelings but it was difficult to see or hear the source of her pain. The role she seemed to need me to take was to clearly frame the boundaries of the session and to try to help her contain her rapidly oscillating range of feelings. Sometimes I had glimpses of the source of her distress but more often I was aware of what seemed to be her manic defence. When she was particularly lucid she wanted me to speak with her about the art-making process, her thoughts about constructing the collage and what she thought she should do to make it like 'modern' art. At the end of each session the work was rolled up like a carpet. It became big and at times it was spread out all over the floor of the studio. Other hospital staff became aware of its construction during Delia's manic rummaging for materials because she would proffer excited descriptions of the collage to anyone who would listen. They tended to think the work was evidence of her inner mental state. However, one of the doctors began to have a suspicion that there was something more significant in the collage and he decided to visit her family home. What he found there made the connection between the artwork and the realities of her outer world strikingly apparent. Suffice it to say that the realities of her home were grim. Although the collage had been difficult to understand, it was not an example of 'symbolic equation' (Segal, 1955) because it made *direct symbolic* reference to Delia's home life and she was reassured and calmer when this was acknowledged. Her thinking seemed to slip in and out of being under internal attack and acknowledgement of the external seemed to help her. Even when made in the very midst of a psychotic episode, the art made by a client can have powerful references to the material realities of the world in which they have to live. This example taught me that although the regular sessions and the collage-making process enabled me to establish a good therapeutic alliance with Delia, without any information about her home life I would have remained mystified and my relationship with her would have been poorer and possibly less effective. Also I would not have seen how her use of materials and the way her collage covered the floor was showing me something materially about her family home.

Discussion

Treatment philosophies for the 'insane' have been and continue to be shaped by several centuries of historical circumstance, including that of the current recession. This chapter has made a case for using and adapting the frames of reference and research that have developed throughout art therapy's history. I do not think this constitutes a dilution of any of the practices that I have described, rather that it is important to understand the evolution of art therapy theory and practice in relation to its wider context and how practitioners have adapted in response to client need.

Most art therapists do not solely use internal frames of reference, the range of needs and the complexity of clients' lives requiring different perspectives and adaptations to practice, including consideration of the impact of mass culture that is increasingly articulated by clients. Discussion with art therapy practitioners in the NHS where I work, with placement supervisors and with students indicate that art therapy with adults and children is often influenced by the material poverty and deprived living circumstances with which clients contend. It seems likely that the proportion of art therapy clients who are seriously ill and who experience deprivation and alienation will have increased since the census I did in 2000, as social, economic and political conditions change, and access to services becomes more difficult as referral criteria thresholds get higher.

For many clients a period of supportive art therapy has facilitated a reality-based strengthening of the ego and an acknowledgement of the fear associated with psychosis. It was in 1997 that Greenwood first described this approach as 'supportive psychotherapy'. This seems right to me. It is possible to discern how this links with the social psychiatry origins of art therapy with its 'side-by-side', respectful ethos and its acknowledgement of an adaptation of theory and practice according to context (Greenwood and Layton, 1987; Wood, 1997a). This is not simply a matter of nomenclature: 'supportive psychotherapy' is in keeping with evidence about therapeutic effectiveness with people who have serious and complex mental disorders (Roth and Fonagy, 1996: 193–4; Parry and Richardson, 1996: 103). It is also linked to what Papadopoulos (2002) has described as 'therapeutic care'. The therapeutic alliance with these clients is subtly different from those forged in other kinds of therapeutic relationships, the therapeutic frame being used as a way of modelling the containment of disordered thinking and feeling processes and the adaptive measures that might be needed to achieve this. For example, although the transference relationship is understood, it is not always appropriate to acknowledge and work with it directly because it risks raising the client's anxiety in ways that could be counter-productive.

I do not see the three periods in the history of art therapy, or the fourth contemporary period identified in this chapter, as discreet paradigms (Kuhn, 1962). Instead they seem to me to be elements in one evolving paradigm for art therapy theory and practice with people who have complex and enduring mental health needs.

From Research into Practice

Throughout this chapter I have indicated how my research has influenced my clinical practice. A summary of important practice elements that I repeatedly consider as a result of the research follow.

- I aim to keep clear communication with other colleagues involved in the client's care because this often provides me with real-world insights that help me genuinely acknowledge the client's living circumstances.
- A safe room in which to work without interruptions, and with art materials (including a computer and art books) is critical. The place of practice becomes recognised and internalised by the client and helps provide a clear frame and therefore a place in which it is possible to be absorbed in art-making. The books and the computer provide links to culture and media that might inspire art-making and provide a sense of connection.

- People are rarely continuously psychotic and so, although their thinking might be under internal attack, they may move in and out of an ability to think even in one session. I have repeatedly seen how clients can compose themselves (and restore their capacity to think) when they compose an image. Consequently sometimes now (more than before) I am quite directive with suggestions about them beginning to make art.
- The same elements of psychotherapeutic work are present in work with these clients as with others but adaptations for client need may mean that a supportive approach or even one of 'therapeutic care' (Papadopoulos, 2002) is the most appropriate.
- With these clients the individual therapeutic relationship or the group processes make themselves felt over time, even though they may not be immediately apparent. Also, although I am sometimes aware of transference or group issues, I might judge that when clients are in the midst of frightening mental processes it is best to be informed by these issues without necessarily voicing them.
- For clients with 'continuing needs' the length of the work is a vexed question; economic pressures may lead to shorter work, but this needs careful consideration. Some briefer interventions may be helpful as part of a rolling system of care, but there are clearly times when brief work would be a false economy.

There is still a lot of art therapy work and research needed in this area. My view is that continuing to consider how the interwoven elements from the profession's history can be researched and linked to evidence from related fields is eminently worthwhile. It can contribute to efforts to develop and defend this powerful way of working in an area of real need.

JACKY MAHONY

10 Artefacts Related to an Art Psychotherapy Group: The Therapist's Art Practice as Research

Abstract

This chapter describes a visual heuristic research project which documents curating an exhibition in order to examine archival material associated with the art-making of an outpatient art psychotherapy group. A narrative account was constructed as part of the autobiographical process and deep, complex and reciprocal communications were found to be facilitated by the therapist's art-making. The research also shows how craft practices can materialise autobiography and the culture of individuals and of an art psychotherapy group. The political implications of how to convey the research are considered.

Key Words

outpatient art psychotherapy; visual arts practices as research; heuristics; exhibitions; curating; art and craft practices; archives; participative art-making.

How it all Began: From Practice to Research

The source of inspiration for my own art-making is the passion I feel for the substance, texture and detail of raw materials derived from the natural landscape. I trained as a studio potter and my art or 'materials' practice involves ceramics and textiles, an urge to make things for use and a love of slow labour. This experience seemed far removed from the more analytic approach that informed my work in NHS psychiatry. I wanted to find out what role this materials practice might have in my clinical practice.

In this chapter I will describe one of the stages of my PhD that explored the relevance of the therapist's art practice to an art psychotherapy group. I will discuss the literature and describe my investigation into the junction between visual arts, art psychotherapy and studio practice, illustrating how the voice I use as author contributed to the findings. This research, carried out with an NHS outpatient group that I facilitated for people with severe and complex mental health difficulties, aimed to examine a process of art-making – including my own, both in and outside the group – which enabled members to bring about positive change in their lives.

The Context of the Research

There are implications for the genre of writing that we choose when we report on our research. I will therefore begin with a summary of debates on the question of *voice*. My art-based route, which attempts to develop an understanding of the role of art in the art psychotherapy process, was coupled with the idea of the *civil voice*. This was crucial to the development of my thinking, including choosing to have visual displays as part of the research process (Plates 10.1 and 10.2).

The 'Civil Voice'

Pressures on art therapy influence the way we approach the building of our body of knowledge, our research approaches and the way we present our ideas (McLeod, 2001). The setting for my group was the NHS (to which I am indebted for supporting part of my research). Within this institution, like many others, medical and scientific ideologies dominate that have enormous influence upon practitioners and consequently users' health and well-being, from which (as I discovered from my research) I had not escaped.

Having drawn attention to the lack of qualitative outcomes studies in psychotherapy and to the resources allocated to quantitative/experimental outcome studies, McLeod introduces the concept of 'voice' and the way social power hinges on who is heard, listened to and who is silenced (2001: 162). The politics of psychotherapy research are, he contends, reproduced in the language and structure of publications. Referring to the NHS's adoption of 'evidence-based' treatments, he discusses the consequences of the view that randomised controlled trials are 'the only valid… source of evidence for the efficacy of psychological treatment' (Roth and Fonagy, 1996: 19). McLeod's concern is that the effect of constructing knowledge about therapy in this way reinforces the power of elite groups in psychotherapy and denies a voice to those with less institutional power (2001: 164). He describes the growing interest in the 'shaping of written knowledge' explored by Bazerman (1988) who uses the style manual of the American Psychological Association (APA) to show how social science disciplines codify intrinsic values and philosophical assumptions in their writing. The APA style manual, representing the voice of behaviourism, established a style which came to be regarded as the 'only proper way to write science' (Bazerman, 1988: 268), and included the now familiar devices adopted in art psychotherapy: for example, third-person viewpoint, standardised sub-headings, name and date referencing style.

McLeod draws upon Gergen's (1997) work that describes modes of transmission of voice in human science scholarship and includes indications of the communicative limitations and author-reader relationship that are invited through their use of registers, dominant themes and images. Gergen identifies several textual traditions which I will summarise.

The Mystical Tradition relates to early mysticism and uses metaphor, evaluative terminology, linguistic construction of realities and mysteries beyond rationality, the senses and observation. Examples are Freud, Jung, Laing and Lacan. The status difference between writer and audience is like priest and disciple. The reader is ignorant but can receive knowledge, becoming special.

The Prophetic Tradition relates to early Greek culture where prophets were emissaries for the gods. The use of apocalyptic warnings and a sense of doom serves moral ends. Examples are Marx, Lasch, Bellah and Baudrillard. The reader-writer status difference places the reader as unenlightened but not priviledged.

The Mythic Tradition also relates to early religion. Moral stories with clear narrative properties lead to a sense of climax or drama. Freud, Piaget, Weber and Foucault all draw on this tradition. The writing in this and the previous traditions is impersonal and monologic.

The Civil Voice uses literal language, reason, and objective evidence. It conveys modesty, respect for the reader and their capacity for good judgement, avoiding direct antagonism. However, a subtext claims superiority in an implicit hierarchy of truth, prestige and power, positioning the reader as competitor.

Gergen argues that, compared to such voices from the distant past, recent years have seen the emergence of postmodern, rhetorical forms, including the autobiographical voice. Informing major movements in scholarship, they have 'gained impetus from the intense critique lodged against the presumptions of scientific discourse as truth bearing' (1997: 162).

For example, the Autobiographer provides an 'experiential lens through which to understand the world' (1997: 163) giving the reader access to another's world, probably of broad significance and often with an educative aspect. Autobiography is often used to reveal underlying assumptions and suppression of the civil world and borrows from mythic and fictive traditions. The reader is invited to identify and share subjectivity with the writer, subverting the writer-reader distance that typified earlier traditions.

The Fictionalist offers experimental writing with the broadest boundaries that can include almost all forms of writing, blurring or destroying the 'fact/fiction binary' (1997: 165). Differing voices, realities and values can be orchestrated in a multivocal text. A high degree of author-reader intimacy and identification is offered, but also the possibility of ironic distance. The writer's traditional privilege of authority is undermined by these two more recent discursive genres.

McLeod proposes that the APA/RCT tradition is part of the civil voice as characterised by Gergen. While it is true that case studies have been notable as a form of discourse adhered to by art psychotherapist writer-practitioners, influenced by the autobiographical genre, a civil voice textual tradition seems to have developed. In view of Gergen and McLeod's discussion of the implications, such rhetoric seems incongruent and restricting. As McLeod puts it: 'The way we write about therapy is a political act… the "civil voice" or APA/RCT genre of writing operates to exclude many important and interesting aspects of the therapy research process by effectively silencing the voices of almost everyone concerned' (2001: 172). My research explores the creative art process in and out of clinical practice and so the way knowledge is conveyed is an important consideration. I am aware, however, that my 'literature review' uses aspects of the civil voice.

The Art Therapy Literature

Research into art psychotherapy groups with adults who have severe and complex problems and who are living in the community is limited. Some authors have described studio-based approaches in inpatient care (e.g. Killick, 2000) but only Greenwood and Layton (1987, 1991) have described a community-based art therapy group with this client population. Most studio-based approaches are a different genre from my own and do not draw on group analysis in the way that I do.

Similarly, there is little written by art psychotherapists about their art. Particularly rare are accounts of personal art practice (Gilroy, 1989; Rawcliffe, 1987; Rogers, 2002) as distinct from art therapists' use of their art for self-exploration and growth (e.g. Allen, 1995; Lanham, 1998; McNiff, 1992). My art-making, whether in the group described in this chapter or in my studio, is not conceptualised as a form of therapy, even if deep personal insight follows.

Art therapists' art-making linked to clinical practice is either seen as a type of reflective countertransference made outside sessions to inform the therapy (e.g. Case, 1994; Rogers, 2002) or as part of therapeutic practice.

There are conflicting views about art-making in sessions: some think that clients might feel neglected (e.g. Wadeson, 1980) but others think there are therapeutic benefits (e.g. Greenwood and Layton, 1987; Saotome, 1998). Significantly, the practice is seen to hold countertransference feedback and reduce transference (Greenwood and Layton, 1987).

Haeseler (1989) argues that therapists can make art in the sessions in the service of clients. She points out that being with someone doing art allows clients' access to their creative process. She suggests that it also puts clients at ease and that the therapist's relationship to art is made clear and accessible, as is their investment in the group. It is also a way of knowing the therapist more fully, hastening formation of the therapeutic alliance whilst maintaining a distance (1989: 70).

There is a lack of discussion of both ceramics (as opposed to working with clay) and textiles in the art therapy literature apart from a few exceptions; these include Henley's (2002) notable exploration of the therapeutic application of claywork.

Maybe this is because the concept of 'crafts' has, in the past, been held in low esteem. For instance, many craft areas appeared to vanish from some art school curricula when the new Diploma in Art and Design was introduced in the early 1960s. (Harrod, 1999: 238). However, Harrod's view is that the crafts embody or reify theory, commenting critically and profoundly on ideas and events in visual rather than verbal form (1999: 464).

Method

I used my art practice as a visual heuristic methodology. Heuristic research emphasises intense interest leading to immersion in the topic. There follows an incubation process outside of the researcher's immediate awareness that arrives at illumination which provides new dimensions to the research. Explication then takes place with a full examination of what has happened; this culminates, when there is familiarity with all the data, in a creative synthesis (Moustakas, 1990: 27). Layers of meaning and depth are created in a wide and deep investigation which uses personal documents including artwork, narrative descriptions, journals and poems to depict the experience (ibid. 39). Exhibition practices, such as those I describe here, are visual arts practices that can be used as methods to generate and analyse data (Sullivan, 2005: 211). 'Materials of creative expression' and 'live experiment with the creative process' can, and were, also used to explore the issues (McNiff, 1998: 54). The direct experience is the evidence. The self of the researcher is present throughout, critical subjectivity being an essential aspect of minimising bias. This includes providing an account of possible influences.

My own art history has its origins in a Scottish ancestry with women's textile practices, a country childhood and time spent playing on my own in 'my' wood. Always making things, my artwork has developed from initial training as studio potter (Plate 10.3) in the Leach tradition to, more recently, developing textural interests and the use of basic materials in textiles. Many objects I make are for use but also are intended to be sculptural.

There is an underlying sense of a secret abundance in the natural landscape and a fascination with raw materials which is the source of inspiration. My early influences are from the conceptual art of the period examined by the exhibition *Live in Your Head: Concept and Experiment in Britain 1965–75* at the Whitechapel Art Gallery which relates to when I first made art (Mahony, 2001). Later training in studio ceramics brought links with Modernism's concepts of 'abstraction, expression and utility' (Stair, 2003: 42, Plates 10.3 and 10.4).

I situate my recent material practices with the textile artists Binns, Bristow and Wilson, whose work was shown in the exhibition *Textures of Memory: the poetics of cloth* (Mahony, 2001). Juxtapositions of emotional and contemplative issues with conventions of utility were shown, exploring material processes that are characterised by the slow labour and detailed making which are associated with objects for use. There are also relationships with the ambiguousness of domesticity, comfort and gender-indexed activities that are associated with loss, separation and death (as shown in Plate 10.5). My interests are related to aspects of Hesse's obsession with materials, particularly regarding repetition and seriality.

Outside the group my work has included simple, pre-industrial technologies such as spinning, knitting, natural dyeing and those of ceramics, which has included making objects for activities such as seed-saving and small-scale milling as well as bird baths and a seat. Transformation of raw materials in ceramics (for instance, making my own clays and glazes using ashes and local clay) by fire has contrasted with spinning directly from a fleece and hardly changing fibres in order to preserve their intrinsic qualities in the final garments.

Archival activities (museum-like) for documentation, display and experimentation were prominent in the art I made in the group and seem to reflect the symbolic processes taking place in the group. Serial activities have also dominated with the making of multiples that appear to be exploring the minutiae of the image or object within the context of the group's life.

During this research my art practice within and outside the group ran parallel to theoretical studies which included reviewing literature, considering relevant artists' work, reflection and my own writings. These formed an interaction, moving back and forth in a constantly developing process. I used notebooks, journals and photography. Digital images in the text were generated from visual forms produced in the studio. Exhibitions or visual displays staged the reciprocal process at intervals and were subsequently reflected on and written about. Looking at the effect of the research on a particular period of my clinical practice, I can see that changes in my thinking and emotions impacted on my art practice outside the group and influenced the art that I made in the group. This then impacted on the art made by the members. Interactions in the group then acted on the research and a continual, simultaneous and iterative progression developed.

The cyclic nature of this process was extremely engaging. Periods in my studio were followed by notes, exhibitions (as shown in Plates 10.1 and 10.2) or displays, texts and thinking, interspersed with exhibition visits and reading. It was the repetitive nature of these activities that provided opportunities for exploration, interaction, reflection and comparison that comprised the research process.

The next section describes an aspect of this process in a narrative about curating an exhibition of all the visual material created in association with a particular period in the life of the art psychotherapy group. Although these kinds of interactions happen in any art psychotherapy group, they can be unseen and unthought about, particularly regarding the interaction of the group and the art works made therein with the therapist's own art practice. Outlining these relationships demonstrates the complexity of the field set up by the research process.

The Group

Referrals for the group came from the Psychological Therapies Team and Community Mental Health Team. Group members may have had a number of admissions throughout their lives. Their histories included childhood sexual abuse, domestic violence, substance misuse, complicated grief reactions, eating disorders, relationship and emotional problems, phobias and compulsions. A number of people had major psychiatric diagnoses including clinical depression, personality disorder, schizophrenia and bipolar conditions. Many people were acutely distressed when they started in the group but, on leaving, several said they thought it unlikely they would need mental health services again. Often they described finding a new direction in their life.

The model I developed is informed by group analytic principles (see McNeilly, 1984) modified for working with serious disturbance in a community setting. It was an ongoing, slow open group in a studio environment, taking place weekly for two and a half hours. There were clear, dynamically structured boundaries focused on complex art-making (one and three quarter hours making: three quarters of an hour discussion). My side-by-side stance as therapist offered parity and privacy in the art-making, the style being relaxed and transparent. Engagement with self-initiated artwork was maximised, including making work to take away. The discussion, with tea, focused on art-making, not content and meaning. I advised staying with the art-making rather than talking.

I maintained clear time boundaries in order to reduce anxiety and focused on the art-making, suggesting that the purpose for each person was to find the most helpful way of using the art materials. Tables were arranged together in the middle of the room so that sitting around them loosely created a 'circle'. I started my artwork immediately, sometimes unpacking the kiln. Members got out their work and art materials as soon as they arrived, often asking each other how they were. Sometimes they chatted and laughed and sometimes a serious discussion started straight away, particularly if something had happened during the week. Sometimes it was silent. Usually it was silent half way through when engagement with the artwork seemed at its height. Complex, self-initiated art-making was sustained over weeks, sometimes much longer. Work might be made to take home or for someone outside of the group; members knew they could make private or exploratory work which would stay in the room. I photographed the work at the end of most sessions, bringing the photos back for group members to see. Everyone was extremely interested to look back at their work in this way as it developed; this enhanced members' engagement with their art-making.

I took part in any talking during art-making whilst also doing my own artwork. This took many forms and included textiles and ceramics, often multiples or series such as cards or small, roughly-cast clay containers. Like the group members, the things I made stayed in the room until finished, when I usually took them home. Members sometimes asked me about my work or commented on aspects of it. I drew attention to links in our art-making only with regard to their formal qualities.

After clearing up we returned to where we were sitting with a cup of tea. While looking at the work still on the table or on a table easel, discussion focused on how people got on rather than speculating, analysing or interpreting what the content might mean. Talking about a piece of work might take the form of a description or interchange about techniques and materials. Sometimes people volunteered interpretations about meaning but I did not encourage this. If someone got upset, I would explore whether or nor the discussion was helping. My focus was on the concrete, practical elements of the art-making process and how this might relate to group members' outside lives. For instance, I often asked what had helped, (or not) in sessions, and how might this translate to their life outside. I asked their opinion on all aspects that related to the group and to each other and made clinical decisions based on such discussion. The group usually became a 'safe haven' for people. This, I would suggest, could be repeated outside.

My style aimed to be informal. I made jokes and tried to be warm. My aim was that members' experience of the group was enjoyable and 'good', based on the belief that the degree of investment in the artwork is a key therapeutic factor.

The Artefacts and the Display

Part of the research process took the form of a private exhibition in an art school studio.[1] This was the culmination of a year's work and one of the 'stages' that included a review of three exhibitions (Mahony, 2001). I was preoccupied with the sensitive, confidential nature of the material and how this might be studied without compromising confidentiality or unduly affecting the therapy process. The reflection that followed resulted in the viewers of the exhibition being restricted to my research supervisors and me. The main purpose of the display was to provide initial information, like a pilot study, prior to further data collection. In this it succeeded beyond my hopes. It also raised some important issues about clinical practice.

The room was booked for three days: one to put out the work, one to arrange and look at it, and one to dismantle it. It was a large, square room with four windows opposite the door, painted white with white blinds and four plinths that had been left there. The space turned out to be very suitable. It had been booked for a time when students would not be around and was therefore quiet and confidential.

1 In the interest of confidentiality and anonymity all recognisable material, including names, places, dates etc., have been removed.

Due to complex security arrangements there were difficulties on the first morning in gaining access, resulting in lengthy negotiations and time-consuming trips. Up till then I had not really considered the effect of exhibiting on the maker. Having arrived to set up the exhibition this was high on my agenda. I felt very nervous. I remembered feelings of vulnerability and a sense of exposure from previous ceramics exhibitions that had been blotted out of my consciousness. I had decided not to involve clients in any way at this stage of the research, the purpose of this private display being to gather together all the artefacts relating to the group and my art practice and to examine them in a formalised space. My research supervisors took part in this exercise in their role as 'extended clinical team'.

The artwork I had brought with me consisted mainly of group members' two-dimensional work, some three dimensional work and a file of photographs of 'work in progress'. I also had files and documents relating to the group, my own artwork – made both in the group and out of it – my personal notebooks relating to my artwork and files relating to my studio and to the research.

I decided quickly that I wanted to see a chronological display of the clients' two-dimensional work and that I would position these on the three walls without windows. There were four current clients and the work ranged back four years. Getting out the work I realised that one person had quite a lot more than the others so I arranged it all in piles, one for each year, in front of each wall. Then I laid it out on the floor: it would just fit. Not having much time to spare, I started putting it up as quickly as I could, using masking tape on the back. After trying it out, I felt that a row of each person's work round the three walls would work visually, showing gaps where there had been no two-dimensional work in a session. It showed individual sessions where there was more than one piece of work. It also showed the overall development of artwork over the four years. When the two-dimensional work was up I considered how to display the three dimensional pieces and my own work. The clients had dated theirs; two people had also signed it, which needed masking out. Mine was not dated but my notebooks enabled the dates to be worked out.

My main concern was that the methods of display would give the work dignity. I felt that the plinths and formal lines of wall-hung work would help and I used nylon thread to get them as exact as I could. The eyes were drawn upwards to look at the top line of work which I felt also helped.

The next day I unpacked three-dimensional work and starting moving it around along with the plinths. I also started unpacking my work, the files and documents and looked at the photographs. The photographs showed what was not there: other clients' work, and the cherished three-dimensional work that had mostly been taken home. Some extraordinary links started to emerge between my work done outside of the group and clients' work. It was only by seeing the work all together in this setting that the links emerged.

I added the three-dimensional work that I had made in the group to the group's artworks. I put up photographs taken at the end of sessions and placed them where there were gaps to give an indication of work that was taking place in those gaps, including that of other clients. I eventually arrived at an arrangement of work on the plinths, including the first pieces of clay work by a client that had been made after I used clay for the first time. One plinth had unfired clay work, two pieces of which were by people no longer in the group and where the clay had been used in a regressed fashion (smearing, hitting, splashing). Most of the other work seemed orderly.

I then had to decide how to display my own artwork made outside of the group. For the duration of this group my work had mainly been textiles. This had involved spinning animal fibres and wool from-the-fleece; dyeing with natural dyes; knitting test squares, swatches, tension squares and garments; making chair pads from hand-spun raw silk filled with fleece; and I had started tapestry weaving as well. That year my studio had finally been built, of which there were photographs and designs. I had already laid out my notebooks that included photographs of some work I no longer have as well as samples of spinning, dyeing and lichen studies. At the time I worried that there were a lot more examples of my work than of the clients but I was never sure if that was actually the case. The four windows in the unused wall acted as frames with a background of the view outside.

During the group I had also finished two sweaters, each taking two years to make. After moving them around I placed them at each end of the walls adjoining the wall with the window. Current work was then in the middle. I decided to have the windows open as there was a breeze that gently moved the work hung there. I hung the two garments to exploit this so they could move freely, hanging them on coat hangers from nylon thread. They moved from side to side and I became aware they were like absent figures. Over the other two windows in the middle I hung offset square objects on nylon thread so that they became diamond shaped (Plate 10.6). The cushion pads in one window were strange objects and in the other window there were tension squares that the light shone through, showing the stitches. They twisted and spun in the wind like mobiles. The movement in these windows was soothing and reminiscent of the spinning, stitching and knitting that made them. A creative process emerged in the process of curating this work in a more obvious way than when I was setting out the clients' work. It seemed like a continuation and culmination of the making process.

In retrospect, this aspect of the display related to my history: I had recurrent nightmares as a child of a window that involved absence and early separation. I had always thought that spinning related to separation. It also seemed that writing this account of the curatorial process was important as I had not realised what was happening at the time. I was finished half an hour before my supervisors arrived and I spent the time looking and photographing the finished result. I was really pleased to see them when they arrived and to show them the visual display.

Findings

Three key themes emerged from curating this visual display: the process of mapping, the links between work, and my role as container of the group.

A 'Mapping' Process

Whilst walking around the room and looking at the work one of my supervisors remarked that it was a chronological mapping focusing on the process not the product: a reflection of art psychotherapy and its attention to interior processes. A face I had embroidered seemed to be placed symbolically in the middle of the group's lines of artwork. We discussed the display methods and agreed that a sense of dignity had been achieved, the wall-hung work and plinths having played an important role in this.

Links

I had come to several realisations through curating the clients' and my artworks and had made particular links between two pieces. One I had made at an Art Psychotherapy Service Art Practice afternoon as a model for a jacket; this was a collage of torn pieces of paper opening out flat to show the construction. The other, a group member's ceramic vase painted with underglaze colours, had been made a year later. However, it had cracked and split open. The group discussed the kiln accident and the group member decided to carry on and work with what had happened. It seemed highly significant as I knew it particularly related to his autobiography and the problems that had brought him to the group, although this was not discussed. Given that the group had not seen my piece, the similarity between the two objects in terms of colours and shape was uncanny. I had set them on adjacent plinths to emphasise the connections (see Figure 10.6). There were other clear resonances between people's work across the four years of the groups's life that was on display.

The Art Therapist as Container

My research supervisors and I talked about my role in the group in relation to the display methods. Group members had started using clay and textiles after seeing me use them in the group; this seemed to have been an important modelling process. We also discussed the lack of mess, remarking on the apparent order of the work versus my experience of chaos when writing my therapist's notes. My approach in the group was aimed at reducing anxiety and it was postulated that the notes were an expression of the anxiety, 'mess' and chaos that I was containing as therapist.

We discussed another 'messy' element that I had kept out of the display: the latex moulds I had made and used for making small, rough, slip cast ceramic containers. These had been an ongoing process in the group for several years. I had put these on another plinth. We also talked about my garments, their relationship to skin and their position in the display. I explained my realisation that they were like absent figures in the room. It was pointed out that I had placed them like 'bookends' which contained each end of the chronological lines of work. Bick's (1968) paper on skin as a container seemed relevant to both disciplines of visual arts and art psychotherapy. The 'gaps' in the layout of the pictures were referred to and how they were a reminder of musical scores, particularly those of John Cage.

It seemed to us that we were looking at and discussing the whole in a way which seemed to address the problem of considering the huge volume of information presented by an ongoing art psychotherapy group and its' art works. Here our conversation was very different to the usual discussions about art psychotherapy products and the meaning of individual pieces of art work in relation to individual psychopathology, transference, a single session and a group's process over time. We were looking at the art and seeing the entirety of its development before us. My supervisors remarked that this might be the first time that an art psychotherapist's personal artwork had been put together with that of her group and that all the related objects and texts could be seen together. We also talked about looking at art work in art therapy groups and how it was often placed on the floor.

This was a temporary display that created a collage-like effect, like thought memories in 'story boards'. It included what was described as 'forensic' work. This was fragments of collected material, put in plastic bags and labelled – actually the contents of some of the cast ceramic containers – which showed what I brought into the group. We discussed the intentionality of making and the intentionality of an exhibition such as this, including the process of putting it up and the status of the work which had to speak for itself without any accompanying texts. I felt I had arrived at a climax of the research yet it was situated in the middle of the project.

Summary

I have presented this narrative in an autobiographical style that borrows on mythic traditions as described by Gergen (1997). This, as he suggests, allows the reader a personal response to the text and retains the fullness of sensitive and subjective experience. Like a visual work it retains a sense of fluidity which avoids closure and, by inviting the reader to identify with the experience, does not infer a status difference between writer and reader.

Findings Arising from the Text

The narrative emphasises the importance of giving dignity to clients' artwork when displaying it, including in an art psychotherapy setting. Seeing all four years' work together made it clear that complex reciprocal exchanges were taking place between my art practice outside the clinical setting as well as inside it, and with the clients' artworks. Resonance was clear in the artwork between all those making art together. It also became apparent that the creative process of curating a visual display can be a continuation of the making process which changes the way an object is experienced and perceived, enhancing and extending understanding of both individual and group processes. Further, the exhibition made it possible to look at a huge amount of information all at once. It enabled us to look at the 'whole' as well as particular parts, as opposed to focusing on the meaning of individual pieces. It clearly showed how 'gaps' in making are as important as making itself. The importance of photography for documentation became clear as an important method of investigation.

The role of the art therapist in an art psychotherapy group was also elucidated. First in terms of modelling, for instance where group members started using particular materials after I had used them. Second, with regard to containment, for instance chaos and mess was only experienced in my notes. The importance of communication through unspoken metaphor in the art therapist's art was illustrated too, in particular with regard to the form and use of particular materials and techniques. (For a fuller account see Mahony, 2010.)

This account of a visual display has shown how communication can be through unspoken metaphors. This is particularly valuable for people who have severe and complex problems who may not be able to tolerate talking or recognise direct communication. Examples include the looking face that I embroidered and placed in the middle of my clients' work and how the two garments I made outside the group acted as 'bookends' to the display, representing containment. My embroidered face was a personal image that the group saw develop very slowly over time from a pair of disembodied eyes to the finished face. The slowness of the process allowed me to monitor its impact on the members and their response to my stitching and choice of imagery. Responses were triggered in the clients; for example, mask paintings and material practices generally became established in the group at this time. The tapestry weavings I made in the group also seem to have had containing functions.

The characteristics of rhythm, repetition and connectivity are echoed in my other activities with art materials in the group. The slowness of the development of my and group members' artworks, the repetition in actual processes (like stitching or casting), and actions as well as repetition of actual objects, all contribute to a fugue-like quality where themes are repeated in slowly developing, complex patterns. There is also an analogy with music in group analysis (Skaife and Huet, 1998: 20), the gaps relating to silence as in John Cage's *Silence* (1978).The artworks and the display seemed to articulate visual and aesthetic concerns related to the group's process and to that of individuals, giving visual form to the group matrix that is described in group analysis (Foulkes and Anthony, 1965: 26). It was like a series of utterances, a discourse, the implications of which may or may not have reached consciousness in individual group members or in the group as a whole. The art was communicating but this was not articulated verbally. Rather the art transmitted information and complex ideas to and fro, creating a multidimensional, operational base for the group. Art is thus a means of accessing deep unconscious material that can be worked on without being fully understood, although it may reach consciousness and provide insight, as my personal experience in the narrative illustrates. This account also illustrates how craft practices can materialise the culture and autobiography of individuals and of a group, embodying complex ideas and offering visual interpretations.

From Research into Practice

The implication of this research is that the art therapist's art practice is an integral part of clinical practice both in and outside clinical groups, even when unseen by the client. This leads me to suggest that clients' experiences can be significantly enhanced by the therapist's carefully considered art-making in art psychotherapy groups. This represents a significant challenge to orthodoxy presented in the literature where the therapist's art practice is often kept separate from the clients'.

The emerging picture is one of deep, complex and reciprocal relationships and communications, implicitly enmeshed in the art-making processes within a group. Despite the difficulties of countertransference, participative art-making by the art therapist in art psychotherapy groups brings these otherwise hidden relationships into the foreground and finds them embedded in the artwork where they can become accessible and be monitored by all concerned. Communication through unspoken metaphor is also emphasised, especially the containment and role modelling of the creative process by the art therapist.

Art practices entrenched in materiality, habitually described as craft, have also been shown to have an important function in art psychotherapy groups, requiring a wide range of media and technologies in a studio environment. I would therefore recommend that far greater consideration be given to the form, genre and characteristics or materiality of the art-making of an art psychotherapy group, including the therapist's art practice taking place outside the group. Profound influences are being transmitted and documented, as well as rich ideas and personal histories that are materialised and transformed in the embodied experience of making art together.

SALLY SKAIFE

11 Maps and Mess: Group Members' Experience of the Relationship between Art and Talk in an Art Therapy Group

Abstract

This chapter describes a research project in which women and their therapist in an art psychotherapy group were interviewed and given questionnaires in order to explore their experience of art-making and interactive talking. Whilst exploration of their interpersonal relationships emerged as the most important therapeutic factor, art was also key, although it was experienced as frustrating due to time limits. The chapter discusses the adaptation the group made to ensure that the art could be a useful resource without compromising the interpersonal work. Implications for practice are discussed, the suggestion being that the distinction between types of art made in art therapy could be used as a means of keeping the group in a state of creative disruption.

Key Words

women; art; psychotherapy; group; interviews.

How it all Began: from Practice to Research

This chapter will describe how, whilst conducting art psychotherapy groups loosely based on models described by McNeilly (1983, 1987, 2006) and Waller (1993) in a university setting, I encountered a problem. Aspects of art-making that I had found important in my personal experience, for example the feeling of becoming anchored in the world through using the art materials and of gaining and losing control of the means of expression that allows in something other that is self-enriching, did not seem to be overtly exploited. Instead art seemed to be engulfed by interactive talking. The art that was made, although often strong, seemed to be mainly used as a springboard for talking; art's existential aspects were overlooked. However, talking in the group enabled group members to learn from one another about the unconscious expectations and fears they brought to relationships that had led them to seek therapy.

My attempts to redress the balance between art and talk in art psychotherapy groups brought me up against dilemmas. I found that if I utilised familiar techniques, such as encouraging self-expression and communication through art and paying attention to the experience of making and of looking, there was not only a conflict between the individual and the group, there was also a conflict with my analytic role. At the time I decided to prioritise the analytic role whilst attempting to create a culture in the group in which group members gave the art enough space. However, I was left wondering if this might result in an inadequate art therapy group and at the same time a poor analytic group. I reassured myself, however, that the group members were certainly benefiting from the group and did not appear to be dissatisfied. How far, though, did I just see what I wanted to see?

The Context of the Research

My concerns that arose from my practice related to issues in art therapy theory. In the early days of the profession conflicts between art and therapy had been acknowledged (Champernowne, 1971; Edwards, 1981) but during the 1980s and 1990s efforts had been made to integrate art and talking (Case and Dalley, 1992; Schaverien, 1992; Waller, 1993). This was understandable, given the need to present a coherent idea of art therapy to clients, employers and other professionals. This integration may have been responsible for, in more recent times, art therapists expressing similar concerns to my own about aspects of art getting hidden (Moon, 1997; McNiff, 1997; Mahony, 2001; Rogers, 2002; Gilroy, 2008). Perhaps as a result, separations have been made between different types of art therapy, some becoming more based in art and others in talk, and in their application to different kinds of clients or therapeutic contexts; for example, art therapy, art psychotherapy and analytic art therapy (Schaverien, 1994, 2000) and theme-based, directive groups, group analytic art therapy groups and group interactive art therapy (Case and Dalley, 2006). This categorisation is supported by the *What Works for Whom* (Roth and Fonagy, 1996) approach of EBP which matches types of therapy with types of client but, in my view, these are considered without any reference to social context with the result that a social and class agenda is hidden. For example, might clients who can reflect on their reasons for being in therapy be given a therapy where there is an emphasis on talking and those who are more disabled be likely to be referred to a more art-based approach?

These thoughts were in my mind prior to conducting a research project with a colleague on her art therapy group. My colleague and I, who both ran art therapy groups in a university setting, were conscious of the need for research-based evidence of the value and effectiveness of art therapy and aware of the sparse literature on art therapy groups. Together we set up the women's art therapy research group in which she was the therapist and I the researcher. We devised an open-ended approach in which I interviewed and gave questionnaires to group members and interviewed the therapist as a means to elicit phenomena in art therapy groups. Lomas and Hallas (1998) are the only art therapy authors, as far as I know, to have interviewed group members, though unlike our research they did not separate the roles of therapist and researcher. They describe a project in which they asked their art therapy group of people with learning difficulties what they had found most helpful about the group. We asked group members this question too in order to address our primary research question: 'How do group members experience the relationship between interactive talking and art in an art therapy group?'

Method

Following ethical approval and financial support for the research from the university, my colleague and I advertised the research group in the prospectus as a time-limited, eighteen months long group which involved research. We had enough responses for my colleague to start assessment, selection and preparation for the group. All seven respondents were women of whom all but one had trained in art; we therefore had a particularly homogenous group which contrasted with the groups we had been running which had given rise to the research questions. The group was to be run in the same way as our previous groups. It was to be once a week for two hours, group members would decide on the structure of the group and the therapist would stay in analytic role and not make her own art work in the group. The art work would be kept in the studio until the group finished.

Before the assessment appointments my colleague and I devised our research questions together which involved our separate as well as our mutual interests. We also devised the first questionnaire to be sent to group members before the group began. At this point we made the decision to cease discussion about the group until it was finished, except for our two formal research interviews. We agreed however, that she would keep a photographic record of the images made in the group and that these would be available to me for the interviews with the group members. The first set of interviews, which included the first with the therapist, took place six months into the group; a year into the group I sent group members a second questionnaire; and a month after the group finished I interviewed group members and the therapist again. A year later I sent out a final, follow-up questionnaire.

Our questions in the interviews and questionnaires were based on three research questions:

1. What could be learnt about the usefulness of art therapy for addressing issues particular to women?
2. What was the role of art in change?
3. What was the relationship between interactive talking and art-making in an art therapy group?

Although all of these questions are interrelated this chapter focuses on the last which, once interviewing began, I found was my primary research question. This resulted in my analysing the data independently.

My colleague and I had decided to use both interviews and questionnaires as a means to get the most data we could without making the research too onerous for us or the group members. The questionnaires aimed to give a space for the group members to think about their answers away from the influence of the researcher. The first introduced members, at an early stage, to a reflective process in relation to the group experience. Allied to this was the first interview where I decided to explore issues relating to the women's experience of time for art-making, time for interactive talking and time for talking about the art work. This was addressed in two ways: first, by direct questions about the time structures and second, by asking questions about what group members were finding helpful and frustrating in the group. In the latter I did not refer to any distinction between art-making and talking. I took note, however, of whether or not they distinguished between the two. I asked about which images they had made, or others had made, that had been significant for them. This was in order to make links between the art and points of change for themselves, individually and for the group, and to address the question about the role of art in the group and its relationship to interactive talking. Asking about significant images resulted in each individual group member and I leafing through the photographs of the images, which led them to tell me their own story in the group.

The second questionnaire mirrored the questions in the interview but in addition I asked directly about what they had learnt about themselves and others and the process through which this happened. I also introduced an idea of art as a skill. This was because I had long wondered if feelings about accomplishment in art-making were present but went unspoken in art therapy groups like this. In the second interview I covered much the same ground as in the first but my questions were looser and I allowed the group members to lead, hoping that more would be revealed. I added one more question about group members' experience of the therapist.

The final questionnaire asked one question: what had group members found most and least valuable about their group experience? This addressed the crux of the research and I asked the women to talk, or rather to write, freely upon it.The questions I asked the therapist in both interviews mirrored those I had asked group members; for example, what she thought group members were finding most helpful or frustrating, and which images she thought were significant in the group process.

Silverman (1993) describes differences in approach to making sense of what is found in interview transcripts. For instance, some regard them as a true reflection of external reality, others as a co-construction between interviewer and interviewee which reveals knowledge about external reality; yet others see the interview itself as the object of study as it is a reflection of the very reality it sets out to explore. When I began the research I hoped to find knowledge about external reality but in the midst of interviews I realised that they were a co-construction of reality. I became aware that my questions led the answers and, much later, I began to appreciate that the interview process itself paralleled the art-making and research process and might reveal something about the role of art in therapy more generally. I became aware that my approach to the interview texts would be steeped in my conscious desire to find what was of interest to me, as well as my less conscious attitude that I embodied through my social and cultural place in the world. Thus the findings discussed here should be seen like a life drawing in which one attempts to stay faithful to what is observed at the same time as inescapably working in one's own selective style. Validity is achieved by a reflexive attempt to be transparent about the method and about the entirety of the research process.

I tried out different ways of interrogating the texts. I went through each group member's interview and questionnaire responses, building up an idea of their individual journey in the group and the significance of their personal response to the research questions. I then looked across the texts to study how often particular aspects of the group were said to be helpful and frustrating and how this varied through the time span of the group. I noted all the comments that related to the usefulness of, or the frustrations with, art. As I went along I categorised the comments, changing the name of the category as more comments were added so as to encompass subtle changes to the category group, as described by Strauss and Corbin (1990). I then amalgamated these into a smaller number of category groups. Having acquired a list of helpful and frustrating features of the art therapy group, I then looked at what had been said in answer to questions about experiences of the group's structure. Lastly I looked at the images group members had chosen as significant.

In describing the findings I have attempted to demonstrate the process of analysis in which I separated comments on art from comments on the group overall in order to see them more clearly. For instance 'not enough space in the group', could refer to many things, including art. I was attempting to redress the problem whereby the art could become subsumed in the group dynamics overall.

Findings

Interpersonal Relating

I found that what was considered by all to be the most helpful factor in the group was what Yalom (1975) refers to as interpersonal learning. This was one of the two factors, group cohesion being the second, of eleven 'therapeutic' factors of psychotherapy groups that Yalom considered most important that had emerged in his research. The category groups that emerged in my research were as follows:

1. Gaining confidence from finding similarity with others.
2. Learning from the feedback given by others.
3. Learning about yourself through differences with others.
4. Learning from listening to other people's stories.
5. Helping others.
6. Being heard and accepted by others.
7. Learning from yourself though the way you relate with others.
8. Learning from transferences.
9. Seeing others change.
10. Being heard specifically by a group of women.
11. Saying what cannot normally be said.

These categories are very similar to those Yalom (1975) describes.

As interpersonal learning in the group seemed to be the most significant therapeutic factor it was perhaps not surprising that the most dominant frustrating factor was irritation with others. For example: 'The group lacks intensity, there is too much talk about "issues", and people are too polite with one another.' Some of the women were thought to talk too much and some were irritated by others who were often absent. The group was also felt to be too homogenous. Sharing the group's time with others was also found to be difficult, as was group members' experience of the therapist not saying enough. All but one comment like this were in the first interview, that is at the six month point.

Over time comments about frustrating factors dwindled. There were practically none in the second interview after the group finished and, even though the last questionnaire asks about the least valuable factors of the group, there are no further comments.

The Pros and Cons of Making Art

Although interpersonal issues were more frequently mentioned, art-making and looking were clearly also important. A common positive experience amongst group members was that they could bring issues from outside the group, work on them through art and then share them verbally with the group. They spoke about art allowing a release from the intensity of the group, a feeling of 'letting go', and that making art in the group allowed thoughts and feelings to flow. Other people's images were also important as they stirred up issues for themselves. There were some things said about how the art was helpful that seemed to address the existential issues I spoke of earlier: for example, the women described becoming aware of their role in making decisions (this referred to how the group set about making art) and that art-making made them feel alive. They spoke too of being part of the group's creativity.

Some responses were particular to this group being predominantly comprised of women who were artists. Group members talked about how they were able to be more experimental with art made outside of the group. They also said that improvements in their confidence and self-esteem that were a result of being in the group helped their art-making elsewhere. However, of the eighteen comments made in the follow-up questionnaire a year after the group ended, only four were about art. Although all these were positive comments this does suggest that the art became secondary to the interpersonal relationship work in the group.

Art was also a source of frustration to the group members. Several people spontaneously spoke about there not being enough time in the group to either talk about the art work or to make it. In the first interviews, when I asked whether the group was meeting up to their expectations, two of the seven group members mentioned frustration with a lack of time for art. Several felt that the group was not long enough for all its parts. One person found the art-making very frustrating, feeling it was just illustrative of what had been talked about. The art materials were also criticised.

Time Structures

I asked in both interviews and in the second questionnaire about how the group was structured and how it used its time, anticipating that this might shed light on why art often becomes submerged in art therapy groups which use talk. Nearly all group members would have liked more time for art-making, on average about fifteen to thirty minutes more, though not all felt strongly about it. One group member said in her interview: 'I like the time I spend painting, it is like a dialogue with yourself, but the time is very short and you're in a hurry.' One woman had a suggestion: 'Perhaps we should try to do one session that is all art work and then the next session just talk about it. It would mean that you could really give some time to the art work.'

There was also frustration about time to look at the art. One person described her eyes wandering over her painting whilst the others were talking about theirs. Someone else said that they found it hard to do something and then not talk about it. Another person spoke about a wish to spend more time looking at people's images in turn, to see the sequence of an individual's work and identify recurring themes. This comment must be seen in the light of she and I doing precisely this in the interview, looking back at her work separately from the work of the rest of the group, which allowed a different sort of meaning-making process to take place from that routinely happening in this group. However, there seemed to be a frustration that there was no room for individual history to be traced via the images within the group.

The desire for longer times for both making and talking about the images requires less time to be spent in an initial talking period, which all agreed was about an hour, one half of the group's time. Most felt that in some way this was necessary. For example, one woman said: 'I think it is fairly important that initial joining of the group again after a week apart, sort of finding out where everyone is… it seems like lots of pressing issues come up in the first hour and it is important to sort of let them work their way <out> somehow rather than cut them short.' However there was some ambivalence about this, some of the women feeling dissatisfied but powerless to change what seemed to have become an established structure:

> I think I would prefer having a shorter period of talking at the beginning of the group and then longer to do the art work and longer to talk about the work. Having said that, I know I probably talk a lot in the first period and the reason this hasn't happened is down to individual discipline.

> I think generally that we tend to spend a lot of time at the beginning where personally I would like us to get on with the painting a bit earlier… but on the other hand there is obviously things that people want to discuss and you don't want to stop that.

In the interview with the therapist, which took place about a month after those with the group members, she reported that the group had discussed their frustration with the time allocation in the group and that a positive change had been made which enabled discussion of the images in much more depth. It is interesting to note, however, that the second questionnaires, distributed six months after the interview with the therapist i.e. a year into the group, show there had been no change to the way the group structured their time. Despite acknowledging the frustration with there not being enough time to make, look and talk about art work, discussing it together in the group and being aware that it was the group's choice to change it, members did not alter the pattern. It seems probable that the time structure they had arrived at was the best compromise, given the two hour time limitation of the group. This concurs with my experience in non-artist, art therapy groups.

The therapist felt that group members' feeling that there was not enough time in the group was the result of it being a women's group and women often feeling that there is not enough 'space' for them. Wadeson (1987) and Case and Dalley (1992) talk about art providing individual space as a special feature of art therapy groups but they also mention a tension about time to look at the work. This is double edged: the individual time spent making provides something which is then diminished when there is no time to really explore the art made. Understanding the art work as belonging to both the individual and the group as in the 'group image' (Skaife and Huet, 1998), an image which is a metaphor for the group dynamic, can be a way of allowing the tension between individual and group to be constructive, grappling with the tensions between the group as a whole process and individuality being a part of the process of group work. However, these views about the role of art make no distinction between the art work and group member/s, a theoretical position which might contribute to art becoming occluded in some art psychotherapy groups.

Does it matter that art becomes hidden? The interviews and questionnaires at the end of the group and at follow-up showed that frustration was not the women's primary experience, a successful compromise about time for making and looking at art in the group having somehow been achieved. The women appeared to have found a way of managing the tensions between the art as both relating to their personal identity and to the group. Looking at what the group members said about their experience of the art-making might help us understand how they managed the tension between individual and group, and between art and talk.

Mess-Making and Mapping

One member of the group, Vanessa, found the art in the group frustrating throughout. Although she was the only one who felt this, what she says is interesting in that she characterises a certain use of art by the others. In the first interview she described the way she made art when not in the group, walking along the beach with her camera and collecting things and then taking them back to the studio to work on:

> I worked with them over and over, and changed the idea, … tearing it apart, pulling it this way, filming it, photographing it, doing it in a dark room, doing it in a light room, all that working through a lot of ideas come, and then your final work when you see it, even then you know yes this is right, this is how it should be, … and then I think months later… it just speaks to me of my frame of mind and what was happening to me at the time.

She went on to talk about the difficulties of communicating feelings clearly in art, both to herself and to others: 'I don't believe you can convey your feelings actually to somebody else, because they are going to read what they want to read. You are forever trying to get there as clear<ly> as you can. … but you need that recognition from other people.' This is what she said was the purpose of art-making:

> There are always questions and not just aesthetic questions and those questions have to be addressed and solved in the artwork… and I think within that problem solving the questions that come up particularly for you in your particular piece of work and the way you answer those problems, all has a lot to say about you…

She then went on to talk about others' art-making in the group:

> From what I saw, I saw a lot of repetition, in eighteen months people coming up with exactly the same things, … I felt there was no pushing in that dynamic, no using of the art to actually get that person to overcome or to work further and actually get around something within their artwork… we talked for about an hour about all kinds of things and then what happened was it was almost like an illustration of what we had been talking about.

What is interesting here is that she described two types of art work, one where it is very difficult to know if it communicates what was intended and the other which communicates more clearly but might just as well have been spoken about; there is no resolution of the issues in the art work itself. What she said about problem solving in art-making is something that does not easily translate into words and, perhaps because of this, there is a conflict with the group's interaction. However, she did talk about this type of art-making in therapeutic terms, describing it as speaking to her of her frame of mind and as an attempt to communicate what is very difficult to communicate. She describes a very physical aspect to art-making, creatively changing the context of materials and moving in and out of spaces; the process seems to determine the time it takes to make art. All these things are antithetical to a boundaried art therapy group where time constraints, art material constraints, and room constraints provide the group with a containment that gives meaning and intensity to what happens within it.

Did the other women feel the same? Despite their frustration with time and experiencing interpersonal learning as the most helpful thing about the group, nearly all found art-making extremely helpful. It was interesting that they spoke about the art-making in the same way as Vanessa: that it was illustrative of feelings that can be verbalised although not necessarily illustrative of what has just been spoken about. Often it is a means by which feelings are brought into the group, worked on and prepared before being shared with the group. One person said in the first interview: 'I couldn't do these paintings at home, it is too unsafe, but to be outside somewhere and with other people with their own kind of difficulties… makes it very safe.'

What appears to have happened is that the group came to a compromise or adaptation about the role and function of art that worked for all but one woman. This they called 'mapping' or 'making diagrams' or 'illustrations' of their feelings, images which seem to contain intense feelings. For example, one person said in the first interview: 'I have often mapped things out, I will often map it out almost in a quite diagrammatic way, sort of do a feeling and the next week do a map of the feeling – you see like a journey.'

Another said in the interview after the group finished:

> The art work I used in a different way than I would if I was making artwork for something else… I would illustrate something that was in my mind… mapping things out… It helped me to place things without talking about them, so I had to really feel where I am in the world.

She added that her artwork changed towards the end of the group when she used more paint and different art materials.

Can we learn more about this split between different sorts of art from looking at the women's images?

Significant Images

In the first interview I asked each individual to show me, from the photographs of the work they had made, an image they felt was the most significant. What was striking about these images was a similar illustrative quality which tells of something outside of the group that was very important about, or to, the person, that she wanted the group to know. The intention behind them, I think, was about belonging in the group. This was synonymous with the interpersonal relating category which related to talking with one another in the group.

Laura's image was of pin figures with speech bubbles and described a situation at work in which she experienced persecutory voices. Sharing this with the group had been important. Sarah's was about her son's potty training, being made of neat clay pieces which she said were 'poo'. She was discussing the parallel between her son's growing up and issues of her own. Lucy had made a pencil drawing of a figure with little people in the arm which she said was about wanting children. Maria had broken little pieces of clay and felt very liberated by not having to make anything; a second piece was an image of her and her husband in bed and she was afraid because he was about to go away. Ella had made a picture of vaginas which felt a radical thing to do in the group. Vanessa mentioned a performance piece which involved the others who had refused to take part.

The work that group members felt was significant for them seemed to be mostly work that could be easily explained in words and seemed to be either about telling other people about something that was important to them, or about gauging others' reactions. In this sense it blended well with the group interactive work, and supports Vanessa's argument that the art work in the group was an illustration of issues that were talked about. When I looked at them though, I found a lot that was not addressed in their verbal explanations. The clay pieces actually looked nothing like poo, and though Ella's painting of vaginas was in fleshy pinks it was hard to decipher vaginas. When I put Maria's clay pieces together with Lucy's arm full of children I noticed that they looked visually alike and then saw an interesting coincidence – these two images had been made in the same session. What group members had made related to embodiment; faeces, vaginas, physical intimacy, birth and death.

Discussion

How does this map-making/mess binary relate to Schaverien's (1992) diagrammatic and embodied images? Schaverien talks of the diagrammatic image as one which is an approximation of a pre-conceived mental image and usually conscious in intent. The way in which Vanessa appears to regard the others' art work seems to be in this category. If this is the case, it confirms the ideas of those who think that art is minimilised in much art therapy (for example, Maclagan, 1995; McNiff, 1997). The way in which Vanessa describes her own work outside of the group is similar to Schaverien's embodied image. The embodied image may start with a pre-conceived mental image or it may be a response to marks already made, but it combines conscious and unconscious elements and both mental and pictorial image develop in an interaction of these.

Some of the images selected as significant in the second interview appeared to be much more embodied in that they made use of the physicality of the art materials, suggesting development of both idea and image through the group members' engagement in the work. However, many of them could still have been considered as maps, as described by group members. The maps and mess division is thus not the same as Schaverien's diagrammatic and embodied image. The images described as significant in this research seemed to relate to literal embodiment in the sense of awareness of being in a body.

This takes us back to Yalom's group research. Yalom and his co-researchers (Yalom 1985) found that there were comments made about what was helpful in the group that had fallen outside his category groups; he later decided these could be grouped together as existential factors. What he found was that group members found it very hard not to collapse existential issues into interpersonal ones. For instance, they would understand one member's realisation of being ultimately alone to be about social isolation. Yalom discovered that group members benefited from acknowledgement of feelings about what is inescapable in being human *alongside* recognition of feelings that can be understood in interpersonal terms, but that this was accompanied by resistance.

Can we understand the underprivileging of the art in this group to relate to this? Does the use of physical materials that parallel bodily parts and substances bring existential material into the group that then receives less attention than material that relates to interpersonal relationships? This resonates with Lomas and Hallas's research (1998) which found that interpersonal relating was most highly valued but that the images spoke of something profound that seemed to become hidden in the group.

There are a series of overlapping binaries (all constructed and fluid) that are emerging in this discussion: talk/ art, embodied/ diagrammatic, maps/ mess, existential factors/ interpersonal factors. What I think is important is that we keep both sides of any binary pair open, allowing a deconstruction of the one that inevitably dominates (Derrida 1988) through acknowledging its uncertainty.

Finally, Jameson (1981), a contemporary socialist philosopher, speaks of an aesthetic form of map-making that can help individuals find their own path within a capitalist society that requires its members to perform its workings. He sees it important that a pedagogy is developed in which individuals develop awareness of their position in the world system. He speaks of mapping our personally experienced relationships to class realities, both near to home and much more widely; of bringing together our embodied experience with the reality of our social position and with conceptual, theoretical frameworks – to make an aesthetic map. With this, Jameson is attempting to bring together the aesthetic and the cognitive, the individual and the group (social) in a way that gives the individual a means to find their way and move forward.

This research revealed that this group found a particular compromise that worked for them whereby they could feel less frustrated with the limitations posed by there being the possibility for interpersonal learning as well as art-making in the group. Whilst the end result was good, and the art could not be sidelined as merely a stepping stone for talking, nonetheless the women's feeling that there was not enough space for art mirrors my own experience as an art therapist. The word 'space' rather than 'time' is probably significant here as it refers more to the quality of the time. The challenge for the art therapist is how to make more of the time that there is in the group for art without compromising the therapeutic benefits of interpersonal learning.

From Research into Practice

Translating this research into practice has led me to think of art not only as integrated with interpersonal learning but also as having a separate existence. Thinking of there being a duality in the group – between art that fits comfortably with interpersonal relating, that is mapping, and art which creates a conflict with interactive work – allows one form of expression to be in discussion with the other. I have found in my own practice that making small adjustments in technique can help this. I try to ensure that the art-making space does not get subsumed by talking and that generally it is given significant space. I actively involve myself as art therapist in the art, either by making my own work or treating the room as a studio rather than as a group analytic space. I talk about art and attempt to encourage critical thinking. These attentions to art can create conflict with interpersonal talking but I now embrace such conflict as providing a disruption which keeps the group in creative movement.

ANDREA GILROY

Commentary: Art Therapy with Adults

The chapters in Part Three about art therapy with adult clients offer different kinds of evidence about the effectiveness of different approaches to art therapy. These gave rise to energetic conversation between the editor and the authors contributing to this part of the book about varying approaches to clinical work that are driven by the demands of EBP and whether it was possible, or desirable, to differentiate between clinical approaches and client populations in the way that EBP requires.

What or Who?

Most art therapy research with people who have severe and complex problems – including those diagnosed as schizophrenic, bi-polar, personality disordered, compulsive, phobic and chronically depressed – has, until recently, comprised qualitative studies of casework (e.g. Greenwood and Layton, 1987; Killick, 1993; Saotome, 1998; see Gilroy, 2006) and an historical overview of art therapy's long history of practice with such clients (Wood, 2000; Chapter Nine). Generally speaking, long-term supportive work is described, although, interestingly, outcome research has begun to establish the effectiveness of short-term art therapy with people diagnosed as schizophrenic. The first to do so was Green, Wehling and Talsky's RCT (1987). This short-term, directed art therapy group led to improvements in clients' self-esteem and ability to get on with others. This was followed by another RCT conducted in China (Peixin et al., 2005) and Richardson et al.'s (2007) seminal RCT that demonstrated the effectiveness of similarly short-term – although on this occasion, interactive – art therapy groups (Jones, Chapter Eight).

This small body of art therapy research contributed to NICE's Clinical Guideline about the treatment of schizophrenia (2009), as Wood described in Chapter Nine. NICE's extensive review of possible treatments for these clients states that 'at present, arts therapies are the only interventions, both psychological and pharmacological, to demonstrate consistent efficacy in the reduction of negative symptoms' (205). This important endorsement of art therapy's effectiveness (as one of the four recommended arts therapies) is based on just six RCTs and demonstrates their 'gold standard' status within EBP. Based on these RCTs, NICE recommends that clinicians and managers should: 'Consider offering arts therapies to all people with schizophrenia, particularly for the alleviation of negative symptoms' (205). It goes on to say that most of the RCTs reviewed 'utilised a group-based approach' (204) and later that:

> The intervention should be provided in groups… Arts therapies should combine psychotherapeutic techniques with activity aimed at promoting creative expression which is often unstructured and led by the service user. (205)

The clinical approach should help people to 'express themselves and to organise their experience into a satisfying aesthetic form' and 'to accept and understand feelings that may have emerged during the creative process (including, in some cases, how they have come to have these feelings) at a pace suited to the person.' (op. cit.). The Guideline is sufficiently broad to suit most art therapists' practice, though perhaps not those who work individually with schizophrenic clients or prefer more directed approaches.

However, should art therapy with people diagnosed as schizophrenic be guided solely by evidence from RCTs – based, as NICE acknowledges, on arts therapies groups that averaged twelve sessions, the optimum length of therapy requiring further research – it would not reflect the knowledge base developed by art therapy practitioner researchers over a substantial period of time. Wood and Mahony (Chapters Nine and Ten respectively) describe, like others before them (Greenwood and Layton, 1987; Killick, 1993), 'real world' or naturalistic, practitioner-based research of long-term clinical work with heterogeneous groups of people who have severe and enduring difficulties. There are resonances between these studies, Mahony's research that described a 'sealing over' of distress through sustained and careful art-making and Wood's supportive approach to her clients. All focus on containment and 'therapeutic care' (Papadopoulos, 2002), much as NICE suggests. Generally speaking these approaches contrast, as contributors noted during our discussion, with the short-term, insight-oriented, interactive art therapy group(s) that Jones conducted in the RCT which took a more exploratory approach with a similar client population, and Skaife's research about another, longer-term art therapy group that took a similar, interactive approach with quite different clients.

This begs a series of fundamental questions for art therapy practice and research. Is best practice in art therapy groups associated with the discovery, insight and interpersonal learning that Skaife respondents said they valued? Would the 'slow labour' and participative working of Mahony's group be effective with Skaife's articulate, self-aware group of research participants, or within the time-limited frame of an RCT? In conversation, Jones remarked that the group he describes in his chapter was the best attended of any in the RCT. In his view this was because, at key moments in the group, he 'went for it because it seemed right' and 'got hold of the horror and wouldn't let it go away.' What was important was the art therapist's ability to be in the 'here and now' with the clients, not the use of a particular treatment approach deemed useful with a client population. Thus, is effectiveness associated with different ways of working or is it linked to the therapeutic relationship and hence to the people involved, no matter the clinical approach? Is it not so much about *what* works with whom as about *who* works with whom?

The Role of Art

And what of the role and function of art in art therapy's effectiveness? Both Wood's and Mahony's research suggests that making art was especially helpful to their clients' ability to contain and manage distress. Mahony's focus was on clients' self-initiated, sustained and complex art-making and how their experience of the group related to their lives outside. Discussion had not engaged with affect-laden interpretation and analysis of the imagery linked to clients' problems. In conversation she explained that her research had discovered that clients had been able to explore their difficulties at a deep level through their art in ways that may not have been conscious. The emergence and containment of powerful material through art-making in an art therapy group *might* therefore be effective in and of itself.

There are interesting resonances between this and other research findings that support the effectiveness of art-making per se in art therapy with clients who have serious mental health problems. For example, Green et al.'s clients reported during their RCT that the art-making process was the most helpful aspect of the group (1987); Schindler and Pletnick's single case design (2006) demonstrated a successful combination of social and interpersonal skills training and focus on art-making during twelve weeks of individual and group art therapy; and Greenwood et al. (2007) evidenced the clinical and cost-effectiveness of long-term, individual art therapy with a client who had not previously responded to other forms of psychological and medical intervention. And, although a laboratory experiment with participants who did not have mental health problems, Bell and Robbins's RCT (2007) demonstrated significant reductions in negative mood and anxiety as a direct consequence of making art. They suggest that this finding supports 'one of the fundamental tenets of art therapy: the idea that the production of art has general mood enhancing properties' (73).

Of course, such research on the role, function and the changing nature of the art in art therapy does not address the effects of the relationship between client and art therapist on the effectiveness of therapy but it does begin to unpack art therapy's active ingredients. However, and as contributors to Part Three of this book discussed, a lack of conversation about artworks' meaning could impede the interpersonal learning that emerged as the most important factor for Skaife's respondents. In this group art-making had allowed a 'letting go' which enabled thoughts and feelings to be brought into the group and to be visually explored before being spoken about. However in this group too it seemed to the researcher that deep, existential issues had remained unspoken but been explored visually in clients' artworks. This relates to the compromise and creative tension between art and conversation in art therapy groups that Skaife researched and to what authors agreed was the paradoxical request that art therapists make to all their clients, regardless of diagnosis: that they make art when in the midst of distressing circumstances. We also agreed that it was crucial that practitioners did not allow making art to be diminished in the face of other, pressing matters. Why is this so important? Because the materiality of art enables an awareness of being a person who is alive and engaged with life. It also allows a sense of place through a real, physical engagement with the world and through the 'labour' involved in making.

Polarities and Policy

This led us to explore Mahony's discussion of the sustained art-making that evolved in her group which contrasted with the diagrammatic 'mapping' of issues that Skaife described and Wood's analysis of art therapy's history in relation to its social and political contexts. We discussed psychoanalytic thinking about class and poverty (see Layton et al., 2006; Ryan, 2009) and how this is positioned in art therapy in relation to the differences between art-based and verbal, analytic approaches that we had been thinking about. In her chapter Wood proposes that art therapy is integrating the different practices that evolved during the profession's history. However, given contributors' discussions about the varying practices they had researched, perhaps intra-professional differences are in danger of being polarised as schools of thought struggle for dominance in the competitive, evidence-based healthcare marketplace. The 'slow labour' of Mahony's textiles and ceramics work suits long-term clinical work but does not sit easily with the 'swift labour' currently required in the NHS. Perhaps what Skaife's research teaches us is that tensions and dilemmas (in art therapy groups of all kinds, including groups of practitioners and researchers) are ever-present and can be creative and productive.

An interest in psychosocial approaches to mental health care is where these and other practitioner researchers come together. We agreed that the descriptions of clients' deprivation and poverty by Jones and Wood were a vital contribution to Part Three of this book. They gave rise to interesting conversation between us about the impact of domiciliary visits on the practitioner researcher, how hard it is to 'stay neutral' in the face of such deprivation and despair and how such interactions shift the power relationship between client and art therapist when the relationship moves outside the office or the studio. We discussed how practitioners relate to clients living in the community and agreed that home visits 'levelled things up' and were useful because they enabled power relations to be addressed at the beginning of therapy. As Jones described in his chapter, an unlooked for outcome of the RCT was an increase in the participation of schizophrenic clients from black and ethnic minorities, thanks to the assertive outreach required to achieve the necessary numbers in the trial. This suggests, as Jones proposed in his chapter, that art therapy services might benefit from more taking more assertive approaches to outreach.

This can be usefully discussed in the context of current policy that acknowledges that the prevention and treatment of mental health problems is not the sole responsibility of the NHS. *New Horizons* (DH, 2009) articulates a framework for multi-agency provision that moves from the treatment and management of mental health problems to their prevention and the promotion of emotional wellbeing in a cross-sectoral way. This describes a psychosocial approach to the multi-faceted difficulties that clients face which are woven together in a complex manner: poverty, education, crime and mental health interact and reinforce one another and require a shift in focus away from the narrow confines of diagnosis and symptoms – notions of 'wellbeing' and attention to the social context do not always sit comfortably with the medical model of psychiatry and the prevailing ethos of EBP orthodoxy. The kinds of evidence required will therefore change. This paradigm shift in mental health care gives art therapists an opportunity to build on the work of these practitioner researchers and do research about the range of art therapy practices encountered in all sectors and to do so using a variety of research methodologies. It *is* possible for art therapists to engage with research as part of their clinical practice, and to generate interesting, innovative and important research that makes a real contribution to art therapy's developing evidence base.

References

E. Adamson, *Art as Healing* (London: Conventure Ltd, 1984).

E. Adelson, and S. Fraiberg, 'Self-Representation in Language and Play: Observations of Blind Children', *The Psychoanalytic Quarterly*, 42 (1973), 539–62.

F. Aldridge, 'Chocolate or Shit', *Inscape: Journal of the British Association of Art Therapists*, 3 (1998), 2–9.

P. Allen, *Art is a Way of Knowing* (Boston, MA: Shambhalla, 1995).

L. Althusser, *Lenin and Philosophy and Other Essays*, translated: B. Brewster (New York: Monthly Review Press, 2001).

A. Alvarez, *Live Company: Psychoanalytic Psychotherapy with Autistic, Borderline, Deprived and Abused Children* (London and New York: Routledge, 1992).

N. Andreason, 'The Scale for the Assessment of Negative Symptoms (SANS): Conceptual and Theoretical Foundations', *British Journal of Psychiatry*, 155 (1989), 49–52.

D. Anzieu, *The Skin Ego* (New Haven and London: Yale University Press, 1989).

E. Ashby, 'See How They Run. A Survey of Art Therapists Working With People Who Have Severe Learning Disabilities and Challenging Behaviour', MRes thesis, Goldsmiths, University of London (2004).

D. Atkinson, *Art in Education: Identity and Practice* (Dordrecht and London: Kluwer Academic Publishers, 2002).

J. Austin, *How to do Things with Words* (Oxford: Oxford University Press, 1962).

A. Aviles, T. Anderson, and R. Davila, 'Child and Adolescent Social and Emotional Development within the Context of a School', *Child and Adolescent Mental Health*, 11 (2006), 32–9.

C. Bagley and B. Cancienne, *Dancing the Data* (New York: Peter Lang, 2002).

B. Ball, 'Moments of Change in the Art Therapy Process', *Arts in Psychotherapy*, 29 (2002), 79–92.

M. Banks, *Visual Methods in Social Research* (London: Sage Publications Ltd, 2001).

P. Barham, *Closing the Asylum* (Harmondsworth: Penguin Books, 1992).

M. Baxandall, *Patterns of Intention. On the Historical Explanation of Pictures* (New Haven and London: Yale University Press, 1985).

M. Baxandall, 'The Language of Art Criticism' in S. Kemal and I. Gaskell, eds, *The Language of Art History* (Cambridge: Cambridge University Press, 1991).

C. Bazerman, *Shaping Written Knowledge: The Genre and Activity of the Experimental Article in Science* (Madison, WI: University of Wisconsin Press, 1988).

C. Bell and S. Robbins, 'Effect of Art Production on Negative Mood: a Randomized Controlled Trial', *Art Therapy. Journal of the American Art Therapy Association*, 24 (2007), 71–5.

J. Berger, *Ways of Seeing* (Harmondsworth: Penguin Books Ltd, 1972).

D. Betts, 'Art Therapy Assessments and Rating Instruments: Do They Measure up?' *The Arts in Psychotherapy*, 33 (2006), 422–34.

E. Bick, 'The Experience of the Skin in Early Object Relations', *International Journal of Psychoanalysis*, 49 (1968), 484.

H. Biemans, 'Video Home Training: Theory Method and Organisation of SPIN' in J. Kool, ed, *Innovative Institutions* (Ryswijk, Netherlands: Ministry of Welfare Health and Culture, 1990).

W. Bion, *Learning from Experience* (London: Hogarth Press, 1962).

W. Bion, *Attention and Interpretation* (London: Tavistock Publications, 1970).

W. Bion, *Second Thoughts* (London: Karnac, 1990).

K. Borchers, 'Do Gains Made in Group Art Therapy Persist? A Study with Aftercare Clients', *American Journal of Art Therapy*, 23 (1989), 89–91.

T. Boronska, 'Art Therapy with Two Sibling Groups Using an Attachment Framework', *Inscape: Journal of the British Association of Art Therapists*, 1 (2000), 2–10.

C. Bowen, and M. Rosal, 'The Use of Art Therapy to Reduce the Maladaptive Behaviours of a Mentally Retarded Adult', *Arts in Psychotherapy*, 16 (1989), 211–18.

J. Bowlby, *Child Care and the Growth of Love* (London: Pelican Books, 1953).

J. Bowlby, *Attachment and Loss, Volume 1: Attachment* (New York: Basic Books, 1969).

J. Bowlby, *Attachment and Loss, Volume 2: Separation, Anxiety and Loss* (New York, London: Hogarth, 1973).

J. Bowlby, *Attachment and Loss, Volume 3: Loss, Sadness and Depression* (New York, London: Hogarth, 1980).

J. Bowlby, *A Secure Base: Clinical Applications of Attachment Theory* (London: Routledge, 1988).

A. Bragge and P. Fenner, 'The Emergence of the "Interactive Square" as an Approach to Art Therapy with Children of the Autistic Spectrum', *International Journal of Art Therapy: Inscape*, 14 (2009), 17–28.

T. Brazelton, B. Koslowski and M. Main, 'The Origins of Reciprocity: The Early Mother-Infant Interaction' in M. Lewis, M. and L. Rosenblum, eds, *The Effect of the Infant on Care* (New York, 1974).

D. Brisset, and C. Edgley, eds, *Life As Theater* (New York: Aldine de Gruyter, 1990).

British Association of Art Therapists, *Newsbriefing*, Spring (2009), 4.

R. Britton, 'The Oedipal Situation and the Depressive Position' in R. Anderson, ed., *Clinical Lectures on Klein and Bion* (London and New York: Routledge, 1996).

C. Brooker, I. Falloon, A. Butterworth, D. Goldberg, V. Graham-Hole and V. Hillier, 'The Outcome of Training Community Psychiatric Nurses to Deliver Psychosocial Interventions', *British Journal of Psychiatry*, 160 (1994), 836–44.

J. Brooker, M. Cullum, A. Gilroy, B. McCombe, J. Mahony, K. Ringrose, D. Russell, L. Smart, B. von Zweigbergk and J. Waldman, *The Use of Artwork in Art Psychotherapy with People Prone to Psychotic States: A Clinical Practice Guideline* (London: Goldsmiths, University of London, 2007). Available at http://cprints gro.gold.ac.uk/112/

A. Brown and M. Latimer, 'Between Images and Thoughts: an Art Psychotherapy Group for Sexually Abused Children' in J. Murphy, ed., *Art Therapy with Young Survivors of Sexual Abuse. Lost for Words* (London: Routledge, 2001).

G. Brown and T. Harris, *The Social Origins of Depression: A Study of Psychiatric Disorders in Women* (London: Tavistock Books, 1978).

R. Buckland and J. Murphy, 'Jumping Over it: Group Therapy with Young Girls' in J. Murphy, ed., *Art Therapy with Young Survivors of Sexual Abuse. Lost for Words* (London: Routledge, 2001).

L. Bunt, *Music Therapy: An Art Beyond Words* (London: Routledge, 1994).

M. Bunting, *Willing Slaves: How the Overwork Culture is Ruling our Lives* (London: Harper Collins, 2004).

D. Burlingham, 'Some Notes on the Development of the Blind', *The Psychoanalytic Study of the Child*, 16 (1961), 121–45.

J. Butler, *The Psychic Life of Power: Theories in Subjection* (Stanford, CA: Stanford University Press, 1997).

G. Butterworth, 'The Ontogeny and Phylogeny of Joint Visual Attention' in A. Whiten, ed., *Natural Theories of Mind. Evolution, Development and Stimulation of Everyday Mindreading* (Oxford: Blackwell Publishers, 1992).

A. Byers, 'Beyond Marks. On Working with Elderly People with Severe Memory Loss', *Inscape: Journal of the British Association of Art Therapists*, 1 (1995), 13–18.

J. Cage, *Silence* (London: Marion Boyars, 1978).

J. Campbell, M. Liebmann, F. Brooks, J. Jones and C. Ward, *Art Therapy, Race and Culture* (London and Philadelphia: Jessica Kingsley, 1999).

CAMHS, *CAHMS Review. Children and Young People in Mind: the Final Report of the National CAMHS Review* (2008)

M. Carr and T. Vandiver, 'Effects of Instructional Art Projects on Children's Behavioural Responses and Creativity within an Emergency Shelter', *Art Therapy. Journal of the American Art Therapy Association*, 20 (2003), 157–62.

C. Case, 'Reflections and Shadows: an Exploration of the World of the Gifted Girl' in C. Case and T. Dalley, eds, *Working with Children in Art Therapy* (London: Routledge, 1990).

C. Case, 'Art Therapy in Analysis: Advance/Retreat in the Belly of the Spider', *Inscape: Journal of the British Association of Art Therapists*, 1 (1994), 3–10.

C. Case, 'Our Lady of the Queen: Journeys Around the Maternal Object' in A. Gilroy and G. McNeilly, eds, *The Changing Shape of Art Therapy. New Developments in Theory and Practice* (London and Philadelphia: Jessica Kingsley Ltd, 2000).

C. Case, 'Animation and the Location of Beauty', *Journal of Child Psychotherapy*, 28 (2002), 327–43.

C. Case, *Imagining Animals: Art Therapy and Primitive States of Mind* (London: Routledge, 2005).

C. Case, 'Playing Ball: Oscillations within the Potential Space' in C. Case and T. Dalley, eds, *Art Therapy with Children: From Infancy to Adolescence* (London and New York: Routledge, 2008).

C. Case and T. Dalley, *The Handbook of Art Therapy* (London and New York: Routledge, 1992).

C. Case, and T. Dalley, *The Handbook of Art Therapy*, Second Edition (London and New York: Routledge, Taylor and Francis, 2006).

I. Champernowne, 'Art and Therapy: An Uneasy Partnership', *Inscape: Journal of the British Association of Art Therapists*, 10 (3) (1971), 131–43.

J. Charon, *Symbolic Interactionism. An Introduction, An Interpretation, An Integration* (NJ: Pearson Prentice Hall, 2004).

J. Chassan, *Research Design in Clinical Psychology and Psychiatry* (New York: Wiley, 1979).

R. Chin, M. Chin, P. Palombo, C. Palombo, G. Bannaasch and P, Cross, 'Project Outreach: Building Social Skills through Art and Video', *Arts in Psychotherapy*, 7 (1980), 281–4.

H. Chipp, *Theories of Modern Art: A Source Book by Artists and Critics* (Berkeley: University of California Press, 1968).

C. Christians, 'Ethics and Politics in Qualitative Research' in N. Denzin and Y. Lincoln, eds, *Handbook of Qualitative Research* (Thousand Oaks, London, New Delhi: Sage Publications, 2000).

T. Clark, *The Sight of Death. An Experiment in Art Writing* (New Haven and London: Yale University Press, 2006).

D. Coghlan and T. Brannick, *Doing Action Research in Your Own Organisation* (London: Sage Publications, 2005).

B. Cohen, J. Hammer, and S. Singer, 'The Diagnostic Drawing Series: A Systematic Approach to Art Therapy Evaluation and Research', *The Arts in Psychotherapy*, 15 (1988), 11–21.

M. Cole and S. Scribner, *Minds in Society: The Development of Higher Psychological Processes* (Cambridge, MA, London: Harvard University Press, 1978).

Commission for Social Justice, *Social Justice: Strategies for National Renewal* (Guernsey: Vintage Press, 1994).

M. Cooper, *Counselling in Schools Project: Phase II* (Glasgow: University of Strathclyde, 2006).

J. Corbin and A. Strauss, *Basics of Qualitative Research: Techniques and Procedures for Developing Grounded Theory. Third Edition* (Thousand Oaks, CA: Sage Publications Ltd, 2008).

A. Coren, *A Psychodynamic Approach to Education* (London: Sheldon Press, 1997).

M. Cox, *Children's Drawing* (Harmondsworth: Penguin Books 1992).

K. Cromarty and K. Richards, 'How do Secondary School Counsellors Work with Other Professionals?', *Counselling and Psychotherapy Research*, 9 (2009), 182–6.

A. Curson, 'The Blind Nursery School Child', *The Psychoanalytic Study of the Child*, 34 (1979), 51–83.

T. Dalley 'Art Therapy in Psychiatric Treatment: An Illustrated Case Study', *The Arts in Psychotherapy*, 6 (1979), 257–65.

T. Dalley, 'Assessing the Therapeutic Effects of Art: an Illustrated Case Study', *The Arts in Psychotherapy*, 7 (1980), 11–17.

T. Dalley, 'Images and Integration: Art Therapy in a Multi-Cultural School' in C. Case and T. Dalley, eds, *Working with Children in Art Therapy* (London: Routledge, 1990).

T. Dalley, 'Back to the Future: Thinking about Theoretical Developments in Art Therapy' in A. Gilroy and G. McNeilly, eds, *The Changing Shape of Art Therapy. New Developments in Theory and Practice* (London: Jessica Kingsley, 2000).

C. Daniel-McKeigue, 'Cracking the Ethics Code: What are the Ethical Implications of Designing a Research Study that Relates to Therapeutic Interventions with Children in Individual Play Therapy?', *The Arts in Psychotherapy*, 34 (2007), 238–48.

J. Davis, *Exchange* (Buckingham: Open University Press, 1992).

S. Deco, 'Return to the Open Studio Group: Art Therapy Groups in Acute Psychiatry', in S. Skaife and V. Huet, eds., *Art Psychotherapy Groups* (London: Routledge, 1998).

M. Denscombe, *The Good Research Guide* (Maidenhead: Open University Press, 2003).

Department for Education and Skills, *Every Child Matters* (London: Stationery Office, 2003).

Department for Education and Skills, *Extended Schools: Access to Opportunities and Services for All. A Prospectus* (London: Department for Education and Skills, 2005a).

Department for Education and Skills, *Excellence and Enjoyment: Social and Emotional Aspects of Learning* (London: Department for Education and Skills, 2005b).

Department of Health. *National Service Framework for Children, Young People and Maternity Services: Change for Children – Every Child Matters* (London: Department of Health, 2004).

Department of Health, *Valuing People Now: A New Three-Year Strategy for People with Learning Disabilities* (London: Department of Health, 2008).

Department of Health, *New Horizons. A Shared Vision for Mental Health* (London: Department of Health, 2009).

J. Derrida, '*Limited Inc.*' S. Weber and J. Mehlman (trans), G. Graff, ed. (Evanston: North Western University Press, 1988).

K. Doerner, *Madmen and the Bourgeoisie: A Social History of Insanity and Psychiatry* (translated from the German *Burger Und Irr*, 1969, reprinted Oxford: Blackwell, 1981).

B. Dick, Action Research Thesis: Thesis Resource Paper: You Want to do an Action Research Thesis (date not known), http://www.scu.edu.au/schools/gem/ar/art/artthesis.html

E. Dissanayake, *Art and Intimacy: How the Arts Began* (Seattle, London: University of Washington Press, 2000).

W. Dryden and J. Yankura, *Daring to Be Myself* (Buckingham: Open University Press, 1992).

J. Dubowski, 'An Investigation of the Pre-representational Drawing Activity of Certain Severely Retarded Subjects within an Institution Using Ethological Techniques', PhD thesis, Hertfordshire College of Art and Design (1983).

J. Dubowski, 'Alternative Models for Describing the Development of Children's Graphic Work: some Implications for Art Therapy' in T. Dalley, ed., *Art as Therapy: An Introduction to the Use of Art as a Therapeutic Technique* (London and New York: Tavistock Publications, 1984).

J. Dubowski, 'Stereotyping and Repetitivity in the Art Work of Severely Mentally Handicapped Individuals: A Psychodynamic Approach', in *Conference Proceedings*, Hertfordshire College of Art and Design (1984), 37–40.

J. Dubowski, 'Art versus Language' in C. Case and T. Dalley, eds, *Working with Children in Art Therapy* (London and New York: Routledge, 1990).

J. Dubowski and J. James, 'Arts Therapies with Children with Learning Disabilities' in D. Sandle, ed, *Development and Diversity* (London and New York: Free Association Books, 1998).

J. Dudley, 'Art Psychotherapy and the Use of Psychiatric Diagnosis: Assessment for Art Psychotherapy', *Inscape. The Journal of the British Association of Art Therapists*. 9 (2004), 14– 25.

T. Eagleton, *The Ideology of the Aesthetic* (Oxford: Blackwell, 1990).

L. Eaton, K. Doherty and R. Widrick, 'A Review of Research and Methods used to Establish Art Therapy as an Effective Treatment Method for Traumatized Children', *The Arts in Psychotherapy*, 34 (2007), 256–62.

B. Edwards, *Drawing on the Artist Within* (Great Britain: William Collins, 1997).

D. Edwards, 'Evaluation in Art Therapy' in D. Milne, ed, *Evaluating Mental Health Practice: Methods and Applications* (London: Groom Helm, 1987).

D. Edwards, 'The Role of the Case Study in Art Therapy Research', *Inscape: Journal of the British Association of Art Therapists*, 4 (1999), 2–9.

D. Edwards, *Art Therapy* (London: Sage Publications Ltd, 2004).

M. Edwards, 'Art Therapy Now', *Inscape: Journal of the British Association of Art Therapists*, 5 (1981), 18–21.

A. Ehrenzweig, *The Hidden Order of Art* (London: Granada Publishing, 1967).

J. Elkins, *Pictures and Tears. A History of People who have Cried in Front of Paintings* (New York and London, Routledge, 2001).

D. Elliot, *The Inner Eye* (Oxford: Catalogue Museum of Modern Art, 1978).

R. Elliott, 'Hermeneutic Single Case Efficacy Design', *Psychotherapy Research*, 12 (2002), 1–21.

J. Ellwood, *Psychosis: Understanding and Treatment* (London: Jessica Kingsley, 1995).

M. Essex, K. Frostig and J. Hertz, 'In the Service of Children: Art and Expressive Therapies in Public Schools', *Art Therapy. Journal of the American Art Therapy Association*, 23 (2006), 59–65.

K. Evans, 'Shaping Experience and Sharing Meaning: Art Therapy for Children with Autism', *Inscape: Journal of the British Association of Art Therapists*, 3 (1998), 17–25.

K. Evans and J. Dubowski *Art Therapy with Children on the Autistic Spectrum. Beyond Words* (London: Jessica Kingsley Publications, 2001).

B. Falk, 'A Narrowed Sense of Space. An Art Therapy Group with Young Alzheimer's Sufferers' in D. Waller, ed, *Arts Therapies and Progressive Illness: Nameless Dread* (Sussex and New York: Brunner-Routledge, 2002).

E. Ferrance, *Action Research* (Providence: Brown University, 2000).

M. Foucault, *Madness and Civilization: A History of Insanity in the Age of Reason* (London: Tavistock Books, 1967, reprinted London: Routledge, 1989).

M. Foucault, *Essential works of Foucault 1954–1984. Volume 3: Power* (Harmondsworth: Penguin Books, 1984).

K. Foulds, 'Ruth', Case Study, Postgraduate Diploma in Advanced Training in Art Psychotherapy, Goldsmiths, University of London (1998).

S. Foulkes and E. Anthony, *Group Psychotherapy: The Psychoanalytic Approach* (Harmondsworth: Penguin, 1965).

L. Fox, 'Lost in Space: The Relevance of Art Therapy with Clients who have Autism or Autistic Features' in M. Rees, ed, *Drawing on Difference. Art Therapy with People who have Learning Difficulties* (London and New York: Routledge, 1998).

S. Fraiberg, *Clinical Studies in Infant Mental Health* (London: Tavistock, 1980).

S. Freud, *The Ego and the Id. Standard Edition, Volume 19* (London: Hogarth Press, 1923).

S. Freud and J. Breuer, *Studies in Hysteria* (London: Penguin, 1991).

L. Gantt, 'The Case for Formal Art Therapy Assessments', *Art Therapy: Journal of the American Art Therapy Association*, 21 (2004), 18–29.

K. Gergen, 'Who Speaks and Who Replies in Human Science Scholarship', *History of the Human Sciences*, 10 (1997), 151–73.

A. Gilroy, 'On Occasionally Being Able to Paint', *Inscape: Journal of the British Association of Art Therapists*, Spring (1989), 2–9.

A. Gilroy, 'Research in Art Therapy' in D. Waller and A. Gilroy, eds, *Art Therapy: a Handbook* (Buckingham, Philadelphia: Open University Press, 1992).

A. Gilroy, 'Changes in Art Therapy Groups' in A. Gilroy and C. Lee, eds, *Art and Music. Therapy and Research* (London: Routledge, 1995).

A. Gilroy, 'Our Own Kind of Evidence' in *Inscape: Journal of the British Association of Art Therapists*, Winter (1996), 52–60.

A. Gilroy, *Art Therapy, Research and Evidence-Based Practice* (London: Sage Publications Ltd, 2006).

A. Gilroy, 'Taking a Long Look at Art. Reflections on the Context of Production and Consumption of Art in Art Therapy and Allied Organisational Settings', *International Journal of Art and Design Education*, 27 (2008), 251–63. Also available at http://eprints-gro.gold.ac.uk/113/

A. Gilroy and C. Lee, eds, *Art and Music. Therapy and Research* (London: Routledge, 1995).

E. Goffman, *Interaction Ritual. Essays in Face-to-Face Behaviour* (New Brunswick, New Jersey: Transaction Publishers, 2005).

A. Goldsmith, 'Substance and Structure in the Art Therapeutic Process – Working with Mental Handicap', *Inscape: Journal of the British Association of Art Therapists*, Summer (1986), 18–22.

I. Got and S-T. Cheng, 'The Effects of Art Facilitation on the Social Functioning of People with Developmental Disability', *Art Therapy. Journal of the American Art Therapy Association*, 25 (2008), 32–7.

C. Gottlieb, *Beyond Modern Art* (New York: Dutton and Co., 1976).

B. Green, 'Group Art Therapy as an Adjunct to Treatment for Chronic Outpatients', *Hospital and Community Psychiatry*, 38 (1987), 988–91.

B. Green, C. Wehling and G. Talsky, 'Group Art Therapy as an Adjunct to Treatment for Chronic Outclients', *Hospital and Community Psychiatry*, 38 (1987), 988–91.

H. Green, A. McGinnity, H. Meltzer, T. Ford and R. Goodman, *Mental Health of Children and Young People in Great Britain* (London: TSO, 2005).

D. Greenwood and D. Loewenthal, 'The Use of "Case Study" in Psychotherapeutic Research and Education', *Psychoanalytic Psychotherapy*, 19 (2005), 35–47.

H. Greenwood, 'Cracked Pots', *Inscape: Journal of the British Association of Art Therapists*, 1 (1994), 11–14.

H. Greenwood, 'Psychosis and the Maturing Ego' in K. Killick and J. Schaverien, eds., *Art, Psychotherapy and Psychosis* (London: Routledge, 1997).

H. Greenwood and G. Layton, 'An Out-Patient Art Therapy Group', *Inscape: Journal of the British Association of Art Therapists*, Summer (1987), 12–19.

H. Greenwood and G. Layton 'Taking the Piss', *Inscape. Journal of the British Association of Art Therapists*, Winter (1991), 7–14.

H. Greenwood, C. Leach, M. Lucock and R. Noble, 'The Process of Long-Term Art Therapy: a Case Study Combining Artwork and Clinical Outcome', *Psychotherapy Research*, 17 (2007), 588–99.

D. Grodner, D. Braff, D. Janowsky and P. Clopton, 'Efficacy of Art/Movement Therapy in Elevating Mood', *Arts in Psychotherapy*, 9 (1982), 217–25.

I. Grubrich-Simitis, *Early Freud and Late Freud* (London: Routledge, 1997).

S. Gudmundsdottir, 'The Teller, The Tale and The One Being Told: The Narrative Nature of The Research Interview', *Curriculum Inquiry*, 26 (1996), 293–306.

M. Haeseler, 'Should Art Therapists Create Artwork Alongside Their Clients?', *American Journal of Art Therapy*, 27(1989), 70–9.

P. Hall, Exploring the Mother-Child Relationship: an Art Therapy Workshop, MA thesis, University of Hertfordshire (1991).

P. Hall, 'Painting Together: An Art Therapy Approach to Mother-Infant Relationships' in C. Case and T. Dalley, eds, *Art Therapy with Children* (London, New York: Routledge, 2008).

J. Hallam, 'Regression and Ego Integration in Art Therapy with Mentally Handicapped People', in *Conference Proceedings*, Hertfordshire College of Art and Design (1984), 8–15.

D. Hardy, 'Creating Through Loss: An Examination of How Art Therapists Sustain Their Practice in Palliative Care', *Inscape: Journal of the British Association of Art Therapists*, 6 (2001), 23–31.

G. Harrison, D. Owens, A. Holton, D. Neilson and D. Boot, 'A Prospective Study of Severe Mental Disorder in Afro-Caribbean Patients', *Psychological Medicine*, 18 (1988), 643–58.

T. Harrod, *The Crafts in Britain in the Twentieth Century* (New Haven: Yale University Press, 1999).

D. Henley, 'Facilitating the Development of Object Relations through the Use of Clay in Art Therapy', *American Journal of Art Therapy*, 29 (1991), 69–76.

D. Henley, 'Art Therapy in a Socialization Program for Children with Attention Deficit Hyperactivity Disorder', *Art Therapy. Journal of the American Art Therapy Association*, 37 (1998), 2–12.

D. Henley, 'Facilitating Socialization within a Therapeutic Camp Setting for Children with Attention Deficits Utilizing the Expressive Therapies', *Art Therapy. Journal of the American Art Therapy Association*, 38 (1999), 40–50.

D. Henley, 'Annihilation Anxiety and Fantasy in the Art of Children with Asperger's Syndrome and Others on the Autistic Spectrum', *Art Therapy. Journal of the American Art Therapy Association*, 39 (2001), 113–21.

D. Henley, *Clayworks in Art Therapy: Playing the Sacred Circle* (London: Jessica Kingsley, 2002).

D. Henley, 'Attachment Disorders in Post-Institutionalized Adopted Children: Art Therapy Approaches to Reactivity and Detachment', *Arts in Psychotherapy*. 32 (2005), 29–46.

J. Henriques, W. Hollway, C. Urwin, C. Venn, and V. Walkerdine, *Changing the Subject. Psychology, Social Regulation and Subjectivity* (London: Methuen and Co. Ltd, 1984. Reissued London: Routledge, 1998).

U. Herrmann, 'A Trojan Horse of Clay. Art Therapy in a Residential School for the Blind', *Arts in Psychotherapy*, 22 (1995), 229–34.

U. Herrmann, 'Blick und Blindheit in der Kunsttherapie', *Kunst & Therapie*, 1 (2006), 42–54.

U. Herrmann, 'Der Blick der Tastenden Hand' in *Verband der Bilden- u. Sehbehindertenpaedagogen u. -paedagoginnen e. V.* eds, *Teilhabe Gestalten* (Würzburg: Edition Bentheim, 2009a).

U. Herrmann, 'Braucht das Selbst ein Bild?' in P. Sinapius, M. Wendlandt-Baumeister, A. Niemann and R. Bolle, eds, *Wissenschaftliche Grundlagen der Kunsttherapie* (Zürich: Peter Lang, 2009b).

R. Higgins, *Approaches to Case Study* (London: Jessica Kingsley, 1993).

R. Hilliard, 'Single Case Methodology in Psychotherapy Process and Outcome Research', *Journal of Consulting and Clinical Psychology*, 61 (1993), 373–80.

P. Hobson, *The Cradle of Thought: Exploring the Origins of Thinking* (London: MacMillan, 2002).

S. Hogan, *Healing Arts: The History of Art Therapy* (London: Jessica Kingsley, 2001).

L. Horowitz, S. Rosenberg, B. Baer, G. Ureno and G. Villasenor, 'Inventory of Interpersonal Problems: Psychometric Properties and Clinical Applications', *Journal of Consulting and Clinical Psychology*, 56 (1998), 885–92.

R. Holtom, 'Measuring Changes Attributable to Art Therapy', *Inscape: Journal of the British Association of Art Therapists*, 15 (1977), 34–6.

H. Hosea, 'The Brush's Footmarks: Parents and Infants Paint Together in a Small Community Art Therapy Group', *International Journal of Art Therapy: Inscape*, 11 (2006), 69–78.

V. Huet, 'Challenging Professional Confidence: Arts Therapies and Psychiatric Rehabilitation', *Inscape: Journal of the British Association of Art Therapists*, 2 (1997), 14–19.

R. Hughes, 'Transitional Phenomena and the Potential Space in Art Therapy with Mentally Handicapped People', *Inscape: Journal of the British Association of Art Therapists*, Summer (1988), 4–8.

M. Hussain-Gamble, B. Leese, K. Atkin, J. Brown, S. Mason and P. Tovey, 'Involving South Asian Patients in Clinical Trials', *Health Technology Assessment*, 8 (2004).

International New Arrivals Partnership, *Out of the Lion's Mouth: A Report on the Work of the Emotional and Trauma Support Team* (Manchester: Children's Fund, 2007).

R. Irwin and A. de Cosson, *a/r/tography. Rendering Self through Arts-Based Living Inquiry* (Vancouver: Pacific Educational Press, 2004).

J. Isserow, 'Looking Together: Joint Attention in Art Therapy', *International Journal of Art Therapy: Inscape*, 13 (2008), 34–42.

M. Jackson, 'Learning to Think about Schizoid Thinking' in J. Ellwood, ed., *Psychosis: Understanding and Treatment* (London: Jessica Kingsley Publishing, 1995).

F. Jameson, *The Political Unconscious: Narrative as a Socially Symbolic Act* (London: Methuen, 1981).

A. Jaworski, and N. Coupland, eds, *The Discourse Reader* (London and New York: Routledge, 1999).

K. Jones, 'Review: 'What Works for Whom': a Critical Review of Psychotherapy Research', *Inscape: Journal of the British Association of Art Therapists*, 3 (1998), 75–7.

D. Kalmanowitz and B. Lloyd, *The Portable Studio. Art Therapy and Political Conflict: Initiatives in former Yugoslavia and South Africa* (London: Health Education Authority, 1997).

R. Karr-Morse and M. Wiley, *Ghosts from the Nursery* (New York: The Atlantic Monthly Press, 1997).

R. Kellogg, *Analysing Children's Art* (California: Mayfield Publishing Company, 1970).

K. Killick, 'Working with Psychotic Processes in Art Therapy', *Psychoanalytic Psychotherapy*, 7 (1993), 25–36.

K. Killick, 'The Art Room as Container in Analytical Art Psychotherapy' in A. Gilroy and G. McNeilly, eds, *The Changing Shape of Art Therapy* (London and Philadelphia: Jessica Kingsley, 2000).

K. Killick and H. Greenwood, 'Research in Art Therapy with People who have Psychotic Illnesses' in A. Gilroy and C. Lee, eds, *Art and Music: Therapy and Research* (London and New York: Routledge, 1995).

K. Killick and J. Schavarien, eds, *Art, Psychotherapy and Psychosis* (London: Routledge, 1997).

K. Kolvin, G. Garside, A.Nicol, A. MacMillan, E. Wolstenholme and I. Leitch, *Help Starts Here* (London: Tavistock, 1982).

T. Kornreich and B. Schimmel, 'The World is Attacked by Great Big Snowflakes: Art Therapy with an Autistic Boy', *American Journal of Art Therapy*, 29 (1991) 77–84.

E. Kramer, *Art as Therapy with Children* (New York: Schocken Books, 1971).

E. Kramer, *Childhood and Art Therapy* (New York: Schocken Books, 1979).

E. Kramer, *Art as Therapy. Collected Papers* (London/Philadelphia: Jessica Kingsley, 2001).

S. Kut Rosenfeld and M. Sprince, 'Some Thoughts on the Technical Handling of Borderline Children', *Psychoanalytic Study of the Child*, 20 (1965), 495–517.

E. Kuczaj, 'Learning to Say "Goodbye": Loss and Bereavement in Learning Difficulties and the Role of Art Therapy' in M. Rees, ed, *Drawing on Difference. Art Therapy with People who have Learning Difficulties* (London: Routledge, 1998).

T. Kuhn, *The Structure of Scientific Revolutions* (Chicago and London: University of Chicago Press, 1962, reprinted 1970).

P. Kymiss, E. Christenson, A. Swanson and P. Orlowski, 'Group Treatment of Adolescent Inpatients: a Pilot Study using a Structured Art Therapy Approach', *Journal of Child and Adolescent Group Therapy*, 6 (1996), 45–52.

J. Lacan, 'The Mirror Stage as Formation of the Function of the I as Revealed in Psychoanalytic Experience' in J. Lacan, *Ecrits: A Selection* (London: Tavistock/Routledge, 1949/1977).

R. Laing, *The Divided Self* (London: Tavistock Books, 1959, reprinted Harmondsworth: Penguin, 1965).

R. Lanham, 'The Life and Soul of the Image', *Inscape: Journal of the British Association of Art Therapists*, 3 (1998), 48–55.

M. Laufer, 'The Body Image, the Function of Masturbation and Adolescence. Problems of Ownership of the Body', The *Psychoanalytic Study of the Child*, XXIII (1968), 114–37.

L. Layton, N. Hollander and S. Gutwill, *Psychoanalysis, Class and Politics* (London and New York: Routledge, 2006).

R. Lee, C. Tiley and J. White, 'The Place2Be: Measuring the Effectiveness of a Primary School-Based Therapeutic Intervention in England and Scotland', *Counselling and Psychotherapy Research*, 9 (2009), 151–59.

M. Levens, *Eating Disorders and Magical Control of the Body* (London: Routledge, 1995).

R. Lev-Weisel and N. Zeevi, 'The Relationship between Mothers and Children with Down Syndrome as Reflected in Drawings', *Art Therapy. Journal of the American Art Therapy Association*, 24 (2007), 134–37.

M. Liebmann, *Art Therapy in Practice* (London and Bristol, Pennsylvania: Jessica Kingsley, 1990).

M. Lindsay, 'The Role of Transference in Art Therapy with a Severely Mentally Handicapped Child' in *Conference Proceedings*, Hertfordshire College of Art and Design (1984), 55–9.

M. Lister and L. Wells, 'Cultural Studies as an Approach to Analysing the Visual' in T. Van Leeuwen and C. Jewitt, eds, *Handbook of Visual Analysis* (London, Thousand Oaks, New Delhi: Sage Publications, 2001).

H. Lomas and P. Hallas, 'It's a Mystery. Accounts of an Art Therapy Group for People with Learning Difficulties' in M. Rees, ed, *Drawing on Difference: Art Therapy with People who have Learning Difficulties* (London: Routledge, 1998).

V. Lowenfeld, *The Nature of Creative Activity* (London: Routledge and Kegan Paul, 1939).

V. Löwenfeld and L. Münz, *Plastische Arbeiten Blinder* (Brünn: Rudolf M. Lohrer, 1934).

E. Lyddiatt, *Spontaneous Painting and Modelling* (New York: St Martin's Press, 1972).

F. Lyshak-Stelzer, P. Singer, P. St. John and C. Chemtob, 'Art Therapy for Adolescents with Postraumatic Stress Disorder Symptoms: A Pilot Study', *Art Therapy. Journal of the American Art Therapy Association*, 24 (2007), 163–9.

K. Mackenzie, D. Chisholm and G. Murray, 'Working with Sex Offenders who Have a Learning Disability', *Inscape: Journal of the British Association of Art Therapists*, 5 (2000), 62–9.

D. Maclagan, 'Fantasy and the Aesthetic: Have they Become the Uninvited Guests at Art Therapy's Feast?', *Arts in Psychotherapy*, 22 (1995), 217–21.

D. Maclagan, 'Anorexia: the Struggle with Incarnation and the Negative Sublime' in D. Sandle, ed, *Development and Diversity. New Applications in Art Therapy* (London and New York: Free Association Books Ltd, 1998).

D. Maclagan, *Psychological Aesthetics* (London and Philadelphia: Jessica Kingsley Ltd, 2001).

D. Maclagan, 'Re-imagining Art Therapy', *International Journal of Art Therapy: Inscape*, 10 (2005), 23–30.

J. Mahony 'Three Commentaries: Looking Experiences at Three Exhibitions', *Inscape: Journal of the British Association of Art Therapists*, 6 (2001), 51–62.

J. Mahony, ''Reunion of Broken Parts' (Arabic al-jabr). A Therapist's Personal Art Practice and its Relationship to an NHS Outpatient Art Psychotherapy Group: an Exploration through Visual Arts and Crafts Practice', PhD thesis, Goldsmiths, University of London, 2010).

M. Mauss, *The Gift. The Form and Reason for Exchange in Archaic Societies*, trans. W. Halls (London and New York: Routledge, 1990)

S. McClelland, Ann and Pat, 'The Art of Science with Clients. Beginning Collaborative Inquiry in Process Work, Art Therapy and Acute States' in H. Payne, ed, *One River, Many Currents. Handbook of Inquiry in the Arts Therapies* (London: Jessica Kingsley, 1993).

S.McDonough, 'Interaction Guidance: Understanding and Treating Early Infant Caregiver Relationship Disorders' in C. Zeanah, ed, *The Handbook of Infant Mental Health* (New York: Guilford Press, 1993).

I. McGregor, 'Unusual Drawing Development in Children: What Does it Reveal About Children's Art?' in C. Case and T. Dalley, eds, *Working with Children in Art Therapy* (London: Routledge, 1992).

J. McLeod, *Practitioner Research in Counselling* (London: Sage Publications Ltd, 1999).

J. McLeod, *Qualitative Research in Counselling and Psychotherapy* (London: Sage Publications, 2001).

J. McLeod, *Doing Counselling Research* (London: Sage Publications Ltd, 2004).

G. McNeilly, 'Group-Analytic Art Therapy', *Group Analysis*, 3 (1984), 204–10.

G. McNeilly, 'Directive and Non-Directive Approaches in Art Therapy', *Inscape: Journal of the British Association Art Therapists*, December (1984), 7–12.

G. McNeilly, 'Further Contributions to Group Analytic Art Therapy', *Inscape: Journal of the British Association of Art Therapists*, Summer (1987), 8–11.

G. McNeilly, *Group Analytic Art Therapy* (London and Philadelphia: Jessica Kingsley Publishers, 2006).

S. McNiff, *Art as Medicine* (London: Shambala, 1992).

S. McNiff, 'Art Therapy: A Spectrum of Partnerships', *The Arts in Psychotherapy*, 24 (1997), 37–44.

S. McNiff, *Art-Based Research* (London: Jessica Kingsley Ltd, 1998).

J. Males, 'Art Therapy Investigations and Implications', *Inscape: Journal of the British Association of Art Therapists*, 4 (1980), 13–15.

M. Marrone, *Attachment and Interaction* (London, Philadelphia: Jessica Kingsley, 1998).

N. Martin, 'Assessing Portrait Drawings Created by Children and Adolescents with Autistic Spectrum Disorder', *Art Therapy. Journal of the American Art Therapy Association*, 25 (2008), 15–23.

J. Matthews, 'Children's Early Representations', *Inscape: Journal of the British Association of Art Therapists*, Winter (1986), 12–17.

J. Matthews, 'How Young Children Give Meaning to Drawing' in A. Gilroy and T. Dalley, eds, *Pictures at an Exhibition, Selected Essays in Art and Art Therapy* (London, New York: Tavistock Routledge, 1989).

J. Matthews, *The Art of Childhood and Adolescence: The Construction of Meaning* (Padstow: Falmer Press, 1999).

J. Matthews, *Drawing and Painting: Children and Visual Representation* (London and California: Paul Chapman Publishing, 2003).

D. Mearns and B. Thorne, *Person-Centred Counselling in Action* (London: Sage Publications, 1988).

D. Meltzer, *Explorations in Autism. A Psychoanalytical Study* (Strath Tay: Clunie, 1975).

J. Meyerowitz-Katz, An Exploration of Art Therapy with Children Under Five. MA thesis, Goldsmiths, University of London (1999).

J. Meyerowitz-Katz, 'Art Materials and Processes – A Place of Meeting: Art Psychotherapy with a Four-Year-Old Boy', *Inscape: Journal of the British Association of Art Therapists*, 8 (2003), 60–9.

M. Milton, 'Evidence-Based Practice: Issues for Psychotherapy', *Psychoanalytic Psychotherapy*, 16 (2002), 160–72.

W. Mitchell, *Picture Theory* (Chicago and London: The University of Chicago Press, 1994).

P. Mollon, *Releasing the Self: the Healing Power of Heinz Kohut* (London and Philadpelphia: Whurr Publishers, 2001).

T. Molloy, 'Art Therapy and Psychiatric Rehabilitation, Harmonious Partnership or Philosophical Collision?' in K. Killick and J. Schaverien, eds, *Art, Psychotherapy and Psychosis* (London and New York: Routledge, 1997).

C. Moon, 'Art Therapy: Creating the Space we Live in', *Arts in Psychotherapy*, 24 (1997), 45–9.

D. Moriya, 'Ethical Issues in School Art Therapy', *Art Therapy. Journal of the American Art Therapy Association*, 23 (2006), 59–65.
C. Moustakas, *Heuristic Research: Design, Methodology, and Applications* (Newbury Park, CA: Sage Publications, 1990).
L. Mulvey, 'Visual Pleasure and Narrative Cinema', *Screen*, 16 (1975), 6–18.
J. Murphy, ed, *Art Therapy with Young Survivors of Sexual Abuse* (London: Brunner-Routledge, 2001).
National Academy of Science (NAS), 'Unravelling the Enigma of Vitamin D: Closing in on Rickets' (Washington: NAS, 2000).
National Institute for Health and Clinical Excellence, *Schizophrenia. Core Interventions in the Treatment and Management of Schizophrenia in Adults in Primary and Secondary Care (Update)* (London: NICE, 2009).
National Institute for Health and Clinical Excellence, *Promoting Children's Social and Emotional Wellbeing in Primary Education* (London: National Institute of Clinical Excellence, 2008).
National Institute for Health and Clinical Excellence, *Promoting Children's Social and Emotional Wellbeing in Secondary Education* (London: National Institute of Clinical Excellence, 2009).
E. Nissimov-Nahum, 'A Model for Art Therapy in Educational Settings with Children who Behave Aggressively', *Arts in Psychotherapy*, 35 (2008), 341–8.
F. O'Brien, 'Bella and the White Water Rapids', *Inscape: Journal of the British Association of Art Therapists*, 8(2003), 29–41.
F. O'Brien, 'The Making of Mess in Art Therapy: Attachment, Trauma and the Brain', *Inscape: Journal of the British Association of Art Therapists*, 9 (2004), 2–13.
E. Och, 'Transcription as Theory' in J. Jaworski and N. Coupland, eds, *The Discourse Reader* (London: Routledge, 1999).
Office of National Statistics, *Mental Health of Children & Young People in Great Britain* 2004 (2004)
Office of National Statistics, *Revised Statistical Publication for Independent School Census* (2007).
E. Omwake and A. Solnit, '"It Isn't Fair" – The Treatment of a Blind Child', *Psychoanalytic Study of the Child*, XVI (1961), 352–404.
M. Onizo and S. Onizo, 'Art Activities to Improve the Self-Esteem among Native Hawaiian Children', *Journal of Humanistic Education and Development*, 27 (1989), 167–76.
A. Oppenheim, *Questionnaire Design, Interviewing and Attitude Measurement* (London: Pinter Publishers Ltd, 1992).
J. Pallant, *SPSS Survival Manual* (Berkshire and New York: Open University Press, 2001).

G. Pankow, 'Psychotherapy: A Psychoanalytic Approach Employing the Concept of Body Image' in M. Dongier and E. Wittkower, eds, *Divergent Views in Psychiatry* (New York/London: Harper and Row, 1981).

E. Panofsky, *Studies in Iconology: Humanistic Themes in the Art of the Renaissance* (New York and London: Harper and Row, 1972).

R. Papadopoulos, *Therapeutic Care for Refugees and Asylum Seekers: No Place Like Home* (London: Karnac Books, Tavistock Clinic Series, 2002).

G. Parry and A. Richardson, *NHS Psychotherapy Services in England: Review of Strategic Policy in England* (NHS Executive: Department of Health, 1996).

H. Payne, ed, *Handbook of Inquiry in the Arts Therapies: One River, Many Currents* (London: Jessica Kingsley, 1993).

M. Peixin, Z. Richang, C. Zhuoji, C. Dahong, M. Liang, L. Jun and L. Yu, 'Group Intervention for Schizophrenia Inpatient with Art as Medium', *Evidence-Based Mental Health*, 37 (2005), 403–12.

T. Pifalo, 'Pulling out the Thorns: Art Therapy with Sexually Abused Children and Adolescents', *Art Therapy. Journal of the American Art Therapy Association*, 19 (2002), 12–22.

T. Pifalo, 'Art Therapy with Sexually Abused Children and Adolescents: Extended Research Study', *Art Therapy. Journal of the American Association of Art Therapists*, 23 (2006), 181–5.

F. Pine, 'On the Development of the Borderline-Child-To-Be', *American Journal of Orthopsychiatry*, 56 (1986), 450–7.

P. Pinel, *Traité Medico-philosophique sur l'Aliénation Mentale ou la Manie* (Paris; 1801), translated by D.D. Davis as *A Treatise on Insanity* (reprinted London: Cadell and Davis, 1806).

S. Pink, *Doing Visual Ethnography* (London: Sage Publications Ltd, 2001).

A. Pleasant-Metcalf, 'The Use of Art Therapy to Improve Academic Performance', *Art Therapy, Journal of the American Art Therapy Association*, 14 (1997), 23–9.

R. Porter, *A Social History of Madness, Stories of the Insane* (London: Weidenfeld and Nicolson, 1987).

E. Pringle, Evidence Based Practice. Exploring the Implications for Research within the Therapy Professions, Unpublished paper presented at the University of East Anglia (1996).

F. Prokofiev, 'Adapting the Art Therapy Group' in S. Skaife and V. Huet, eds, *Art Psychotherapy Groups: Between Pictures and Words* (London: Routledge, 1998).

F. Prokofiev, 'The Emergence of Meaning and the Emergence of Self in Art Therapy', MA thesis, Goldsmiths, University of London (2002).

J. Prosser, ed, *Image-Based Research. A Sourcebook for Qualitative Researchers* (London: Falmer Press, 1998).

P. Proulx, *Strengthening Emotional Ties through Parent-Child-Dyad Art Therapy* (London, Philadelphia: Jessica Kingsley, 2003).
G. Pugh and J. Statham (2006), 'Interventions in Schools in the UK' in C. McAuley, P. Pecora and W. Rose, eds, *Enhancing the Wellbeing of Children and Families through Effective Interventions: International Evidence for Practice* (London: Jessica Kingsley Publications, 2006).
S. Rabiger, 'Art Therapy as a Container' in C. Case and T. Dalley, *Working with Children in Art Therapy* (London: Routledge, 1990).
M. Rapley, *The Social Construction of Intellectual Disability* (Cambridge: Cambridge University Press, 2004).
T. Rawcliffe, 'A Few of my own Experiences of Painting in Relation to Marion Milner's Book, "On Not Being Able to Paint"', *Inscape: Journal of the British Association of Art Therapists*, Summer (1987), 20–2.
I. Ray 'Rebuttal of Pliny Earle in 1879' in Warner *Recovery from Schizophrenia: Psychiatry and Political Economy* (London and New York: Routledge, Kegan and Paul, 1985).
P. Reason and J. Rowan, eds, *Human Inquiry, A Sourcebook of New Paradigm Research* (Chichester, New York: John Wiley and Sons, 1991).
M. Rees, 'Making Sense of Marking Space. Researching Art Therapy with People who have Severe Learning Disabilities' in A. Gilroy and C. Lee, eds, *Art and Music. Therapy and Research* (London and New York: Routledge, 1995).
M. Rees, ed, *Drawing on Difference. Art Therapy with People who have Learning Difficulties* (London and New York: Routledge, 1998).
S. Reid, E. Fry and M. Rhode, 'Working with Small Groups in Primary Schools' in D. Daws and M. Boston, eds, *The Child Psychotherapist* (London: Mansefield Library, 1977).
C. Renne, P. Dowrick and G. Wasek, 'Considerations of the Participant in Video Recording' in P. Dowrick and S. Biggs, eds, *Using Video: Psychological and Social Applications* (Chichester: John Wiley and Sons, 1983).
P. Richardson, K. Jones, C. Evans, P. Stevens and A. Rowe, 'Exploratory RCT of Art Therapy as an Adjunctive Treatment in Schizophrenia', *Journal of Mental Health*, 16 (2007), 483–91.
C. Robson, *Real World Research* (Malden: Blackwell Publishers, 2002).
M. Rogers, 'Absent Figures: a Personal Reflection on the Value of Art Therapists' own Image-Making', *Inscape: Journal of the British Association of Art Therapists*, 7 (2002), 59–71.
M. Rosal, 'Comparative Group Art Therapy Research to Evaluate Changes in Locus of Control in Behaviourally Disordered Children', *Arts in Psychotherapy*, 20 (1993), 231–41.

M. Rosal, S. McCulloch-Vislisel, and S. Neece, 'Keeping Students in School: an Art Therapy Program to Benefit 9th Grade Students', *Art Therapy. Journal of the American Art Association*, 14 (1997), 30–6.

G. Rose, *Trauma and Mastery in Life and Art* (New Haven: Yale University Press, 1987).

G. Rose, *Visual Methodologies: an Introduction to the Interpretation of Visual Materials* (London: Sage Publications Ltd, 2001).

A. Roth and P. Fonagy, *What Works for Whom: a Critical Review of Psychotherapy Research* (New York: Guildford Press, 1996).

J. Rubin, *Child Art Therapy* (New York: Van Nostrand Reinhold, 1978).

M. Rutter, *Helping Troubled Children* (London: Penguin Books, 1975).

J. Ryan, 'Elision and Disavowal: the Extrusion of Class from Psychoanalytic Discourse and Practice', *Sitegeist: a Journal of Psychoanalysis and Philosophy*, 3 (2009), 27–41.

A. Sandler and D. Wills, 'Preliminary Notes on Play and Mastery in the Blind Child', *Journal of Child Psychotherapy*, 1 (1963), 7–19.

J. Saotome, 'Long-Stay Art Therapy Groups' in S. Skaife and V. Huet, eds. *Art Psychotherapy Groups. Between Pictures and Words* (London: Routledge, 1998).

N. Sarra, 'Connection and Disconnection in the Art Therapy Group: Working with Forensic Patients in Acute States on a Locked Ward', in S. Skaife and V. Huet, eds. *Art Psychotherapy Groups. Between Pictures and Words* (London: Routledge, 1998).

E. Saunders, J. Saunders, 'Evaluating the Effectiveness of Art Therapy through Quantitative Outcomes-Focused Study', *Arts in Psychotherapy*, 27 (2000), 99–106.

J. Schaverien, 'The Scapegoat and the Talisman: Transference in Art Therapy' in T. Dalley, C. Case, J Schaverien, F. Weir, P. Nowell Hall, D. Halliday and D. Waller, *Images of Art Therapy* (London: Tavistock and Routledge, 1987).

J. Schaverien, *The Revealing Image* (London: Routledge, 1992).

J. Schaverien, 'The Retrospective Review of Pictures: Data for Research in Art Therapy' in H. Payne, ed, *Handbook of Inquiry in the Arts Therapies: One River, Many Currents* (London: Jessica Kingsley, 1993).

J. Schaverien, 'Analytical Art Psychotherapy: Further Reflections on Theory and Practice', *Inscape: Journal of the British Association of Art Therapists*, 2 (1994): 41–9.

J. Schaverien, 'Researching the Esoteric' in A. Gilroy, and C. Lee, eds, *Art and Music. Therapy and Research* (London: Routledge, 1995).

J. Schaverien, 'Transference and Transactional Objects in the Treatment of Psychosis' in J. Schaverien and K. Killick, eds, *Art, Psychotherapy and Psychosis* (London: Routledge, 1997).

J. Schaverien, 'The Triangular Relationship and the Aesthetic Countertransference in Analytical Art Psychotherapy' in A. Gilroy and G. McNeilly, eds, *The Changing Shape of Art Therapy. New Developments in Theory and Practice* (Jessica Kingsley Publishers: London and Philadelpia, 2000).

J. Schaverien, 'Art and the Active Imagination: Reflections on Transference and the Image', *International Journal of Art Therapy: Inscape*, 10 (2005), 39–52.

V. Schindler and C. Pletnick, 'Role Development Applied to Art Therapy Treatment of an Artist Diagnosed with Schizophrenia', *Art Therapy. Journal of the American Art Therapy Association*, 23 (2006), 126–31.

A. Schore, *Affect Regulation and the Origin of the Self* (Hillsdale New Jersey: Lawrence Erlbaum Associates, 1994).

A. Schore, 'The Effects of Early Relational Trauma on Right Brain Development, Affect Regulation, and Infant Mental Health', *Infant Mental Health Journal*, 22 (2001), 201–69.

H. Segal, 'Notes on Symbol Formation', paper read at the Medical Section of the British Psychological Society 1955, first Published *International Journal of Psychoanalysis*, 38 (1957), 391–7. Reprinted in *The Works of Hannah Segal* (New York: Jason Aronson, 1981).

K. Sharmaz, *Constructing Grounded Theory: A Practical Guide Through Qualitative Analysis* (London: Sage Publications Ltd, 2006).

L. Sheppard, J. Rusted, D. Waller and F. McInally, *Evaluating the use of Art Therapy for Older People with Dementia: A Control Group Trial* (Brighton: Alzheimer's Society, Brighton Branch 1998).

D. Silverman, *Interpreting Qualitative Data: Methods for Analysing Talk, Text and Interaction* (London, California, New Delhi: Sage Publications, 2001).

R. Simon, *The Symbolism of Style: Art as Therapy* (London: Routledge, 1992).

R. Simon, *Symbolic Images in Art as Therapy* (London: Tavistock/Routledge, 1997).

H. Simons, *Case Study Research in Practice* (London: Sage Publications Ltd, 2009).

V. Sinason, 'Smiling, Swallowing, Sickening and Stupefying: the Effect of Sexual Abuse on the Child', *Psychoanalytic Psychotherapy*, 3 (1988), 97–111.

V. Sinason, *Mental Handicap and the Human Condition: New Approaches from the Tavistock* (London: Free Association Books, 1992).

S. Skaife, 'Making Visible: Art Therapy and Intersubjectivity', *Inscape: Journal of the British Association of Art Therapists*, 6 (2001), 40–50.

S. Skaife and V. Huet, *Art Psychotherapy Groups: Between Pictures and Words* (London and New York: Routledge, 1998).

S. Skaife and V. Huet, 'Introduction' in S. Skaife and V. Huet, eds, *Art Psychotherapy Groups: Between Pictures and Words* (London: Routledge, 1998).

S. Skaife, and V. Huet, 'Dissonance and Harmony; Theoretical Issues in Art Psychotherapy Groups' in S. Skaife and V. Huet, eds, *Art Psychotherapy Groups: Between Pictures and Words* (London: Routledge, 1998).

A. Sluckin, 'Humans are Conversational from Birth: Systemic Therapy, Developmental Psychology and the Artistic Metaphor', *Human Systems*, 10 (1999), 11–23.

N. Springham, 'Through the Eyes of the Law: What is it About Art that Can Harm People?', *International Journal of Art Therapy: Inscape*, 13 (2008), 65–73.

M. Stack, 'Humpty Dumpty had a Great Fall', *Inscape: Journal of the British Association of Art Therapists*, 1 (1996), 1–13.

M. Stack, 'Humpty Dumpty's Shell: Working with Autistic Defence Mechanisms in Art Therapy' in M. Rees, ed, *Drawing on Difference. Art Therapy with People who have Learning Difficulties* (London: Routledge, 1998).

J. Stair, 'Rational Primitives', *Crafts*, 180 (2003), 40–3.

P. Stanley and M. Miller, 'Short Term Art Therapy with an Adolescent Male', *Arts in Psychotherapy*, 20 (1993), 397–402.

D. Stern, *The Interpersonal World of the Infant* (London: Karnac Books, 1985).

D. Stern, *The Motherhood Constellation: a Unified View of Parent-Infant Psychotherapy* (New York: Basic Books, 1995).

D. Stern, 'The Process of Therapeutic Change Involving Implicit Knowledge: Some Implications of Developmental Observations for Adult Psychotherapy', *Infant Mental Health Journal*, 19 (1998), 300–7.

D. Stern, The Nature of the Therapeutic Alliance in Parent Infant Psychotherapy, lecture given at University College, London, 8 June 2002.

E. Stirling, Art Therapy in Mainstream Scottish Primary Schools, MA thesis, Goldsmiths, University of London (2001).

J. Stott and B. Males, 'Art Therapy for People who are Mentally Handicapped' in T. Dalley, ed, *Art as Therapy. An Introduction to the Use of Art as a Therapeutic Technique* (London: Tavistock Publications, 1984).

A. Strauss and J. Corbin, *Basics of Qualitative Research: Grounded Theory Procedures and Techniques* (London: Sage, 1990).

G. Sullivan, *Art Practice as Research: Inquiry in the Visual Arts* (London: Sage Publications Ltd, 2005).

J. Symington and N. Symington, *The Clinical Thinking of Wilfred Bion* (London: Routledge, 1996).

B. Tedlock, 'Ethnography and Ethnographic Representation' in N. Denzin and Y. Lincoln, eds, *Handbook of Qualitative Research* (Thousand Oaks, London, New Delhi: Sage Publications, 2000).

L. Thomas, 'From Re-Presentations to Representations of Sexual Abuse' in D. Sandle, ed, *Development and Diversity* (London and New York: Free Association Books, 1998).

T. Tibbetts and B. Stone, 'Short-Term Art Therapy with Seriously Emotionally Disturbed, *Arts in Psychotherapy*, 17 (1990), 139–46.
R. Tipple, 'Art Therapy with People who have Severe Learning Difficulties' in D. Waller and A. Gilroy, eds, *Art Therapy: A Handbook* (Buckingham: Open University Press, 1992).
R. Tipple, 'Challenging Assumptions: The Importance of Transference Processes in Work with People with Learning Difficulties', *Inscape. Journal of the British Association of Art Therapists*, Summer (1993), 2–9.
R. Tipple, 'Communication and Interpretation in Art Therapy with People who have a Learning Disability', *Inscape: Journal of the British Association of Art Therapists*, 2 (1994), 31–5.
R. Tipple, 'The Interpretation of Children's Artwork in a Paediatric Disability Setting', *Inscape: Journal of the British Association of Art Therapists*, 8 (2003), 48–59.
C. Trevarthen, 'Emotions in Infancy: Regulators of Contacts and Relationships with Persons' in K. Scherer and P. Ekman, eds, *Approaches to Emotion* (Hillsdale, New Jersey: Lawrence Erlbaum Associates, 1984).
C. Trevarthen, 'Development of Early Interactions and the Affective Regulations of Brain Growth' in C. von Evler and H. Forssberg, eds, *The Neurobiology of Early Infant Behaviour* (New York: MacMillan, 1989).
C. Trevarthen, 'Intrinsic Motives for Companionship in Understanding: their Origin, Development and Significance for Infant Mental Health', *Infant Mental Health Journal*, 22 (2001), 95 –131.
C. Trevarthen, 'New Preface to Conversations with a Two-Month Old and Conversations with a Two-Month Old' in J. Raphael-Leff, ed, *Parent-Infant Psychodynamics, Wild Things, Mirrors and Ghosts* (London, Philadelphia: Whurr Publishers, 2002).
E. Tronick, 'Dyadically Expanded States of Consciousness and the Process of Therapeutic Change', *Infant Mental Health Journal*, 19 (1998), 290 –299.
S. Tuke, *Description of the Retreat. An Institution near York for Insane Persons* (1813, reprinted London: Process Press, 1996).
H. Vandgrover, 'Dancing Together, at a Different Pace with the Same Partner: Teachers and Art Therapists in Schools', *Special Issues in Special Education and Rehabilitation*, 13 (1998), 22–31.
H. Wadeson, *Art Psychotherapy* (New York: John Wiley and Sons, 1980).
H. Wadeson, *The Dynamics of Art Psychotherapy* (New York: John Wiley, 1987).
D. Waller, 'A Consideration of the Similarities and Differences between Art Teaching and Art Therapy' in T. Dalley, ed, *Art as Therapy* (London: Tavistock/Routledge, 1984).
D. Waller, *Becoming a Profession: The History of Art Therapy in Britain 1940–1982* (London and New York: Tavistock/Routledge, 1991).

D. Waller, *Group Interactive Art Therapy: its use in Training and Treatment* (London and New York: Routledge, 1993).

D. Waller, ed, *Arts Therapies and Progressive Illness: Nameless Dread* (East Sussex and New York: Brunner-Routledge, 2002).

D. Waller, 'Art Therapy with Children; How it Leads to Change', *Clinical Child Psychology and Psychiatry*, 11 (2006), 271–82.

R. Warner, *Recovery from Schizophrenia: Psychiatry and Political Economy* (London and York: Routledge, Kegan and Paul, 1985).

D. Warren, *Blindness and Early Childhood Development* (New York: American Foundation for the Blind, 1984).

C. Welsby, 'Seen and Unseen: Art Therapy in a Girl's Comprehensive School' in C. Case, and T. Dalley, eds, *Art Therapy With Children: From Infancy to Adolescence* (Routledge: Hove, 2008).

M. Weber, *The Protestant Work Ethic and the Sprit of Capitalism* (1904), first English translation T. Parsons, 1930; reprinted (London and New York: Routledge, 2001).

H. Wengrower, 'Arts Therapies in Educational Settings: an Intercultural Encounter', *Arts in Psychotherapy*, 28 (2001), 109–15.

D. Westen, C. Novotny and H. Thompson-Brenner, 'The Empirical Status of Empirically Supported Psychotherapies: Assumptions, Findings and Reporting in Controlled Clinical Trials', *Psychological Bulletin*, 130 (2004), 631–63.

M. Wilkinson, *Coming into Mind: The Mind Brain Relationship: A Jungian Clinical Perspective* (London: Routledge, 2006).

J. Willats, 'Children's Drawing Development' in J. Willats, *Art and Representation: New Principles in the Analysis of Pictures* (New Jersey and Chichester: Princeton University Press, 1997).

P. Williams, 'Psychoanalysis and Cognitive Therapy: What Can Be Learnt From Each Other?' Conference Paper, *International Society for the Psychological Treatment of Schizophrenia and other Psychoses: UK Chapter* (Essex University, 1999).

D. Winnicott, The Theory of the Parent-Infant Relationship in D. Winnicott, *The Maturational Process and the Facilitating Environment* (London: Karnac Books, 1990).

D. Winnicott, *The Child. the Family and the Outside World* (Harmondsworth: Penguin, 1964).

D. Winnicott, Ego and Integration in Child Development, in *The Maturational Process and the Facilitating Environment* (London: Karnac Books, 1990).

D. Winnicott, *Playing and Reality* (London: Tavistock Publications, 1971).

D. Winnicott, *Deprivation and Delinquency* (London: Tavistock, 1984).

D. Winnicott, *Psychoanalytic Explorations* (London: Karnac Books, 1989).

D. Winnicott, *Therapeutic Consultations in Child Psychiatry* (London: Maresfield Library, Karnac Books, 1996).

R. Winter, 'Some Principles and Procedures for the Conduct of Action Research' in O. Zuber-Skerrit, ed, *New Directions in Action Research* (London: Falmer Press, 1996).

R. Winter and C. Munn-Giddings, *A Handbook for Action Research in Health and Social Care* (London: Routledge, 2001).

J. Woddis, 'Art Therapy: New Problems, New Solutions?' in D. Waller and A. Gilroy, eds, *Art Therapy: a Handbook*' (Buckingham, England: Open University Press, 1992).

J. Wolff, *The Social Production of Art* (Basingstoke: Macmillan Press, 1993).

S. Wolff, *Children Under Stress: Understanding the Emotionally Disturbed Child* (London: Penguin, 1969).

C. Wood, 'A Personal View of Laing and his Influence on Art Therapy', *Inscape: Journal of the British Association of Art Therapists*, Winter (1991), 15–19.

C. Wood, 'The History of Art Therapy and Psychosis' in K. Killick and J Schavarien, eds, *Art, Psychotherapy and Psychosis* (London: Routledge, 1997a).

C. Wood, 'Facing Fear with People who have a History of Psychosis', *Inscape: Journal of the British Association of Art Therapists*, 2 (1997b), 41–8.

C. Wood 'Gathering Evidence: Expansion of Art Therapy Research Strategy', *Inscape: Journal of the British Association of Art Therapists*, 4 (1999a), 51–61.

C. Wood, 'Class Issues in Therapy', in M. Liebmann et al. eds. *Art Therapy, Race and Culture* (London, Bristol & Pennsylvania: Jessica Kingsley, 1999b).

C. Wood, '*Art, Psychotherapy and Psychosis: The Nature and Politics of Art Therapy*', PhD thesis, University of Sheffield (2000).

C. Wood, (2000), 'The Significance of Studios', *Inscape: Journal of the British Association of Art Therapists*, 5 (2001), 40–53,

C. Wood, 'Convivencia' *Art Therapy Online* (available at http://eprints-gojo.gold.ac.uk, 2010).

World Health Organisation (WHO) *'Social Justice and Equity in Health. Report from the Program on Social Equity and Health'*, Leeds: 22–6 July, 1985.

K. Wright, *Vision and Separation between Mother and Baby* (London: Free Association Books, 1991).

UNICEF, Report Card 7: Child Poverty in Perspective: an Overview of Child Well-being in Rich Countries, in UNICEF, *Report on Childhood in Industrialised Countries* (Florence: UNICEF Innocenti Research Centre, 2007).

I. Yalom, *The Theory and Practice of Group Psychotherapy* (New York: Basic Books, 1975).

I. Yalom and G. Elkin, *Every Day Gets a Little Closer: a Twice-Told Therapy* (New York: Basic Books, 1974).

O. Zuber-Skerrit, 'Introduction: New Directions in Action Research' in O. Zuber-Skerritt, ed, *New Directions in Action Research* (London: Falmer Press, 1996).

Notes on Contributors

ELIZABETH ASHBY qualified as an art psychotherapist in 1996 and works for an NHS Trust in the Midlands. She works as a Lead Art Psychotherapist with older adults and people who have learning disabilities, and in private practice, and is concerned about the development of the profession, our evidence base and our status among the health professions. As part of her professional development she completed the Masters in Research in Art Psychotherapy at Goldsmiths, University of London in 2004 and subsequently felt the need to begin further research in 2007 in the context of a PhD, also at Goldsmiths. Liz is a member of the editing group starting the process of writing guidelines for art therapists working with people with learning disabilities within the Art Therapy and Learning Disability Special Interest Group.

BARRIE DAMARELL manages a team of arts therapists and counsellors for the Plymouth learning disability partnership and is Professional Lead for the Arts Therapies for Plymouth Teaching Primary Care Trust. His research interests include the significance of place in the artworks of people with learning disabilities and the role of sculptural thinking in art psychotherapy practice.

ANDREA GILROY trained originally as a painter, qualified as an art therapist in the mid-1970s and worked in acute psychiatry and with people who have learning disabilities. She has taught at Goldsmiths, University of London since 1979 and is currently Reader in Art Psychotherapy and Head of the Department of Professional and Community Education (PACE), teaching across a range of programmes in art therapy and art education and supervising research students. Her research interests include the development of an evidence base for art therapy, the interface between the theories and practices of visual art/visual culture and the theory and practice of art therapy and the development of art therapy in different countries around the world. Her publications include *Pictures at an Exhibition: Selected Essays on Art and Art Therapy* (Routledge, 1989) with Tessa Dalley; *Art Therapy: A Handbook* (Open University Press, 1992) with Diane Waller; *Art & Music. Therapy and Research* (Routledge, 1995) with Colin Lee; *The Changing Shape of Art Therapy: New Developments in Theory and Practice* (Jessica Kingsley Publications, 2000) with Gerry McNeilly; and *Art Therapy, Research and Evidence-Based Practice* (Sage, 2006).

UWE HERRMANN trained in art therapy, social pedagogy and fine art in Britain and Germany. He developed the art therapy service at a state school for the blind in Germany in 1991, where he continues his clinical practice with the visually impaired. He completed an MA in Art Psychotherapy at Goldsmiths, University of London, where he is currently completing his PhD research on art therapy and congenital blindness. He is a lecturer and Deputy Course Leader on the MA Programme in Art Therapy at Kunsthochschule Berlin-Weissensee, Germany, and has published several papers on art therapy and blindness.

HILARY HOSEA works as an art psychotherapist with children, adolescents and families in an NHS Child and Family Centre in Norfolk. After graduating in Art History at Essex University she worked as a primary school teacher and then trained as an art therapist at St Albans School of Art & Design. She completed an MA in Art Psychotherapy at Goldsmiths, University of London.

KEVIN JONES studied Fine Art at Loughborough College of Art after which he became a starving painter and community artist/activist. In 1987 he trained as an art psychotherapist at Goldsmiths, University of London and worked within adult mental health services in the NHS. In 2001 he qualified as a Psychoanalytic Psychotherapist with the Institute for Psychotherapy and Social Studies completing his MA in Psychotherapeutic and Social Studies. No longer starving, he works as a lecturer in Art Psychotherapy at Goldsmiths and has a private practice in art psychotherapy and individual psychoanalytic psychotherapy.

JACKY MAHONY trained, worked and exhibited as a studio potter for a decade before qualifying as an art psychotherapist at Goldsmiths, University of London. She completed her MA in 1992 and her PhD in 2010, both at Goldsmiths. She worked as an art psychotherapist in the NHS for twenty years, including nine years at the Henderson Hospital Therapeutic Community, and was Professional Head of Art Psychotherapy for Oxleas NHS Trust until 2003. She taught at Goldsmiths having contributed for a number of years to Foundation, Postgraduate Diploma and MA programmes. Her publications include *Treatment of Addiction: Current Issues for Arts Therapies* (Routledge, 1999) with Diane Waller.

FRANCE PROKOFIEV has worked as an art therapist in primary schools since 1992 and has a particular interest in art therapy groups for children and in long-term individual work with children whose difficulties are preverbal. She is a visiting tutor at Goldsmiths, University of London and the Northern Programme for Art Psychotherapy and is currently researching part-time in the field of art therapy with children, extending her understanding of ways of finding meaning in image-making.

SALLY SKAIFE is Programme Co-Ordinator of the Masters in Art Psychotherapy at Goldsmiths, University of London. She is past chairperson of British Association of Art Therapists, and was a member of the editorial group of *Inscape* for twenty years. She has numerous publications including joint editorship of *Art Psychotherapy Groups: between Pictures and Words* (Routledge, 2008). She has completed her PhD and runs an art psychotherapy group with refugees and asylum seekers who are victims of politically orchestrated torture.

ELIZABETH STIRLING retired from primary education in 1990. She then studied Fine Art (BA, University of Newcastle-upon-Tyne, 1994), Art Therapy (Postgraduate Diploma in Art Therapy, Queen Margaret University, Edinburgh, 1996) and Art Psychotherapy research (MA in Art Psychotherapy, Goldsmiths, University of London, 2000). As a result of these studies, fifteen years as head teacher and six years' experience as an art therapist in schools, she investigated the potential of school staff/art therapist collaboration in an art therapy participative action research project.

ROBIN TIPPLE studied painting and printmaking at Norwich School of Art and Reading University. After working as a mural artist in a London Hospital he trained as an Art Therapist at Goldsmiths, University of London (1983–4). He subsequently went on to work with learning disabled adults and children. His work with children included work in a therapeutic community for children who had experienced neglect and abuse, physical and sexual. He has written about expression and painting, using the theory of the transference, and interpretation, in relation to work with learning disabled adults. More recently he has written about Art Therapy Assessments in Paediatrics and the use of brief Art Therapy to help adolescents with Asperger's Syndrome. Robin is completing his PhD, researching his work with children who have an Autistic Spectrum Disorder at Goldsmiths where he also teaches on the MA in Art Psychotherapy.

CHRIS WOOD is the Director and Team Leader for the Northern Programme for Art Psychotherapy in Sheffield which provides training and research within a partnership between Sheffield Care Trust and Leeds Metropolitan University. She is happy to be in a position to continue to combine work in higher education with therapeutic practice in the public sector. She is interested in the uses of contemporary art and popular culture, in the relationship between mental health and politics and in the many ways in which people with long-term mental health problems manage to live well. She is concerned to contribute to the evidence base for art therapy.

Index

ABA Design *see* research
Adamson, E. 213
Adelson, E 40–1, 58
Aldridge, F. 21
Alvarez, A. 22
American art therapists 142
American Association of Art Therapists Conference (2008) 209
American Psychological Association (APA) 233, 234, 235
anti-psychiatry movement 218
anxiety attacks 45
Art-based Communication Strategies 170–2
art making as visual research method *see* research
art-making process, cognitive & emotional development in 27
art therapy
analytic 253
and body image 42
collaborative role of 88, 104, 105, 159, 169–70
different approaches to 219
ethnic minority clients in 13
historical research into 211–13
image analysis in 44
non-directive 43, 114
psychodynamic approach to 92, 140, 162, 166
psychotherapeutic approaches to 219
responses to psychosis 218–27 *passim*
roots in Social Psychiatry 220
art therapy for children
assessment of 102–4
integration into nursery and primary education 103
in transition from nursery to primary education 81–93 *passim*
psychodynamic 107
supporting curriculum for excellence 101
who have suffered sexual abuse 21, 38, 108
with developmental deficits 21, 25
art therapy groups
experiential 201, 205
interactive 196
outpatient psychotherapeutic 235, 239, 241
psychotherapeutic 251–67 *passim*
women's research 253
Art Therapy in Practice 219
Art Therapy Race and Culture 219
Arts in Psychotherapy 192
Arts Therapy, efficacy of 223
artwriting 10
Ashby, E. 184
Asperger's Syndrome 146, 147 *see also* Autistic Spectrum
attachment theory 22, 23, 36, 65, 114 *see also* attunement; Bowlby's attachment theory
Attention Deficit Hyperactivity Disorder (ADHD) 108, 146
attunement 114 *see also* Stern, D.
authoritarianism 203
autism 146, 147, 158, 162
Autistic Spectrum 93, 108, 160 *see also* Asperger's Syndrome

autistic subjects 139, 140
Autobiographer, the 234
autobiography 231, 234

Baudrillard, J. 234
Baxandall, M. 145
Bazerman, C. 233
behaviourism 233
Bell, C. 272
Bellah, R. 234
Biemans, H. 70
Binns, P. 237
Bion, W. 22, 105, 121, 132, 133, 197
bipolar conditions 239, 269 *see also* depression; manic-depressive psychosis
body-self concept 40
body-self reflections 58
Borchers, K. 193, 205
Boronska, T. 87
Bowen, C. 182
Bowlby, J. 22, 92
  attachment theory of 65
Bowlby Centre, The 222
Brannick, T. 89, 90
Breuer, J. 205
Bristow, M. 237
British Association of Art Therapists (BAAT) 84, 88, 163, 209, 218, 223
  Code of Ethics of 87
Britton, R. 133–4
Brooker, C. 224
Burlingham, D. 51 (hypothesis of aggression and disaster)
Butterworth, G. 131
Byers, A. 177
Byrne, P. 213

Cage, J. 246, 249
Canadian Art Therapy Association (journals of) 192
Case, C. 21, 22, 87, 261
case studies
  approaches to 7–9
  research into 25
Cassirer, E. 122
Central Office for Research Ethics Committee (COREC) 112
ceramics 232, 236, 238, 240, 242–4, 246
challenging behaviour 13, 159–63
Child and Adolescent Mental Health Services (CAMHS) *see* National Health Service
child-centred approach to education 112
Children's Fund 87
Christians, C. 74
chronological mapping 245
civil voice 232, 235
Clark, T. 10
class 207, 215–17, 273 *see also* social and class agenda
clay modelling 41–2, 48
client anxiety 125
Cochrane Collaboration 5
Coghlan, D. 89, 90 (Spiral of Action Research Cycles)
Cognitive Behavioural Therapy (CBT) 4, 108
cognitive psychology 143
Cole, M. 136
collaboration
  art therapists with educational staff 83, 85, 88, 111–13
  art therapists with health professionals 169
collaborative research models 43
Commission for Social Justice 216
communication
  intrapsychic 181
  mother-infant 70
  of artwork 181, 262–3
  of conscious thought 132
  symbolic 28
  through unspoken metaphor 248–9

with people with learning difficulties 170–2, 181–3, 185
Community Mental Health Teams (CMHTs) *see* National Health Service
containment 22, 109, 170–2, 197, 208, 220, 225, 228
art-therapist as container 246–7, 248
coordination & fine motor control 33
Corbin, J. 9, 256
Coren, A. 92
counter-transference 28, 162, 163, 177, 178, 235, 236 *see also* transference
vulnerability of art therapist to 37
'crafts' 236, 250
crime 274
Cromarty, K. 112
Curson, A. 51

Dalley, T. 50, 87, 103, 193, 261
depression 239, 269 *see also* bipolar disorders; psychosis (manic-depressive)
post-natal 70
deserving and undeserving poor 215, 216 *see also* poverty
developmental deficits 20, 35, 37, 38 *see also* art therapy for children
repair of 34, 113
developmental stages of art in children 28
diagrammatic images 119–20, 122, 123, 127, 130, 131, 185
discourse analysis 147–54 *passim*
discursive and nondiscursive symbolism 120
disgrace 214
disorganised attachments 20
Dissenyake, E. 64, 68
Doerner, K. 213
Downik, P. 123
Downs Syndrome 182
drama therapy 160
dramaturgical accounts 145
dream inspiration 53
dual diagnosis (mental health and learning disabilities) 118, 169
Dubowski, J. 31, 120, 161, 162, 182
dyadic interaction 92

Eaton, L. 108
education 274
Edwards, B. 82
Edwards, D. 43, 191, 192, 194, 205, 209
Edwards, M. 213
effects of culture and media 220–1, 228
Ehrenzweig, A. 27, 31
ekphrasis 10
Elkins, J. 10
Ellwood, J. 224
Embase (online database) 192
Emin, T. 221
emotional and behavioural difficulties in children 82, 83, 86, 108
Emotional and Trauma support fund 87
ethics and politics in qualitative research 74
Ethics committees 70 *see also* Central Office for Research Ethics Committee
ethnicity 201–9 *passim*
ethnographic & participative approaches to research 61, 69
Evans, K. 182
Evidence Based Practice (EBP) 3–6, 190, 192, 194, 201, 204, 209, 253, 269–70, 274
evidence based treatments 233

Falk, B. 177
father-child relations 53–4, 56
Ferrance, E. 89
Fictionalist, The 234
Fonagy, P. 221

Foucault, M. 156, 234
Foulds, K. 174–5
Fox, L. 162, 176
Fraiberg, S. 40–1, 58, 65
French Revolution, The 214
Freud, S. 64, 121, 205, 233, 234

'gaze, the' 63, 73, 74
gender and sexuality 204, 207
Gergen, K. 233, 234, 235, 247
Gilroy, A. 43, 192, 193, 200, 205
Green, B. 193, 205, 269, 272
Greenwood, D. 8
Greenwood H. 177, 178, 227, 235
Grubrich-Simitis, I. 205
Guideline Development Group 223

Haeseler, M. 236
Hall, P. 62
Hallam, J. 161, 162, 176
Hallas, P. 253, 266
Harrod T. 236
Hegel, G. 121
Help Starts Here 87
Henley, D. 28, 41
Henzell, J. 213
hermeneutic approach *see* research
Hesse, E. 237
heuristics *see* research
hierarchies of power 206
History of Scientific Revolutions 212
Hogan, S. 215
Holtom, R. 190, 192, 193, 204, 209
Huet, V. 175
Hughes, R. 161
Hurst, D. 221
Hussain-Gamble, M. 209

image-making and cognition link 118
inclusion 102
Industrial Revolution, The 214
infant psychotherapy 62 *see also* parent-infant psychotherapy
Inscape (journal)192
internal object, the 197
International Society for the Psychological Treatment of Schizophrenia 222
interpersonal learning 257–8, 267
intersubjectivity 23
intrapsychic boundaries 52

Jackson, M. 224
James, J. 31, 120
Jameson, F. 266
Journal of the American Art Therapy Association 192
Jung, C. 233

Kellog, R. 132
Killick, K. 20, 177, 178, 192, 225
Kohut, H. 110
Kramer, E. 41
Kuhn, T. 212
Kut-Rosenfeld, S. 24, 35
Kymiss, P. 108

labelling 85, 102
Lacan, J. 58, 233
Laing, R.D. 218, 225, 233
Lasch, C. 234
Laufer, M. 49
Layton, G. 235
Leach, B. 236
learning difficulties *see* learning disabilities
learning disabilities 117, 119, 124, 131
  dual diagnosis (with mental health problems) 118, 169
  mild and moderate 125, 182
  policy and provision for people with 183–5
  psychotherapeutic approaches to working with people who have 161

severe 13, 27, 159–64, 167, 170–2 *see also* challenging behaviour
liaison (teachers & therapists) 111–13 *see also* collaboration
Likert Scale 96
Lindsay, M. 161
Lister, M. 74
Live in Your Head: Concept & Experiment in Britain 1965–75 236
Lomas, H. 253, 266
'Looked-After' system 21
Lowenfeld, V. 41
Lowenthal, D. 8
low-self worth 45

Mackenzie, K. 182
madness *see also* psychosis
association of disgrace with 214
association of poverty with 214
historical themes in treatment of 214–15
Males, J. 182, 191, 192, 196, 205
map-making 265, 266
mapping 263
mark-making behaviours 161
Marx, K. 234
maternal deprivation 22, 31
maternal mirroring 109
Matthews, J. 26, 29, 68
McDonough, S. 70, 72
McLeod, J. 2, 4, 7, 43, 45, 69, 75, 233, 234, 235
McNeilly, G. 251
Medline (online database) 192
Meltzer, D. 50
mental health
dual diagnosis (with learning disabilities) 118, 169
problems in children 107
severe and complex difficulties 192, 194, 232, 235, 248, 269 *see also* schizophrenia; depression
Meyerowitz-Katz, J. 22, 36, 64
MIND (charity) 216
mind-body dualism 214
Mindroom (charity) 86
mixture-making 30
modelling 109, 248
Modernism 236
moral treatment 214–16, 219
Mulvey, L. 74
Munn-Giddings, C. 104
music therapy 160

National Health Service (NHS) 160, 165, 183, 184, 189–92, 204, 206, 219, 227, 274
Children and Adolescent Mental Health Services (CAMHS) 79, 107
Community Mental Health Teams (CMHTs) 194, 195, 206, 239
managers 227
Paediatric Service 139
Primary Care Trusts 183
psychiatry outpatient group 232, 233
Research and Development Departments 112
National Institute for Clinical Health and Excellence (NICE) 5, 182, 209, 220, 222, 223, 270
NICE Clinical Guideline 270
neuro-developmental discourse 141
neurological discourse 139
neurotic patients 42
New Horizons 274
New Labour 212
NHS Psychotherapy Services in England: Review of Strategic Policy in England 221
non-figurative artwork 26
non-marking movements 117, 119, 120, 122 124–5, 128–30, 132–7 *see also* pointing
Nowell-Hall, P. 213
'now moments' 67, 71, 77, 110, 114

object relations theory 161
O'Brien, F. 35
Office of National Statistics Report on Children's Mental Health 86
Omwake, E. 41, 48, 57
Oppenheim, A. 163
Out of the Lion's Mouth 87

paediatricians 140, 144
Pankow, G. 41–2, 47, 52
Papadopoulos, R. 227
parent-infant psychotherapy 61, 63, 64, 65 *see also* infant psychotherapy
Parisian Asylums 214
Parkinson's disease 177
Parry, G. 221
Participative Action Research 81, 88, 89–93, 96, 104
passive and aggressive body concepts 51–2, 56
pathology 142
Perseus and Medusa myth 55
phantasy 143
phenomenological reduction 45
phenomenological research approach 117, 122
Piaget, J. 234
Pifalo, T. 108
Pine, F. 24
Pinel, P. and *Traitement Morale* 214
Pink, S. 73–4
Place to Be, The 87
Pletnick, C. 272
pointing 131 *see also* non-marking movements
Pollock, J. 27, 29, 30, 31
Poor Law (1834) 215
Post Traumatic Stress Disorder 108
poverty 211, 215–17, 222, 273, 274
  association with madness 214
practitioner research *see* research
pre-nursery school children 62
pre-verbal disturbances 24
'primary relatedness' 66
Pringle, E. 190, 192
Pringle, A. 62
Prokofiev, F. 87
Psychinfo (online database) 192
psychoanalysis 121–2, 219, 225
  with the blind 42
psychodynamic discourse 139, 141
psychodynamic material 126
psychological disturbance in blind clients 40
Psychological Therapies Teams 239
psychosis 211, 212, 213, 217 *see also* madness
  art-therapy responses to 218–21, 222, 224, 225, 227
  history of 213
  manic-depressive 225
psychosocial intervention 219, 220
psychotherapeutic interventions 82 *see also* therapeutic interventions
psychotic anxieties 197, 206, 207
psychotic terror 212

Quakers 215
qualitative research *see* research
quantitative research *see* research

Rabiger, S. 109, 162, 176
Randomised Controlled Trials (RCTs) 1, 4, 107, 182, 189, 200, 223, 269, 270, 271–3
  American Psychological Association style/tradition 233, 234, 235
Ray 215
Reagan, R. 212
Rees, M. 161, 177, 178, 182
Renne, C. 123
research *see also* Randomised Controlled Trials
  ABA Design 8
  Analysis of Covariance (ANCOVA) 195

case study 25
collaborative models of 43
hermeneutic approaches to 8, 13
Participative Action Research 81, 88, 89–93, 96, 104
phenomenological approaches to 117, 122
practitioner 2, 3
qualitative data, analysis of 164
qualitative research, ethics and politics in 74
quantitative methods 122, 164, 193, 206
video interaction technique 61, 69, 72, 75–6, 79
visual, art based 10, 11, 39
visual heuristic approach 236
retrospective review sessions 44, 49
Revealing Image, The 122
Richards, K. 112
Richardson, P. 193, 196, 197, 201, 221, 269
Robbins, S. 272
Rosal, M. 182
Rose, G. 133
Roth, A. 221
Royal College of Psychiatrists 'Mind Odyssey' (2001) 209
Rubin, J. 41

Sandler, A. 57
Saunders, E. 108
Saunders, J. 108
Schavarien, J. 26, 28, 44, 58, 117, 122, 127, 138, 192
and diagrammatic images 119–20, 123, 132–4
Schindler, V. 272
schizophrenia 13, 42, 189, 194, 196, 197, 207, 209, 216–17, 239, 269, 270
Schizophrenia Guidelines 222
scopophilia 74
sculpture 39, 43, 45, 48, 58
as substitute for organisational. function of sight 41
self-representation through 40
self-harming behaviours 51, 162, 168–9
semiosis 139
sensory-filter 56–7
service provision 165–8, 174–5, 179–80
see also working conditions
severe learning difficulties 159–80
severe learning disabilities 13, 27 (see also)
Sharmaz, K. 9, 10
Sheppard, L. 178
Silverman, D. 256
Simon, R. 29, 117, 120, 127, 133
Simons, H. 7
Sinason, V. 135, 175, 177
Skaife, S. 157
Sluckin, A. 62, 70
social and class agenda 253 *see also* class
social constructivism 122
Social Psychiatry 215, 216, 218, 219, 223, 227
Solnit, A. 41, 48, 57
Special Educational Needs Coordinators (SENCOs) 112
speech art theory 145
Sprince, M. 24, 35
squiggle game 141, 145, 147–54
Stack, M. 162, 175
Statistical Package for Social Sciences 164
Stern, D. 23–4, 33, 36, 63, 65–6, 76–8
and art processes 38
and parental attunement 66, 77
stigmatisation 85
Stott, J. 182
Strauss, A. 9, 256
Studies in Hysteria 205 *see also* Freud, S.
styles of imagery 127
subjects 143–6
suicide
thoughts of 54
threats of 45

supportive intervention 81
supportive psychotherapy 227
Sure Start 79
Surrealism 218
symbolic equations 226
Symbolism of Style, The 120
Symington, J. 121, 133
Symington, N. 121, 133
syntagm 157

tactile mirror 56, 58
Talsky, G. 269
Tavistock Clinic 86, 222
Tedlock, B. 69
textiles 232, 236, 238, 240, 242–4, 246
practices 237
textual traditions 233–4
Textures of Memory: The politics of cloth 236
Thatcher, M. 212
Theoretical Advances in Art Therapy Conference (2002) 209
theories of exchange 145
therapeutic interventions 87 *see also* psychotherapeutic interventions
Thomas, L. 35
Tipple, R. 27, 78, 162, 182, 183
transference 92, 161, 178, 189, 200, 228, 229, 236 *see also* counter-transference
dynamics of 122
'good grandmother' 65–6, 78, 109
Trevarthen, C. 65, 70, 92
Tuke family, the 215

unemployment 217, 222
UNICEF Report, The (1987) 86
utterances *see* vocalisations

Valuing People Now 183
verbal analytic therapy 41
verbal imagery 145
verbalisations *see* vocalisations
verbal pointing 145
victims of domestic violence 71
video interaction technique 61, 69, 72, 75–6, 79
Video Interactive Guidance 63, 69–70, 72
video recording influence of 123
visual heuristic research 236–7
visual research (art-based) 10, 39
'vitality affects' 63, 110
vocalisations 124, 131, 135–7, 145
categories of 130
Vygotsky, L. 121, 122, 136

Wadeson, H. 261
Waller, D. 82, 103, 176, 192, 196
Warner, R. 213, 215, 217
Warren, D. 41
Wasek, G. 123
Weber, M. 234
Wehlig, C. 269
Wells, L. 74
Welsby, C. 87, 103
Wengrower, H. 105
Westen, D. 5, 6
What Works for Whom? 253
Wills, D. 57
Wilson, A. 237
Winnicot, D. 64, 66, 73, 77, 92, 141
Winter, R. 89, 104
Woddis, J. 175
working environments 85, 165–8, 174–5, 179–80 *see also* service provision
World Health Organisation (WHO) 216, 217
Wright, K. 134

Yalom, I. 257, 266
Young British Artists 221

Zuber-Skerrit, O. 89

www.ingramcontent.com/pod-product-compliance
Ingram Content Group UK Ltd.
Pitfield, Milton Keynes, MK11 3LW, UK
UKHW020122290926
15471UKWH00003B/217

9 783039 119943